D0720627

# THE EMPLOYEE STRIKES BACK!

# John D. Rapoport
# and
# Brian L. P. Zevnik

COLLIER BOOKS

MACMILLAN PUBLISHING COMPANY

NEW YORK

Collier Macmillan Canada
Toronto

Maxwell Macmillan International
New York   Oxford   Singapore   Sydney

# THE EMPLOYEE
## *Strikes Back!*

COPYRIGHT © 1989 BY JOHN D. RAPOPORT AND BRIAN L. P. ZEVNIK

Collier Books
Macmillan Publishing Company
866 Third Avenue, New York, NY 10022

Collier Macmillan Canada, Inc.
1200 Eglinton Avenue East, Suite 200
Don Mills, Ontario M3C 3N1

Library of Congress Cataloging-in-Publication Data
Rapoport, John D.
    The employee strikes back!/John D. Rapoport and
Brian L. P. Zevnik.—1st Collier Books ed.
    p.    cm.
    ISBN 0-02-036150-5
    1. Employees—Dismissal of—Law and legislation—
United States—Popular works.   2. Emploee rights—United States.
I. Zevnik, Brian.   II. Title.
KF3319.6.R37    1990
344.73′012596—dc20
[347.30412596]              90-5967          CIP

Macmillan books are available at special discounts for bulk purchases for sales promotions, premiums, fund-raising, or educational use. For details, contact:

Special Sales Director
Macmillan Publishing Company
866 Third Avenue
New York, NY 10022

Designed by Claudia Carlson

First Collier Books Edition 1990

10  9  8  7  6  5  4  3  2  1

Printed in the United States of America

A Wellington Press Book

To the real power behind the pen
without whom there would have been
no book, my wife, Georgene

—B.L.P.Z.

To Joan, James, and Sara with love

—J.D.R.

# Contents

# Introduction

I t seemed so simple in the old days. The employer employed. The worker worked. The former paid. The latter spent. The party of the first part fired. The party of the second part looked for another job.

There's no such thing as simple anymore. Employee rights have exploded on the work scene. The sparks are everywhere, not just in changing attitudes. Fundamental trends like downsizing, technological advances, increased international competition, changing social mores, conservative political backlash—they all add up to a firefight on the firing front.

And the headlines add fuel to the flames. Sexual harassment is a sexy topic. Drug testing is all the rage. Polygraphs and parental leave have Congress and state courts in an uproar. Privacy problems have everyone covering up. Even the Supreme Court calendar is becoming speckled with employee rights cases, workplace confrontations, employer versus worker donnybrooks.

Every day, hundreds, maybe thousands, of workers are discriminated against in all types of work situations in all types of companies. They may lose out on a job because of race, or age, or sex. Or they're asked to acquiesce to demands they shouldn't have to. Or they're passed over for a plum spot because they're up against someone's relative. Or they're disciplined in a shabby manner or fired for no good reason, or evaluated in a purely subjective manner.

In part this occurs because employees don't know their rights. This book is designed to help fix that, to help them—you—to assert your legal rights to fair, equitable, honest treatment. It's not the ultimate weapon, but it's a good start.

## Lies, damned lies, and statistics

Wrongful discharge is the traditional tent in which most employee rights cases reside. It's been estimated that half of the approximately three million individuals fired each year *do not* have a specific statutory or contractual right to demand an independent review of their discharge. Of course, that means that half *do*. As you read, keep that in mind. Also remember as you look over the following numbers that all numbers can be turned any which way but loose.

The accepted axiom today is that you can make statistics mean whatever you want. But you'll get a better feel for what's going on in wrongful discharge and employee rights these days when you see some numbers to illuminate the words.

- By one estimate, there were twenty-five thousand wrongful terminations cases pending in 1988.
- California, a trendsetter not only in beach togs and umbrella drinks but in employee rights as well, saw wrongful discharge suits rise 22 percent in 1987, with average damage awards to employees in the $400,000 range.
- The Research Institute of America says that lawsuits under statutes protecting employment rights account for the largest single group of civil filings in federal courts.
- A Michigan autoworker won almost half a million dollars after being fired for filing a worker's compensation claim; an Oregon salesclerk cashed in on harassment and discharge claims worth over one hundred grand; a computer manager in California chalked up about $300,000 for being fired for dating a competitor; a computer programmer in San Francisco got just under half a million after being terminated for refusing a drug test.
- An East Coast executive won a whopping initial award of over $10 million for being wooed, won, and then dismissed by a *Fortune* top ten firm.
- Estimated price tag for *privacy suits* lost by employers—$316,000.
- In 1986 and 1987, 130,000 EEOC actions against employers generated $173 million in employee "benefits."
- One publication estimated that in the mid-eighties, 95 percent of termination cases decided by federal and state appellate courts were won by the plaintiffs.

What do all these numbers mean to you? Well, the good news is that there are more precedents being set that could benefit you, employee lawyers are becoming more expert in helping you, and employers are more likely to follow the law and to settle out of court when you catch them red-handed. The bad news is that court calendars are jammed, judges and juries are more jaundiced, employer lawyers are more expert, and corporate headquarters are more careful to cover their corporate hindquarters in sensitive legal areas.

Add another grain of salt to any euphoria that those big-buck results may engender in your financial heart of hearts. Hyperlegis (Latin, *hyper* = over, *legis* = law) may scream at you from the headlines and hum a siren tune as a call to action to solve your own personal workplace problems. But don't jump in. Read this book to get a feel for the reality of the situation. For every $100 thousand award, there are dozens of employee losers still paying their lawyer's bills. The whole experience can be an awful drain—on finances, on time, on psychic and physical energy. One manager who rejected legal recourse said it would have been like suing his own father. Another was sure he'd get blacklisted. So don't let the stats blind you to the down-side risks of employee litigation.

## It wouldn't be lawyerly if it didn't have caveats

You can't expect this book to immediately catapult you to untold riches by revealing unknown secrets for beating the American legal system with employee lawsuits. If anyone claims they can do that for you, please give them our address. Maybe they could write a book for us. But don't believe them.

You can believe this, though. The grounding you'll get in legal employment matters in this book will help you recognize just what rights you have—and don't have—in the workplace. While you're absorbing that background, keep these caveats in mind.

Some of the "legal victories" you'll read about are not conclusive. They may be in their initial stages where the "victory" consists of the court deciding that the employee does indeed have a case which should be heard by the judicial system. No "judgment" is made on how the case will turn out. Why read about them? Well, if the court decides someone else has a case based on certain circumstances, you may have one too.

Another red flag. Certain cases will be appealed and may drag on for years. They may be settled out of court with neither side admitting to a loss. They may fall through one of the many cracks in our legal system.

Another thought to keep in mind as you read through these cases is the *overlapping nature of all litigation*. You may scratch your head and say, "Didn't I just read about that?" At times it will seem like a case of Siamese lawsuits, all joined together at one claim or another. Rarely is a case based strictly on one issue. A wrongful discharge case may include charges of sexual harassment or discrimination. Libel or negligence in record keeping can be thrown in the pot to stir up the legal brew.

You will, in fact, see some landmark cases pop up in several areas. Don't look at it as redundant. Look at it as comprehensive. When you and your lawyer discuss your particular situation, he or she will want to have any ammunition you can provide. Pick a cliché: You want to get all your cards on the table. You don't want to put all your eggs in one basket. You want to touch all the potential litigation bases. You want the big picture.

Okay, forget the clichés. Here's what you really want: The best analysis of whether or not you have a case, and the best chance to win in court if you do. That's why knowing all the links between different aspects of different cases, no matter how repetitive, is important.

So when you come to a case that seems to have absolutely nothing to do with your situation, don't turn up your nose and turn the page. It could have a lot to do with you, as a precedent setter, as an idea generator, as a strategy instigator, as an "add-on" to bulk up your basic case.

## Legal winds of change

Another caveat: As you read about the wide-ranging changes in employee rights, you'll notice years are used to label landmark cases and important legislation. Dates are a little misleading. Changes are occurring as we write this book, and as you read it.

Some state court or local judge or federal jury somewhere in this country is right now making a decision that will have an impact on employee rights. That means you have to be as fluid as the law. Nothing is final. Use the information you pick up here as a format for analyzing and assessing, not a preset program in which to plug your own variables in order to have a lawsuit pop out.

To give you an idea of just how fast such changes can occur, a major pro-employer decision was handed down while this text was being printed. It involved a case you'll see in chapter 1 and basically puts a monetary cap on damage awards likely to be awarded to dismissed workers.

Legally, it said that an employee fired without due cause may only sue on the basis of breach of an express or implied contract. Practically, it would seem to put a damper on open-ended jury awards for punitive and emotional damages under tort law, which covers wrongful acts other than breach of contract.

That universality of change is another reason for the liberal use of words like "may, can, should, might." Almost nothing in the "rules" is cast in stone, except maybe for the Ten Commandments. And as you recall, even they were shattered.

Finally, you may have missed the traditional disclaimer in the front of this book. Don't view what you read here as legal advice. You've seen all the caveats already, and you'll read in chapter 13 just how important it is to work with a lawyer who specializes in this area. That's where your actual legal counsel must come from— a legal counsel.

We have included a number of legal trappings in the text. You'll see many important cases referred to by the names of the parties involved. (Not all cases are cited.) Look in the index for the citations, if you want to do further research or direct your lawyer along appropriate lines of inquiry. There are also charts, checklists, Equal Employment Opportunity Commission (EEOC) guidelines, and such that should give you a better handle on exactly what you'll be facing in the event you do decide to launch an employee lawsuit. Plus, you'll find a whole bunch of Employee Rights Alerts sprinkled in the text, giving you added direction and advice, as well as key phrases and sentences italicized for emphasis.

One final thought on the practical aspects of the book. You'll find numerous references to "we" (hurrah, that's us employees) and "they" (boo, hiss, that's the employer contingent). Permit us the exaggeration of coloring the relationship strictly black and white. In reality, it's nowhere near so clear. But because the two go together like soup and sandwich, you'll see a lot of info on *employer* defenses and strategies, so you'll know what to expect from the "other side."

## The more things change, the more they remain the same

To get your current employee rights adrenalin flowing, take a gander at the list of "rights" reportedly from a time long past. Despite all the negative feelings that you may have about your job, it could be worse. If you had been an office worker back in the 1850s, you might have been subject to some of these management tactics:

- *Reduced office hours*—clerical staff need *only* be present from 7:00 A.M. to 6:00 P.M.
- *Dress rules*—clothing of a *sober* nature. No bright colors. Only hose in good repair to be worn. No overshoes or top coats in office; but in harsh weather hats and scarves were allowed.
- *Religious "accommodations"*—daily prayers in the main office. No exceptions.
- *Teamwork*—each member of the staff was advised to bring four pounds of coal to work every day during cold weather to fuel the stove so generously provided by the company. Junior members of the firm were responsible for the elbow grease to keep the office clean.
- *"Break" rules*—no leaving the room without permission. The bathroom was the garden below the second gate. To be kept "clean" by those who used it. Work was not to cease during the half-hour lunch "break."
- *Socializing*—no talking during working hours. No tobacco, wine, or spirits anytime, although management recognized the "human weakness" associated with them.
- *Resources*—staff provided their own writing instruments, although a sharpener was available on request.

You think you have it bad? Well, maybe you do. Read on.

# THE EMPLOYEE STRIKES BACK!

# CHAPTER 1

# Changes in the Workplace: A Little Background Music

Before we get into the first act of employee rights, let's just set the stage with some legalistic ground rules. We know we promised to go light on the legalities, so we'll be brief here. But you should know a little bit about . . .

. . . Our judicial system and the local, state, and federal courts that make it up. Your lawyer will point you in the right direction when you start considering the filing of motions and charges. Basically, though, the usual progression is from a jury trial in front of your peers to an appeals court in front of judges to a state supreme court, which may very well throw the ball back into the initial court's court and tell them to take another whack at it. In general, employees do best in front of sympathetic juries—who hand out generous awards—and worst in front of appeals judges—who hew more closely to the letter of the law.

. . . The differences between state and federal, in terms of constitutional, statutory (laws or regulations), and judicial (precedents set in court) demands. Usually federal laws are more general in scope and supersede those of the states, except when the state regs are tougher. For example, the federal Age Discrimination in Employment Act (ADEA) kicks in at forty years old on the national scene, while some states have prohibitions against age discrimination that start at younger ages.

The Supreme Court underlined that difference in its landmark pregnancy entitlement case you'll see in chapter 4. One part of the decision said that Title VII and the Pregnancy Discrimination Act (PDA) do not preclude states from enacting laws consistent with, but beyond, federal statutes.

. . . And speaking of Title VII and PDA, your "legal" knowledge bank should receive constant deposits from the Glossary, where employee rights terms and abbreviations are defined. For example, *wrongful discharge* gets tossed around throughout the book. Basically, that's when an employer fires an employee in violation of some law, precedent, or acknowledged right. *Just cause* fits in right behind wrongful discharge. If an employer indicates he will only dump you based on just cause, then he better have a darn good reason for the termination. Or how about *public policy* or *in the public's best interest.* That refers to protecting the public at large from getting stiffed. So it's in the public's best interest if an employee blows the whistle on shoddy products or illegal corporate tactics. Several courts define public policy more extensively for you in chapter 2.

. . . There'll be a lot of initials throughout the book, and references to laws like those you'll see in figure 1 a little further along in this chapter. The most important initials for you and your rights are EEOC, as in Equal Employment Opportunity Commission. That's usually the first place to go to have your wrongs righted. That's also why we devote an entire chapter (12) to the "Agency."

. . . The last concept you should know about is the first: *Employment-at-will,* E-A-W—the employer-cherished traditional concept of employment-at-will which, in twenty-five words or less, states that either the employer or the employee can end the employment relationship at any time or for any reason—or for no reason at all. (Twenty-four words—made it!)

That's a little simplistic. Here's some complexity. Some say the roots of E-A-W go all the way back to the master/servant relationship in Roman times. It first saw the light of day in an American court in Tennessee in the case of *Payne* v. *Western & Atlantic R.R.* (1884).

That state court volunteered that employers could dismiss their employees at will, for good cause, no cause, or even a morally wrong cause, without being guilty of a legal transgression.

Such a decision followed rather smoothly from the so-called Wood rule, an allegedly authoritative treatise written in 1887 by Horace Gray Wood on the American master/servant relationship. That "rule" suggested that unless an individual was hired for a specific period, either party could terminate the relationship.

Modern legal experts have slam-danced all over the "cases" Wood used to support his rule. But American lawyers and judges of the period felt no such compunction and embraced the concept with open arms. Of course, what did they know about being employees anyway?

The Supreme Court gave E-A-W its stamp of approval in an oft-cited case (*Adair* v. *United States*) when it declared that the right of the employee to quit the service of an employer, for whatever reason, is the same as the right of an employer, for whatever reason, to dispense with the services of an employee. (*Adair* v. *United States,* 208 U.S. 161, 175, 1908)

Some chinks in the E-A-W armor were carved out by exceptions over the years resulting from federal union-labor legislation and the equal employment opportunity (EEO) movement to protect minorities and the disadvantaged. But the real bombardment didn't get started until the 1980s. That's when *public policy and express/implied contracts* threw a King Kong–sized monkey wrench into the entire employer/employee relationship. At that point, we were already way behind the rest of the world in the field of employee rights.

## Rights 'round the globe

Americans may be in the forefront of many revolutions, but employee rights is not necessarily one of them. Organizations and countries around the globe have been riding on this bandwagon for years.

- France, 1928. Protective statute reflecting doctrine called "abuse of rights." Prohibits termination for illness, industrial injury, *pregnancy*, political beliefs, personal dislikes.
- Japan, 1947. Labor standards law demands good cause for firing. Requires employers and unions to develop work rules that define cause for discipline and discharge.
- West Germany, 1951. A comprehensive statute prohibits *socially unwarranted dismissals*.
- Canada, 1978. Statute protects workers with one year of service

from unjust dismissal and mandates government supervised conciliation.

## Back in the U.S. of A.

But we are slowly but surely catching up, with a bushel of important legislation. And while it probably won't do any good to memorize those laws per se, you should know something about the major ones that have an impact on the employment scene (and which you will be reading about in the rest of this book). For a brief overview, see figure 1.

It will also do you some good to study the steps that you'll need

### Figure 1. Laws that Impact Employment-at-Will

■ The Labor-Management Relations Act and National Labor Relations Act prohibit discharge on account of an employee's union membership, organizational activities, or other protected concerted activities.

■ The federal Occupational Safety and Health Act prohibits discharge on account of an employee's refusal to work in an unsafe workplace or for otherwise exercising rights under the act related to an employer's compliance with health and safety standards.

■ The Fair Labor Standards Act prohibits discharge for exercising rights under the act's wage and hour standards.

■ The Employee Retirement Income Security Act (ERISA) prohibits discharge for exercising rights covered by the act, such as preventing an employee from collecting benefits under a plan covered by the act.

■ The Consumer Credit Protection Act prohibits discharge on account of a wage garnishment related to a single instance of indebtedness.

■ A federal law, Protection of Jurors' Employment, prohibits the discharge of any "permanent employee" for serving on a federal jury.

■ Title VII of the Civil Rights Act of 1964 prohibits discharge based on race, sex, color, religion, or national origin.

■ The Age Discrimination in Employment Act (ADEA) prohibits the discharge of an employee forty years of age and over where the dismissal is age-based.

- The Pregnancy Discrimination Act prohibits discharge because of pregnancy, childbirth, or related medical conditions.
- The Vocational Rehabilitation Act prohibits employers who are federally funded or who contract with the federal government from discriminating in employment against qualified handicapped persons on the basis of their handicap.
- The Vietnam Veteran's Readjustment Assistance Act prohibits an employer from refusing to reemploy an inducted person who satisfactorily completes his or her military service and who remains qualified to perform the job. This act further prohibits an employer from discharging a reemployed veteran within one year after reemployment without good cause.
- The Energy Reorganization Act prohibits discharge for assisting or participating in any proceeding to enforce the act or the Atomic Energy Act of 1954.
- The Clean Air Act and the Water Pollution Control Act prohibit discharge for exercising rights with respect to an employer's compliance with those acts.
- The Bankruptcy Reform Act prohibits discharge of an employee solely because the individual filed for bankruptcy.

to know to deal with the major legal body that enforces many of those laws. That entity is the Equal Employment Opportunity Commission, often referred to as the Agency, as well as a plethora of unmentionable monikers by employers targeted for action. You'll find the entire chapter 12, as well as much of the appendix, deals with this sometimes infamous agency.

Many employee lawsuits originate after a visit to your friendly neighborhood EEOC office. All these initials, EEO and EEOC, will figure heavily throughout the book, in the procedural steps you'll need to take and the cases you'll need to be familiar with. You should also keep in mind the difference between *common law* as interpreted, expanded, and changed by the judiciary, and *statutory law* as enacted by legislation and enforced by the EEOC.

## States add to the confusion

Being up on your federal legalities is one thing, but the world of state legal systems is a universe unto itself.

One of the biggest variables in the world of employment law exists in the states, specifically the fifty different ones (plus the good old

District of Columbia). Different courts in different jurisdictions with different traditions can (and have) come up with wildly different conclusions to very similar cases. Some states are laying out the red carpet for employee rights; others are circling the wagons.

Take California, for example. Its state codes and regulations in many cases go way beyond federal and other states' statutes. Landmark U.S. Supreme Court decisions on drug testing, maternity leave, and public policy exceptions to E-A-W have originated in the home state of Disneyland.

California state codes, for example, forbid discrimination on the basis of the usual suspects (race, sex, color). But they go further. Protection against marital status discrimination extends to *whom* an employee marries, demands accommodation efforts when *coemployees* marry, and may be interpreted to cover marriages to *competitors*.

California employers also can't discriminate against their workers who:

- File claims or testify before labor commissions
- Suffer a work-related injury or file worker's compensation
- Appear as a witness or serve on a jury
- Refuse to submit to a polygraph
- Participate in an alcohol rehabilitation program
- Engage in political activities or complain about safety conditions at work

Then there are the municipal ordinances. Los Angeles and San Francisco, to name two, prohibit discrimination or discharge on the basis of sexual preference or orientation.

The California Supreme Court was also the scene of a case in which one of the basic questions was whether it is fair that an employee has the freedom to quit at any time, but the employer doesn't have the same freedom to discharge. The case was seen by some as a backlash against E-A-W awards that seem excessive or unfair, and the results—capping awards—will likely make it harder—not easier—to sue and win big damages in California. (*Foley* v. *Interactive Data Corp.*, 174 Cal. App. 3d 282, 1985)

There are numerous other examples of how the legal roller coaster careens from state to state.

In Pennsylvania, a computer operator was dismissed for persistent lateness. He brought in a note from his shrink claiming that he suffered from a "neurotic compulsion for lateness." Nice try, but no cigar. It's not a handicap recognized by law, doesn't limit a major life activity, or require accommodation so he can earn a living.

Back in California again, a UPS driver was fired for insubordination. He refused to honk his horn to alert deliverees to his deliveries, as required by company policy. Stuff that firing, horned in a California court: State law prohibits motorists from honking for anything but safety reasons. Refusal to honk was protected by "concerted activity" part of federal law. Public policy, you know. Or you will know, by the next chapter. (*Garcia* v. *N.L.R.B.*, No. 85-7262, 9th Cir., 1986)

Even within states, the legislative/judicial relationship sometimes muddies legal waters and throws consistency to the winds. One state court threw out a sex/age discrimination claim because other statutory remedies were available for such allegations. Another allowed state and federal claims to be combined. And still another deferred authority to a state legislature.

The point is not that you know all the ins and outs of each state's leanings or grapplings with employee rights. Just be aware that one of the big variables in analyzing your own situation is the fact that different states have different traditions in handling employee litigation.

## Last word on a state "first"

Despite all the hoopla surrounding employee rights and wrongful discharge over the last decade, it wasn't until mid-1987 that the first state—Montana—passed a comprehensive statute protecting at-will employees from wrongful discharge.

You have two good reasons for reviewing how Montana has tackled this problem. One, your state may follow its lead. And two, you may be able to use certain aspects of its regulations to bulwark your own contentions.

In brief, the Montana law covers all employees in the state and prohibits employers from discharging workers without good cause. The bases for judging whether a discharge is wrongful are:

- There are no job-related grounds for dismissal, such as failure to perform satisfactorily, disruption of operations, or other legitimate business reasons.
- Retaliation for the employee's refusal to violate a public policy.

- Retaliation for employee reporting a violation of public policy.
- Employer violating the express provisions of its own written personnel policy.

An employee may sue within one year for lost wages, fringe benefits covering a period of four years after date of discharge, plus interest and punitive damages if there is convincing evidence that the employer engaged in fraud or acted maliciously in discharging the employee.

Employees must first, however, exhaust internal procedures for appealing the discharge. And the Montana statute exempts claims that are subject to another state or federal law, employees covered by a written collective bargaining agreement, and those with written employment contracts with specific terms.

## Out with the old, in with the lawsuit

So if employment-at-will is crumbling under the weight of employee rights, where's the beef coming from? Here are the most familiar "exceptions" on which suits are based.

### #1 Public policy

The theory behind this exception is that if some action isn't in the public's best interest, it shouldn't be condoned. So an employer should not be able to use the powers of discipline and discharge to force an employee to, for example, violate the law. Public policy grounds have been used to win damages for employees who were fired because they refused their employers' orders to commit perjury and because they cooperated in criminal investigations of their companies. In many cases, this exception has been expanded to protect whistle-blowers who report improper activity (criminal actions, falsifying reports) and employees who seek to take advantage of legally granted rights, such as worker's compensation.

Because of the raft of legislation and negative publicity that has been generated by public policy cases, this is probably the toughest E-A-W exception to prove these days, mainly because employers are so careful not to abuse it. It follows that landmark cases in this area are generally older. Here are a couple.

- A union business agent back in 1959 refused to make false

statements before a grand jury. Fired, he won his case even though E-A-W was still going strong then, because public policy proved stronger. (*Petermann* v. *International Brotherhood of Teamsters,* 134 Cal. App. 2d 184, 344 P.2d 25, 1959)

- A woman in 1975 felt it was her duty to serve on a jury, but her manager told her to avoid it. She didn't. He fired her. She sued and won damages. (*Nees* v. *Hocks,* 272 Ore. 210, 536 P.2d 512, 1975)

- An oil company employee asserted he was being forced to fix prices at certain levels with his dealers in 1980. After getting two strikes against him in trial and appellate courts, the California Supreme Court put him back in the game with this assertion of public policy:

  ". . . the employer's authority . . . does not include the right to demand that the employee commit a criminal act to further its interest. . . . an employer may not coerce compliance with such unlawful directions by discharging an employee who refuses to follow such an order." (*Tameny* v. *Atlantic Richfield Co.,* 27 Cal. 3d 167, 1980)

- Other public policy exceptions to E-A-W have involved employees who (a) refused to commit perjury; (b) refused to illegally alter equipment; (c) reported violations of state laws; (d) were terminated when pension vesting was imminent.

That last one involved another well-known case. A model employee garnered every pay raise and promotion he was ever eligible for in his thirteen-year-career with a department store chain. His pension was due to be vested after fifteen years. He was fired, with no reason given, after unlucky year number thirteen.

When pushed to the courtroom wall, the employer didn't even deny that it fired him because of the pension issue. It just said it could fire him at any time. The ruling: An employer can't promise a pension, allow an employee to toil in its vineyards for thirteen years, and then toss him out like a bottle of bad vinegar. (*Savodnik* v. *Korvette's, Inc.,* 488 F. Supp. 822, E.D.N.Y., 1980)

This case also underlined the importance of longevity, which you'll see pop up over and over. It's become axiomatic that the longer you've toiled in that vineyard, the more sympathetic a jury is likely to be toward you.

If you think you may have a public policy case, ask yourself two questions. Did the discharge violate a well-established law or public policy? Is there any other remedy besides a lawsuit that is already in place to protect your interests, or that of "society"? Then read chapter 2.

## #2 Employment contracts—express and implied

Typically, you'd point to a provision in a policy manual or an employee handbook and claim that it amounted to a binding promise of continued employment. Where discipline is concerned, an ex-employee often claims that he or she was not given the benefit of the full disciplinary and termination process described in company policies.

The main targets of litigation in the implied contract area are company publications, like policy manuals, employee handbooks, and application forms. You know it. And so do employers. You should be alert to their defenses, which may cause you to look elsewhere for cracks in their armor. Here are some typical defenses you may run into.

- A statement in an application or employee handbook that expressly states that you are an at-will employee, such as "we hope for a mutually satisfactory relationship between you and this company; but both parties are free to terminate the relationship at any time for any reason or for no reason at all." Some employers have become so sensitive to the at-will uproar that they've created statements so blatantly proemployer that they've resurrected memories of the yellow dog contracts of the 1920s. Named to conjure up images of a cowardly animal cowering in front of a domineering master, yellow dog contracts required job applicants to steer clear of all union inclinations or activities. They were outlawed in the thirties.
- Any clause that "reserves the right" for the employer to lay off or terminate at its discretion, or to deviate from standard policy. (Note: If your employer reserved that right to deviate, and did in your case, check to see if he's acted similarly with anyone else. If not, you might have some ammunition for a discrimination charge, or at least some evidence of unfair treatment or bad faith.)
- A statement in a benefits section of your employee handbook that "nothing in this agreement gives the employee any right to

continued employment, nor does anything restrict the right of the employer to discharge at any time for any reason."

- Any discipline or discharge clause that contains the phrase "as warranted by individual circumstances."
- A disclaimer in the employee handbook to the effect that "We do not intend to enter into a contract on the basis of this publication." (Note: Position counts in disclaimers like this. If they're buried in the text or not in a prominent place, at the beginning of the manual, in conspicuous print, you may be able to discount the force of the disclaimer.)

Then there are the statements, claims, phrases, procedures to look for that are on your side in proving a contract. Here are a few.

- A clause that proffers "permanent employment" status on a probationary employee who satisfactorily completes his or her probation, especially when it makes the employee eligible for additional benefits.
- It's not only written documents and verbal promises that may form the basis of a legally enforceable commitment to you. Standard personnel practices may be interpreted as requiring just cause for discharge.

Two landmark contract cases were decided in 1980, a real bellwether year for employee rights litigation.

In one, a discharged employee claimed that a supervisor's manual put out by his employer created an express contractual obligation when it stated that "good cause" was required for a discharge. Good or just cause is a common standard often mixed into wrongful discharge suits. If you can prove the concept should have been applied to your case—and wasn't—you're in fat city. (*Touissant* v. *Blue Cross/ Blue Shield*, 408 Mich. 579, 292 N.W. 2d 880, 1980)

In the other, an eighteen-year veteran employee was summarily dismissed and not granted a hearing, as was required by written company policy. He won his case too. (*Cleary* v. *American Airlines*, 111 Cal. App. 3d 443, 168 Cal. Rptr. 722, 1980)

### #3 Undue stress and outrageous behavior

The employer's *outrageous behavior* causes *undue emotional distress* for the employee. Another growing exception to employment-at-will is that an employer cannot intentionally subject an employee to undue emotional stress. Many suits of this kind claim the employer inflicted the distress trying to force the employee to resign. Constructive discharge often falls in this category, as does retaliation.

A precedent-setting case here involved a restaurant manager who was trying to solve a case of theft, apparently committed by an employee. The manager informed his waitresses that they would be fired, one by one in alphabetical order, until someone confessed. A waitress whose name began with *A* was fired, filed suit, and won. The basis of this judgment was the employer's "extreme and outrageous conduct." (*Agis* v. *Howard Johnson Co.*, 355 N.E. 2d 315, 1976)

The courts generally reserve their damage awards for acts that, in the words of one decision, "go beyond all possible bounds of decency." Still, some employers manage to reach that extreme.

For example, a veteran of twenty-eight years with a Pennsylvania steel company was fired after he was caught stealing four paint brushes. That was outrageous enough to justify a damage award to the employee, said a federal judge. The employee previously had a spotless record, and other employees had been given lighter penalties for similar offenses. Plus, this employee was one month short of qualifying for a major increase in his pension benefits. Did someone cry "public policy"?

A famous retaliation case involved a woman who went to night school to earn a teacher's certificate and worked the graveyard shift at a rubber company. When she applied for a higher paying job, the foreman told her she'd have to be "nice" to him.

She told him to go scratch, and he sharpened his claws at her expense, giving her the worst assignments, forcing her to do menial jobs, ridiculing her at every turn, and finally firing her at 2:00 A.M. one morning. A court agreed with her charges of retaliation. (*Monge* v. *Beebe Rubber Co.*, 114 N.H. 130, 316 A.2d 549, 1974)

## #4 Broken promises

Often referred to in legal jargon as *promissory estoppel*, the typical case is that of an employee who gives up a good job and/or accepts a transfer on the basis of an employer promise, only to be eventually fired from the new position. This type of case requires that the employee suffer some detriment because he or she relied on the promise.

⸢e⸣ in this area involved a publishing employee who ⸢sought⸣ greener pastures by a competitor. In his new com- ⸢pany's b⸣ook, it said employees would be discharged for just and ⸢good c⸣ause only, and only after every step was taken to salvage ⸢or rehab⸣ilitate the employee.

⸢In f⸣act, when this manager wanted to axe one of his underlings, ⸢he⸣ was told to go by the book—the employee handbook. He later ⸢c⸣laimed he was not only convinced by assurances that the book would be followed, but he turned down other employment offers too.

When he himself got the boot years later, the court found in his favor because he relied on oral promises and the written handbook, which added up to an implied contract. (*Weiner* v. *McGraw-Hill, Inc.*, 57 N.Y. 2d. 458, 443 N.E. 2d 441, 1982)

A number of "promising" phrases have become infamous in legal circles as the basis for employee lawsuits. Here are just a few which, if you've heard them aimed in your direction, should be filed away in your suit bank.

- "Nobody gets fired around here without a good cause."
- "You'll have a job here as long as you exhibit good behavior."
- "You won't be fired if you just do your job."
- "You'll be here for your career as long as you don't screw up."
- "You'll be with this company as long as you do your job."
- "Don't worry, this is a job in which you can stay and grow."

## #5 *Good faith and fair dealing*

A requirement of good faith and fair dealing in executing a contract, in this case an employment contract, is becoming more and more common. Usually this exception to E-A-W is sung in concert with other claims, like promissory estoppel.

Words, both written and verbal, are important aspects of developing your assertion that you were not the subject of a good faith deal. For example, just how specific did your employer make its intentions known in, say, the performance appraisal system? Was the whole evaluation a good faith process?

Perhaps the most well-known performance appraisal case actually turned on words that were not said. A Michigan worker was called on the carpet during a performance appraisal and told to shape up. But there was no mention of shipping out. That was a key management mistake because when the worker was forced to walk the unemployment plank, he instituted a traditional negligence suit and sought recovery on a state wrongful discharge claim, as well as a federal age discrimination claim.

The court threw out the age claim, and assessed 83 percent of the blame for the dismissal on the employee himself. However, based on the failure of the appraiser to tell this twenty-three-year veteran he would be canned if he didn't remedy his job deficiencies, the company had to shoulder 17 percent of the blame. That translated to over $60,000 in damages awarded to the worker. (*Chamberlain* v. *Bissell, Inc.*, 547 F. Supp. 1067, 30 F.E.P. 347, W.D., 1982)

A landmark age discrimination case combined both contracts and the good faith and fair dealing concept. Three executives who had long careers with a department store chain were ignominiously discharged. They claimed ADEA (Age Discrimination in Employment Act) violations, breach of contract, and breach of implied covenant of good faith and fair dealing. Their reward: about $2.3 million. (*Cancellier* v. *Federated Department Stores*, 672 F.2d 1312, 9th Cir. 1982, cert. denied 103 Sup. Ct. 131, 1983)

Past history and future expectations entered into two other important "bad faith" cases. In the first, a twenty-five-year employee was singing happy tunes when he learned his company had made a big cash register sale in his sales territory. His contract called for him to get a piece of the action, to the tune of about $100 grand.

The only action he got was a swift boot out the door shortly before he was due to collect his commission. Ring up this one for the employee, said a Massachusetts court. (*Fortune* v. *National Cash Register Co.*, 373 Mass. 96, 364 N.E. 2d 1251, Mass. Sup. Jud. Ct., 1977)

In the second, a candy firm employee saw his sweet thirty-two-year career melt in front of his eyes with a pink slip. Given his long-term employment and solid history of merit increases and promotions, he figured he had an implied contract to require good faith for discharge. A court thought he figured right. (*Pugh* v. *See's Candies*, 116 Cal. App. 3d 311, 171 Cal. Rptr. 917, 1981)

## Stranger than true

Now you've seen a handful of important cases that affect those general employee rights. Before you go on to the specifics, consider these, ah, unusual cases. Off-beat cases have two characteristics.

They make headlines. They don't set precedents. But they do make interesting reading, and you'll get an idea of just how litigious our society really is. Plus you'll be the hit of the cocktail party with your interesting bons mots to complement the hors d'oeuvres. But don't count on these cases contributing to yours.

Example: A fast-working left-handed check-out girl was asked to become a switch-hitter when computerized scanners invaded her supermarket. A battle raged. She was forced to sign an agreement to check out right-handed. But she continued to work from the port side. A county circuit court jury in Illinois, consisting of all right-handers, handed her over $100,000 for her employer's left-handed discrimination. Did someone say appeal?

Example: Retaliation by *employers* is often an important component of an *employee* rights case. But even if your sympathies lie with the underdog worker, some horror stories contain a large measure of role reversal.

Seems an executive needed a secretary and hired a competent-looking female with a decent résumé and an ability to type. An alleged ability, as it turned out. After a two-week business trip, the boss returned to find *nada* was accomplished by his new hiree. On top of that, she refused to type.

Fired, she cried sexual harassment. That charge was dropped when it was discovered that she had previously lodged similar charges against—her father and brother.

At that point her retaliation shifted into high gear. The campaign included crank calls with a high-tech touch. She sicced an automatic dialing device on her former employer that inundated him with as many as twelve hundred calls a day.

Then, eschewing technology, she hired a cab, told the driver the ex-employer would pay if he drove her to his house in the suburbs, and then proceeded to strip naked in his front yard.

She also charged the harried former boss with rape (he was in a meeting with several people at the time she alleged that it had occurred). When that didn't fly, she then turned on the cop investigating the case and accused him of taking similar liberties with her. He was suspended until the charges were proved false. Want to cop a plea?

# CHAPTER 2

# The Public Be Damned, and You Be Fired

I t was the wide-ranging concept of serving the public's best interests that served as an early generator for the impetus to alter
employment-at-will. The courts were trying to protect "whistle-
blowers," workers who reported company misdeeds and were often
made to suffer for it, as well as employees fired for refusing to break
the law or for trying to take advantage of privileges to which they
were legally entitled. Public policy eventually opened the umbrella
of legal protection to other areas of employee rights.

Being one of the oldest and strongest of all employee rights claims,
public policy has also become one of the rarest. It's simple. Forget
morality. Think publicity. There has been such a public outcry on
public policy cases that it's almost impossible anymore to catch employers with their public policy pants down.

But if you do, and you suffer because of it, boy do you have a
case.

Back in the halcyon days of E-A-W as king of the workplace,
managers clung to the "my way or the highway" attitude. If an
employee crossed them, it was time for the employee to drive away.
Company loyalty superseded any public concerns. But a series of
landmark cases trashed many of those notions.

In general the public policy exception to E-A-W has determined that you can't be fired

- While whistle-blowing, reporting safety hazards, or reporting violations of the law
- For exercising a legal right, such as filing a worker's compensation claim
- When meeting a legal obligation, such as serving on a jury or giving a court-requested deposition
- For refusing to take part in an illegal act, such as altering test results mandated by law
- As a result of a discriminatory motive in a situation covered by law, such as ERISA, in circumstances where an imminent bonus or pension vesting is the trigger for the firing

## Getting up to speed on federal laws

The best way to explain public policy is to explain the cases that have succeeded with that concept as their basis. But first a quick brushup on some of the actual laws that apply, which you saw enumerated in figure 1 in the last chapter.

For one, you've got a federal statute that protects workers when they miss work for required jury duty: "No person shall discharge, threaten to discharge or intimidate any permanent employee by reason of such employee's jury service, or attendance or scheduled attendance in connection with such service, in any court of the United States."

Three sanctions ride along with this statute. They are:

- Liability for damage for loss of wages or benefits suffered by employees
- Injunctions against violations and order for further relief, including reinstatement
- Civil penalties, plus appointment of counsel and award of attorney's fees under certain circumstances

Then there is the Occupational Safety and Health Act, enacted in 1970 to assure safe and healthful workplace conditions, which includes a provision protecting employees who have filed complaints under the act from retaliatory action by employers. It is that act which has served as the underpinning to many a public policy case, especially involving whistle-blowers.

Example: Four carpenters complained about job safety. When their employer was slow in responding, they nailed their boss with a report to the Occupational Safety and Health Administration (OSHA). The company hammered back with a discharge notice two days later. The court: Give them back pay, never violate the act's nonretaliation requirement again, post notices about employee rights, remove dismissal notices from carpenters' records, and don't hinder them from finding new jobs. (*Donovan* v. *Freeway Construction Co.*, 551 F. Supp. 869, D.R.I., 1982)

Example: Several machinists complained to OSHA about poor ventilation when they were welding. Company response: Intense investigation into who had blown the whistle on the company. Then suspension of air-conditioning in one section of the facility. Then revocation of phone privileges. Finally, a termination notice for the machinists based on their returning late from lunch—once. The court: Give them back pay with interest, with no reduction for unemployment compensation collected, avoid future violations, and cleanse their employment records of the adverse references to termination.

Another federal statute that enters the whistle-blower fray is the Energy Reorganization Act. While this act does provide protection against retaliation and discipline, it applies only to safety matters in nuclear power plants and hospitals that handle radioactive matter. Several other federal statutes, including the Toxic Substance Act, Clean Air Act, and Water Pollution Control Act, contain prohibitions against retaliation to whistle-blowers.

In fact, both houses of Congress introduced bills in 1988 for whistle-blowers' protection. The Uniform Health and Safety Whistle-Blowers Protection Act of 1988, H.R. 4305, was introduced in the House of Representatives on March 30, 1988. The bill prohibits discharge or other retaliatory action against private sector employees who disclose or demonstrate an intent to disclose employer activity that the employee reasonably believes is a violation of federal law, creating a danger to the health and safety of employees or the public. The discrimination prohibition also applies to refusing to participate in such an activity or assisting in a proceeding with respect to such an activity. The bill was referred to the Committee on Education and Labor.

The Senate version of the bill, S. 2095, was introduced on February 25, 1988. The Senate bill would also create uniform protection and administrative procedures for whistle-blower complaints, centralizing enforcement in the Labor Department.

The icing on the cake may very well be the False Claims Act Amendment of 1986. It's basically a bounty bill, with rewards of a percentage of the government's "take" in successful cases. It makes whistle-blowing in public policy cases a lot more profitable for wronged employees.

## Figure 2. Specific State Whistle-Blower Law: Michigan

In 1981, Michigan adopted a whistle-blower protection act that specifically forbade retaliation against employees who reported wrongdoing or who agreed to cooperate with public agencies.

### Michigan Whistle-Blowers' Protection Act

Major provisions of the law include:

*M.C.L.A. 15.362:* An employer shall not discharge, threaten, or otherwise discriminate against an employee regarding the employee's compensation, terms, conditions, location, or privileges of employment because the employee, or a person acting on behalf of the employee, reports or is about to report, verbally or in writing, a violation or a suspected violation of a law or regulation or rule promulgated pursuant to a law of this state, a political subdivision of this state, or the United States to a public body, unless the employee knows that the report is false, or because an employee is requested by a public body to participate in an investigation, hearing, or inquiry held by that public body, or a court action.

*M.C.L.A. 15.363:*

■ A person who alleges a violation of this Act may bring a civil action for appropriate injunctive relief, or actual damages, or both within 90 days after the occurrence of the alleged violation of this Act.

■ An action commenced pursuant to subsection (1) may be brought in the circuit court for the county where the alleged violation occurred, the county where the complainant resides, or the county where the person against whom the civil complaint is filed resides or has its principle place of business.

■ As used in subsection (1), "damages" means damages for

injury or loss caused by each violation of this Act, including reasonable attorney fees.

■ An employee shall show by clear and convincing evidence that they or a person acting on their behalf was about to report, verbally or in writing, a violation or a suspected violation of a law of this state, a political subdivision of this state or in the United States, to a public body.

*M.C.L.A. 15.364:* A court, in rendering a judgment in an action brought pursuant to this act, shall order, as the court considers appropriate, reinstatement of the employee, the payment of back wages, full reinstatement of fringe benefits and seniority rights, actual damages, or any combination of these remedies. A court may also award the complainant all or a portion of the costs of litigation, including reasonable attorney fees, if the court determines that the award is appropriate.

## When state and federal laws collide

Generally, you'll find most public policy cases revolve around state decisions. A growing number of state courts are recognizing exceptions to E-A-W when a dismissal clearly flies in the face of a statutorily derived public policy. Some states even have specific whistle-blower laws, as you can see in figure 2, Specific State Whistle-Blower Act. Although state courts have produced a crazy quilt of renderings, one thing is clear: Legal authorities are very quick to pick up on public interest aspects as exceptions to employment-at-will.

That crazy quilt has been made crazier still by state/federal differences which have sometimes jumbled the public policy arena of employee rights even more.

Case in point: A patent attorney had become a pain in the neck with his complaints about job safety. Fired, he argued that the company had violated the public policy that supports health and safety on the job.

The company's view, as you might expect, differed. Yes, it said, both federal and state regulations applaud such policies. But here's the catch. The state's job safety law, adopted as a counterpart to federal OSHA, provides a specific means for employees to file complaints that allege unsafe practices. That law also protects those who make such complaints from retaliation, and in some circumstances even protects those who refuse to work in unsafe conditions. But it doesn't protect employees who fail to use established channels and instead establish themselves as common pains.

Hold on, said a state appeals court. It may do just that. The reason: differences between state and federal laws. The former *does* give employees the right to file suit, *in addition to* using established complaint avenues. The latter doesn't. So the court said the plaintiff did have a right to pursue his lawsuit (not that he would win it, just that he had a public policy basis to sue). (*Hentzel* v. *Singer Co.*, 188 Cal. Rptr. 159, 138 Cal. App. 3d 290, 1982)

## Getting down and dirty with state public policy cases

Back in 1983, the Wisconsin Supreme Court acknowledged the existence of a public policy exception to employment-at-will for the first time. But it said the exception didn't apply in the wrongful discharge case under consideration.

A secretary contended that her dismissal went against the policy of state statutes that prohibited (*a*) injury in reputation, trade, business, or profession, and (*b*) the use of information to keep a person from working.

The court said that wrongful discharge is actionable when the termination clearly contravenes the public welfare and gravely violates paramount requirements of public interest. The public policy must be evidenced by a constitutional or statutory provision. Unfortunately for the secretary, it wasn't here. (*Brockmeyer* v. *Dun & Bradstreet*, 113 Wisc. 2d 561, 1 E.A.W.R. 1127, 1983)

The Illinois Supreme Court took a slightly different angle, but a similar bold step, in a landmark 1980 case. It attested to the existence of the E-A-W concept, but ruled exceptions should be made.

The public interest case that forced the issue involved a sixteen-year veteran employee who was fired for giving police information about the alleged criminal activities of a coworker.

Reasoned the court: Public policy is what is right and just and what affects the citizens of the state collectively. No policy is more basic than the enforcement of the criminal code. So this man shouldn't be penalized for helping out. The court ruled in favor of the fired worker. (*Palmateer* v. *International Harvester Co.*, 421 N.E. 2d 876, Ill., 1980)

# So you think you may have a public policy case

Here's a roundup of different types of public policy cases.

## Let's try "jury" cases first

In a case celebrated as the first landmark public policy exception case to employment-at-will, a union rep was "coached" in what answers he should give when he took the witness stand before a grand jury. He balked and was fired. The court: To uphold a firing under those circumstances would be to encourage criminal conduct and contaminate the honest administration of public affairs. (*Petermann* v. *International Brotherhood of Teamsters*, 174 Cal. App. 2d 184, 344 P.2d 25, 1959)

A secretary in Hawaii was fired and told to return immediately to the mainland. Her superior was afraid she would testify in a federal antitrust investigation that involved him. No can do, ruled the court. (*Parnar* v. *American Hotels, Inc.*, 652 P.2d 625, Ha., 1982)

An Oregon woman received her jury notice and told her boss she wanted to serve. He fired. She sued. The court said: If employees could be fired at-will for serving on juries, the system would be in considerable jeopardy. (*Nees* v. *Hocks*, Ore. 210, 536 P.2d 512, 1975)

You'd think with all the hoopla and the focus on the jury duty issue, no employer would get caught blocking the way to court today. But as recently as 1987, a U.S. District Court awarded a clerk back pay and attorney's fees because it found she had been fired for complying with a jury notice.

The story went this way. Clerk, on the job for about eighteen months, gets jury summons. What're you gonna do, says boss. Go, says clerk. You can't be here at work and there too, says boss. Good point. So on the days covered by the summons, she went to court. But she also missed other days of work during the same period which weren't covered by summons. She claimed family reasons for those absences. The court held that the clerk must prove that she would not have been fired except for her jury duty. She did. (*Johnson* v. *Appliance T.V. Center*, 2 Indiv. Empl. Rts. Rep. 481 M.D.S.C., 1987)

## How about some protected activity cases?

A California worker applied for membership in a union. His boss fired him for doing so. That was judged a direct violation of the right of concerted action guaranteed by the National Labor Relations Act. (*Glenn* v. *Clearnan's Golden Cock Inn*, 192 Cal. App. 2d 793, 13 Cal. App. 769, 1961)

A secretary in Oklahoma was about to type a letter to a prospective employee. The description of the job was remarkably like hers. The salary wasn't. She was upset and told her boss so. Ditto upper management. Then she took her complaint to her clerical colleagues. That was the last straw for the company, which fired her for disruptive behavior.

The National Labor Relations Board ruled her reinstated. Basis: There was no evidence she knew that the salary was confidential, she learned about it during the normal course of work, and her discussions with other workers were protected under the *concerted activity* umbrella.

■ *Employee Rights Alert:* You can't be fired for discussing salaries and wage rates, or for not abiding by a policy you knew nothing about, or for any labor law protected activity.

Several farm workers met with a lawyer to discuss an employment contract. They were fired. No good, said the court. The California Labor Code gives them the right to do so under freedom of association and designation of representatives of their own choosing. (*Montalvo* v. *Zamorra*, 7 Cal. App. 3d 69, 1970)

An injured thumb sent an employee to the hospital. The boss told the employee not to file a claim, and fired the worker when that demand was refused. The court: Can't do that, boss. (*Frampton* v. *Central Indiana Gas Co.*, 260 Ind. 249, 1973)

## How about a couple of specific law violations?

An x-ray technician was told by superiors to conduct a medical procedure he was not legally licensed to perform under state law. He refused, was dismissed, sued, and won. (*O'Sullivan* v. *Mallon*, 390 Atl. 2d 149, 1987)

A Michigan chemist refused to falsify certain pollution control samples. He was fired, sued, and won. (*Trombetta* v. *Detroit, Toledo & Ironton R.R.*, 81 Mich. App. 498, 265 N.W. 2d 385, Mich. App., 1978)

- *Employee Rights Alert:* In many states, the concept of public policy as an exception to E-A-W has expanded like crazy. Here are some other instances of winning causes in such cases:

  - An employee was fired for giving truthful testimony in federal court
  - A medical claims employee who refused to falsify patients' records was fired
  - A nursing supervisor who didn't obey an order to reduce staff overtime was let go
  - A long-time employee who tried to correct what he thought was misleading information sent to stockholders was told his services were no longer needed

But the best-known heroes in the public policy area are the whistle-blowers in the landmark cases that have fed the expansion of exceptions to E-A-W.

## Whistle(blow)ing in the wind

Federal whistle-blowers often become the subject of feature stories and get elevated to modern folk hero status. On the other hand, private industry whistle-blowers are often submarined, lost in the corporate shuffle, or surreptitiously blackballed for their acts.

Perhaps the highest profile case involved Karen Silkwood, the nuclear industry worker who charged her employer with flawed safety procedures. When she died in a car crash while the investigation was still going on, a public hue and cry ensued. Eventually her story was told on the big screen and a million dollar suit by her estate settled the charges that she and her home were contaminated by company negligence.

Two decades ago an Air Force analyst shot down a series of cost overruns at a huge defense contractor. He was castigated as a troublemaker and blacklisted. He had broken the norm of loyalty.

Another famous fired whistle-blower fought for thirteen years to be reinstated. When asked if it was all worth it, if he would have "whistled" if he could do it all over again, he said he'd rather become "a tap dancer or something." Another whistle-blower likened what he did to setting his own house on fire in public.

On the other hand, for many it's a question of conscience. Said one blower: I'll sleep like a baby now.

Aye, there's the rub—whether 'tis nobler to suffer in silence or to set up the potential for being (*a*) driven from your job, if not your entire profession, (*b*) forced to undergo financial setbacks and worries, (*c*) placed in isolation by former colleagues and friends, (*d*) saddled with debts, (*e*) branded as a traitor and discriminated against.

## Banking on public interest

A major case that reflected state-oriented whistle-blowing occurred over a decade ago in a West Virginia bank. A young loan officer discovered that the bank was overcharging people who prepaid installment loans. Such a practice was a direct violation of state consumer laws. So he reported it to his superiors and to outside examiners.

He was fired for the fuss, and found himself blacklisted as well, finally landing a job in a coal mine before finding another bank that would take him. When he finally got his case heard, the West Virginia Supreme Court sided with him and ruled he had suffered for blowing the whistle on an overtly illegal practice. (*Harless* v. *First National Bank in Fairmont*, 246 S.E. 2d 270, W.Va., 1978)

■ *Employee Rights Alert:* The bank employee had an ace in the form of a specific state law which had been breached. Regulations, statutes, and previous legal decisions always give you a much stronger hand than just a vague "public interest" claim.

Public health provided healthy grounds for another public policy case that fell under a state statute umbrella. A quality-control director in a frozen foods company held his tongue at first when he noticed certain vegetables were being replaced in certain products. But when he saw that meat was underweight in other frozen food dishes, he blew the whistle.

Hoping the company would investigate, he reported the practices. Instead they iced him by firing him. His lawsuit held up in court, because those practices were a violation of the state food and drug act. (*Sheets* v. *Teddy's Frozen Foods, Inc.*, 179 Conn. 471, 1980)

## Whistle-blowing in the states

To give you a taste of how different states approach the question of whistle-blowing, consider these. We've included only passages you should take special note of. The first segment of the Hawaii law is fairly standard for all states in this area.

*Hawaii:* Under the Whistleblowers' Protection Act, private and public employers can't discharge, threaten, or discriminate against an employee regarding compensation, terms, conditions, location, or privileges of employment because the employee reports (verbally or in writing) a violation or suspected violation of a local, state, or federal law or rule to a public body (or participates in an investigation by a public body), unless the employee knows that the report is false. . . . Employers must post notices to keep employees informed of their rights under this law. . . . The rights created by this law don't limit employees' common law rights relating to discharges in violation of public policy.

*New Hampshire:* The employee is protected only if he or she brings the allegation to the attention of a supervisor, allowing a reasonable opportunity to correct the violation, unless the employee has specific reason to believe that reporting such a violation to the employer won't correct the violation promptly. . . . An aggrieved employee who has first sought relief through any grievance procedure provided by the employer may obtain a hearing with the commissioner of labor, who may order reinstatement of the employee, payment of fringe benefits, restoration of seniority rights, and any appropriate injunctive relief. This law doesn't diminish any rights an employee has under a collective bargaining agreement or common law. No employer is required to compensate an employee for participation in an investigation or hearing. Employers must post a notice informing employees of their rights under this law.

*Connecticut:* Employees who knowingly make a false report aren't protected and can be dismissed. An aggrieved employee can bring a civil action in superior court for reinstatement, back pay, and lost benefits after exhausting administrative remedies. Suit must be filed within ninety days of the alleged discriminatory treatment or the final administrative action, whichever is later. The court can award prevailing employee costs and attorney's fees.

*California:* It's unlawful for an employer to make, adopt, or enforce any rule, regulation, or policy, or to retaliate against an employee for disclosing information to a government or law enforcement agency where the employee reasonably believes the information discloses a violation of state or federal law or regulation. *Exceptions:* Confidential relationship of lawyer-client or physician-patient, or trade secrets.

Review figure 3 to see how states generally stack up on this issue.

## Figure 3. Whistle-Blower Laws: State Protections Against Retaliation

The following states have statutes that affect whistle-blowing, safety, and retaliation.

| | |
|---|---|
| Arkansas | safety |
| Arizona | whistle-blower—public sector only |
| California | whistle-blower—public and private sectors |
| | safety |
| Colorado | whistle-blower—public |
| Connecticut | whistle-blower—public and private |
| | safety |
| | right-to-know law |
| Delaware | whistle-blower—public |
| | also under right-to-know law |
| Florida | whistle-blower—public |
| Hawaii | whistle-blower—public and private |
| | safety |
| Illinois | whistle-blower—public |
| Indiana | safety |
| Iowa | whistle-blower—public |
| | safety |
| Kansas | whistle-blower—public and covers anyone reporting abuse of an adult |
| | safety |
| Kentucky | whistle-blower—public |
| | safety |
| Louisiana | whistle-blower—public and private |
| Maine | whistle-blower—public and private |
| | safety |
| Maryland | whistle-blower—public |
| | safety |
| Massachusetts | right-to-know law |
| Michigan | whistle-blower—public and private |
| | safety |
| Minnesota | whistle-blower—covers only those required to report suspected child abuse |
| | safety |
| Missouri | whistle-blower—public |
| Montana | right-to-know law |
| Nebraska | whistle-blower—public and private |
| Nevada | safety |

| | |
|---|---|
| New Hampshire | whistle-blower—public and private |
| New Jersey | whistle-blower—public and private |
| | right-to-know law |
| New Mexico | safety |
| New York | whistle-blower—public and private |
| North Carolina | safety |
| Ohio | whistle-blower—public |
| Oregon | whistle-blower—public |
| | safety |
| Pennsylvania | whistle-blower—public |
| | right-to-know law |
| Rhode Island | whistle-blower—public and anyone who |
| | reports dumping of toxic waste |
| | safety |
| South Carolina | safety |
| Tennessee | safety |
| Texas | whistle-blower—public |
| | right-to-know law |
| Utah | whistle-blower—public |
| | safety |
| Vermont | safety |
| Virginia | safety |
| Washington | whistle-blower—public |
| | safety |
| Wisconsin | whistle-blower—public |

■ *Employee Rights Alert:* Many state whistle-blowing laws insist that the employee afford the employer a reasonable opportunity to correct a violation or condition before making a disclosure to a public body.

## Questions for a whistle-blowing case

If you think you may have been the object of whistle-blowing retaliation, here are a few questions to ask about your situation that will give you a better handle on it.

■ Was there any connection you can establish (timing, verbal or written) between your blowing the whistle and your being blown off the job?

■ Were any standard steps not followed in your dismissal, such as progressive discipline or probation?

- Were you given documenting evidence of the purported reason for firing, such as a string of prior performance appraisals or proof of rules breaking?
- Did anyone in management ever bring up your whistle-blowing activity, especially in a performance review or in a carrot-and-stick manner?
- When you originally complained, did you get a reasonable and professional (and written) response which jibed with company procedures?
- Were you the object of any retaliatory actions, such as silent treatment, verbal abuse, loss of perks, demotion, unwarranted discipline, etc.?
- Did the company attempt to stymie your efforts to use either regular grievance channels or a neutral appeal avenue when you didn't get satisfaction?
- Were your whistle-blowing activities conveyed to any future employers or in any way publicized to your detriment (e.g., leaked to fellow employees as the cause of job losses in your hometown)?
- Were you discharged while your claims or complaints were still pending?
- Does your company have a history of being a target of whistle-blowers, and were there other cases still being investigated when you were terminated or retaliated against?

## When public policy doesn't carry the day

A salesman uncovered a serious potential product defect. He squawked about it to management, which took the product off the market. The company also took the salesman off the job for making a nuisance of himself. Sounds like a pretty cut-and-dried case of public policy transgression, doesn't it? Maybe today. But as late as the mid-seventies, such a case produced a court-upheld firing based on the E-A-W theory. (*Geary* v. *U.S. Corp.*, 379 A.2d 174, 1974)

We can see you scratching your head and saying—"Hold on there, pal. What's the difference between this case and the fellow who gave the police info on an alleged crime? If it's in the public interest to report crimes, isn't it also in the public interest to keep unsafe products off the market?"

The answer to your second question is "yes." The answer to your first? Timing is everything. Back in 1974, the Pennsylvania Supreme Court labeled exceptions to E-A-W as excursions into uncharted territories. Today, those exceptions, especially public policy ones, have been well mapped out.

As strong as the public policy interest concept is, it has tasted defeat in court. Some states are less inclined than others to recognize "gray area" cases as exceptions to E-A-W. And when it's not abundantly clear that an employee's behavior was covered by a specific law, courts have been known to fall back on the technically correct.

For example, an accountant reported apparent discrepancies in his company's financial reports. He claimed he was observing the public standards of his profession. The court: No basis in law on which to base a public policy decision here.

Another employee accused his company of falsifying sales information, and various offices of misusing corporate funds. The court: Too vague to decide whether a law or government regulation had been violated.

■ *Employee Rights Alert:* If you go the public policy route, make sure you have a vehicle. Courts almost invariably require some statutory authority, like a federal or state regulation or law, to abandon E-A-W—not just a gut feeling or a hunch or circumstantial evidence that even Perry Mason or Matlock would have trouble crafting into a victory. Most courts will support the public policy claim only if clear evidence of a specific company transgression of expressed public policy is offered.

Example: Another number cruncher claimed he was fired for trying to keep an accurate set of books. He too contended he was trying to meet standards. But he cited the accuracy demanded by the Foreign Corrupt Practices Act. The court responded favorably to this accountant: If an employee is trying to obey the law, the company shouldn't stand in the way. (*Thompson* v. *St. Regis Paper Co.*, 53 U.S.L.W. 2059, Wash., 1984)

One employee tossed in public policy concerns as part of her sexual harassment case. When the judge heard the two combatants had actually been lovers for many years, he declared no public policy was at stake in breaking up the working relationship along with the personal one.

Even when an employer's conduct is found to be "extreme and outrageous," that doesn't automatically drag public policy in. In the well-known restaurant case mentioned earlier, in which a manager fired his waitresses in alphabetical order for suspected theft, the action itself was lambasted by the court, but its link to public policy was dismissed. Be assured, however, that particularly egregious treatment of employees in the discharge process will in many cases push courts to the limit of their authority in creating remedies.

## More losses for public policy claims

An employee claimed he was fired for failing to sign a false statement. His contention: Such a signing violated the principles of honesty in business relationships. The court: A worthy principle, to be sure, but too broad and general to serve as a public policy claim. (*Delaney* v. *Taco Time International, Inc.*, 670 P.2d 218, Ore. App., 1983)

In another court, nepotism didn't qualify for protection under the public mantle. The court: It may be wrong, but it's not illegal.

■ *Employee Rights Alert:* You can't build a case merely on a company practice that's somewhat objectionable. It's not always whether the company is right or wrong, but what legal boundaries it may have strayed over.

Another public policy loser was an Arizona mining employee who complained about job safety violations. Fired, he cited the National Labor Relations Act and the Mine Safety and Health Act and claimed he was dismissed in violation of those two established public policies.

A judge ruled his safety complaints had already been taken to the review commission of the Mine and Health Administration—and had been settled. So the worker switched tactics and complained that he had been denied the progressive discipline outlined in the employee handbook. He was thwarted again when a judge ruled a collective bargaining labor contract prevails over an employee handbook when their authorities conflict. That contract mentioned neither the discipline program nor the handbook. Since the employee had already taken advantage of the grievance procedure spelled out in the contract, his second suit caved in too. (*Olguin* v. *Inspiration Consolidated Copper Co.*, No. 83-2366. 53 U.S.L.W. 2139, D. Ariz., 1984)

■ *Employee Rights Alert:* Watch your technicalities. If you're required to follow certain procedures, whether federal law or bargained contract, go that route first. Otherwise your clout in court will collapse.

That necessity to know your legal options was emphasized in a midwestern case where an airline mechanic had reported safety violations to both management and the FAA. Fired, he sought relief under the whistle-blower umbrella. A court ruled that the Federal Aviation Act did not protect whistle-blowers, and no state laws governed air travel safety. (*Rachford* v. *Evergreen International Airlines*, 596 F. Supp. 384, N.D. Ill., 1984)

Public interest isn't always everything it's cracked up to be. For example, you might not consider it in your best interest, or that of your colleagues, to be stationed at the next desk over from a convicted murderer.

That's sort of how some federal employees in a Social Security Administration office felt about an individual who had knocked off the paramour of his girlfriend in a fit of jealous rage. He wanted his job back. His associates balked.

A federal court of appeals, which of course didn't have to go to work every day with this fellow, saw no public interest problem here. He worked only on the phone. He'd never threatened anyone in the workplace. And he wouldn't interfere with the efficiency of the business. So coworkers' subjective fears weren't enough to justify firing him. Private employees take heart. Remember this was a federal employer/employee case, and they play by a different set of rules in many instances than the rest of the employment world. (*Horner* v. *Hardy*, No. 87-3125, Fed. Cir. App., 1987)

One closing point. As we've emphasized before, almost all wrongful discharge cases, and in fact most employee rights cases, depend on more than one claim. Public policy is a common one to include on a case menu.

For example, the landmark *Monge* case which you'll read about in chapter 4 wasn't just a sexual harassment suit. The plaintiff also claimed that her firing was abusive, and the court ruled that such an abusive discharge was contrary to public policy because it was not in the best interest of the economic system or the public good.

Or consider this one. A grocery store manager was caught between a rock and a hard place: company policy dictated he take cash to the bank at night after closing; but he feared traveling through a high-crime area to get there, especially since the services of the store's security guard, who rode shotgun on deposit runs, had been terminated. The other option was to lock the money in the store safe. The manager chose that route instead of the one that led through the dark streets. His timing was awful. That night the safe was robbed. So he was fired for breaking company policy.

How does public policy creep in here? Well the court ruled that failing to provide a guard for the trip to the bank may very well have been an OSHA safety violation. And everyone knows how strong a public policy interest exists in OSHA.

Public policy is not only a strong weapon for E-A-W exceptions, but pulls the added fillip of tort, failing to live up to a legal obligation, into wrongful discharge suits. That's why you'll find it woven into the fabric of so many cases, just like these two, as you read through the rest of the book.

# CHAPTER 3

# When You're Promised a Gold Mine, but Instead Get the Shaft

P romises won't pay the rent. But they may be used to force your employer to recognize your rights as an employee. The applicability of promises begins right from your initial hiring interview and extends to your final farewell conversation.

One important consideration to keep in mind. To turn those broken promises into weapons in an employee-rights case doesn't require that they be written. Time and again, courts have held that verbal promises, implied agreements, and even standard operating procedures, can contribute to the existence of an employment contract that must not be breached.

You remember that good faith and fair dealing concept from chapter 1. That covenant to deal fairly and in good faith lies at the base of all employment agreements. Each side is expected to live up to its part, to its "promises." Combined with those expectations is the concept of "total." Judges and juries today view the overall circumstances of each case, not a single verbal commitment or a solitary written phrase. It's the whole ball of wax that counts.

Remember the landmark bonus case where the company had a written at-will agreement, and fired a salesman before he could collect a substantial bonus "promised" to him by his contract? The company claimed it was within its rights. Wrong, said a court. It's not just the formal language that counts. Take into account the twenty-five years of good service by the employee, plus the implied covenant of good faith and fair dealing. In that light the company couldn't win. And it didn't.

One other piece of all promise cases is the concept of *promissory estoppel*, where an individual relies on a promise to his or her detriment. To paraphrase *Miranda*, anything employers say can and will be used against them in a court of law.

Many of the cases revolving around broken promises fall within the hiring, rather than the firing, cycle. That's when most promises are made. But they also can be found in benefit packages, employee handbooks, and even company practices or procedures, as well as in promotion and relocation processes.

We've divvied up the promise cases in this chapter according to their main topics. They range from *fraud* to *oral agreements;* from concepts like *consideration* to big picture trends like *facts and circumstances;* from practical employment activities like *relocation* and *probation* to the often-abused *hiring hype.* Make a mental note of any cases or circumstances that sound familiar and file them away for future reference.

## Fraud flexes its muscles

Cases of promises linked to fraud are among the strongest in employee rights. You probably remember the celebrated "sexual discrimination" case of television newscaster Christine Craft back in the early 1980s. Why the quotes? Because the bulk of the damage awards that two different juries tried to bestow (both judgments were eventually overturned) on Ms. Craft were not for sexual discrimination, but for fraud. The jurors believed that the TV station had misrepresented its terms of employment to induce Craft to jump ship and sail into their employment harbor in Kansas City.

The case went something like this. Craft agreed to take the job only if she didn't have to undergo an appearance makeover. The station agreed, but later urged her to consult clothing and makeup artists. The urging became more insistent, including a recommendation for a wardrobe change.

Then a poll found Craft the least popular local female news anchor, due mainly to her appearance. The station reassigned her to reporter duties, with no loss of pay or benefits. She resigned and sued. Basis of case: sexual discrimination, Equal Pay Act, fraud.

The first jury found no pay equity violation and issued only an advisory sexual discrimination opinion. But it awarded her half a million dollars for fraud! Legal volleyball ensued. The first award was found excessive. A second jury hung up another six-figure award, but that was also overturned. (*Craft* v. *Metromedia*, 572 F. Supp. 868, W.D. Mo., 1983)

■ *Employee Rights Alert:* The Craft case underlines an important jury attitude, to wit, how willing an employee's peers are to assess damages against employers who are accused of fraud or deceit in their employment practices.

Fraud, however, is not an easy contention to prove in the workplace environment. Broadly speaking, you may have the makings of a fraud case if your employer:

■ Made a material representation to you that he or she knew was false, or in reckless disregard of whether it was true (as you'll see in chapter 11, similar standards apply in libel cases)
■ Expected you to act on that statement
■ Knew you'd suffer damage as a result

On top of that, you must have relied on that statement as the basis for your action, and you can't have known the statement was false, or had any reasonable method to find that out.

A California employer was alleged to have concealed the risk of exposure to asbestos in one of its plants, a misrepresentation of workplace hazards. A worker developed a work-related disease, and still the company failed to disclose the risk, at which point the health problem was aggravated. The company penalty: While worker's compensation covered treatment of the original health problems, the company had to shoulder the costs of the aggravation part. (*Johns-Mansville Products Corp.* v. *Superior Court*, 165 Cal. Rptr. 858, 1980)

## Heap big promises—heap big problems

Mention the word "promise" to an employment lawyer and the first case likely to pop into his or her head is a famous Michigan case back in 1980.

The operative phrase in this case was "you'll have a good career here as long as you do your job." That "promise" suggested the employee couldn't be fired without just cause. Combined with other statements, it produced a legitimate expectation that the company would fulfill its promise. It didn't, and it lost its case in court. (*Touissant* v. *Blue Cross/Blue Shield*, 408 Mich. 579, 601-3, 292 N.W. 2d 880, 885-88, Mich., 1980)

Neighboring Minnesota was the site of another well-known promise story which underlined the "detrimental" aspect of such cases. After pharmacy school, a young man worked for several years in a drugstore. He applied for a pharmacist position at a hospital clinic, came through two personal interviews with flying colors, and was offered the job over the phone.

He accepted and asked for a two-week grace period to give notice. That fortnight turned into a hell period when the hospital tried to check his references and couldn't get confirmation. So it hired another pharmacist. Pull the plug on that decision, ordered a court, which also awarded lost compensation. He relied to his detriment on the hospital's promise and suffered. Now the hospital had to. (*Grouse* v. *Group Health Plan, Inc.*, 306 N.W. 2d 114, Minn., 1981)

## Add up all the facts and circumstances

An Ohio man found himself back in court after a lengthy criminal court trial. A salesman, he had been arrested and charged with kidnapping, rape, and related charges. He pleaded innocent in court and in front of his boss. The boss suspended judgment pending the outcome of the trial, but also suspended the salesman.

The first trial ended in a hung jury. When a new trial was declared, the plaintiff didn't want to continue and so dropped the charges. But when the salesman went to reclaim his job, he found a pink slip waiting. His beef: You promised to reinstate me if there were a favorable resolution to my trial. His boss: The resolution was not really favorable.

So the salesman found himself back in court. He pointed to a pair of "promises" broken as proof of contract breached. One was the internal grievance procedure detailed in the employee handbook which was never applied to him. The other was the verbal assurances of his reinstatement upon favorable resolution, promises on which he relied and by which he suffered.

A judge and appeals court couldn't find any grounds for an exception to E-A-W. But the state supreme court saw a legitimate factual question being raised, which should be decided by a jury, as well as a possible source of damages in promises on which the salesman had relied. So although the salesman didn't win in court, he at least won his day in court.

That decision spotlighted a "facts and circumstances" approach to promise cases as exceptions to employment-at-will. First, all the ifs should be considered. If the promise had been made. If the salesman relied on it. If he suffered because of that. Then the state supreme court wanted the trial court to take a look at the big picture, including the nature of the job, the company's normal pattern of discipline and grievances, applicable company policies—the whole works. Only then was a determination to be made. (*Mers* v. *Dispatch Co.*, 120 L.R.R.M. 3029, Ohio, 1985)

Another judge took a similar big picture approach when he ruled for an employee who had relied on a promise that his employment relationship would end only for good cause. In this case, the judge noted (and so should you) four pieces of the big picture promise.

First, the company had maintained a publicly announced policy of encouraging long-term employment. Second, the company had an established practice of firing employees only for cause. Third, the employee had been given verbal promises that he would be dismissed only for cause. Fourth, there were similar promises in the employee manual. (*Frazier* v. *Colonial Williamsburg Foundation*, E.D. Va., 1983)

The so-called facts and circumstances approach can also help overcome written documents. A major car company found that out in a landmark decision that involved a union man turned manager.

In its initial job application, the company had spelled out its employment-at-will philosophy, and the worker had read and signed it. But some years later he resigned from the union to accept a management position. Shortly thereafter he was fired, and fought back. His contention: The company's general pattern of actions and policies indicated that he was reasonably assured of a job until he reached retirement age.

A court agreed. While it was true he had signed the application, the company had made both oral and written statements which suggested a promise of lifetime employment. The accumulated effect of those words, plus company actions, was strong enough to overcome the written disclaimer. (*Schipani* v. *Ford Motor Co.*, 302 N.W. 307, 309, 1981)

---

## Little frog, big pond equals trouble

Words and traditional practices also helped overcome a written contract in the case of a basketball coach who got bounced from the employment lineup.

Seems our coach was a big success on the small college level, so a major university launched a recruiting program aimed at corralling his services. He allowed himself to be wooed and won, signing a one-year contract renewable at the option of the university president.

By the time the newly anointed coach took the reins, both the president and athletic director had jumped ship. Things went downhill from there. The new athletic director testified later he had misgivings from the beginning. Practices were disorganized. The coach was unfamiliar with major college hoop regulations. Friction developed between the coach and his assistants and players. Community support plummeted, with average home attendance at late-season games less than the number of season ticket holders. The crowning blow: a basement-finish 4–24 record. Fired, the coach looked for a new job but couldn't get a bite. So he sunk his teeth into his former employer, charging violation of contract terms and breach of implied covenant of good faith and fair dealing in executing it.

Despite the one-year-with-university-option written agreement, the initial jury jumped on the coach's team and awarded him damages for the claimed three lost years of employment, plus allowance for future earning capacity.

An appeals court rejected the future earnings part, but did agree that evidence at the trial indicated the coach had been promised a longer tenure. The original athletic director had given him assurances that the school traditionally gave a new coach four years to prove himself. A member of the search committee made a similar statement. Thus, the court opined, oral promises like those can modify a written promise like the letter contract. (*Lindsey* v. *University of Arizona*, No. 2 CA-CV 87-0125, Ariz. Ct. App. Div. 2, 1987)

## Concept of consideration

There is another legal twist that is leaving old E-A-W notions twisting in the wind. It's called the concept of consideration and it goes something like this.

Employment involves a mutual exchange of benefits, especially when both parties are interested in job security. The merging of those common interests creates a contract situation which doesn't necessarily abide the traditional concepts of contract law, like those Professor Kingsfield espoused so nobly in *The Paper Chase*.

What you may end up with are some special "rules" involving the legal concept of consideration. In the broadest sense, the employer offers, the employee accepts, and voilà, you've got an exchange of mutual benefits that creates a contract. Of course, nothing is quite that simple in the field of law.

Here's an example. The New Jersey Supreme Court found it a quid pro quo situation when an employer gets a loyal and motivated work force in exchange for increased job security and the promise of "due process" in discipline and performance appraisal.

In this particular case, a civil engineering group leader became involved in a series of internal building problems at his company which he couldn't solve. The general manager lost faith in him and asked for his resignation.

The engineer refused and was fired. His courtroom contention: The company manual suggested discharge only for just cause and only after a series of set procedures. His situation sported neither. Two courts rejected his arguments.

But after the engineer's death, his heirs pressed on with a new argument based not on the *personnel* manual as a binding *personal* contract, but as a *general* contract, with the entire work force. In that view, as a collective agreement, a fair reading would be that no member to the agreement could be terminated without just cause.

In fact, said the court, that's just the kind of give-and-take between employer and employee that traditionally binds a contract. The employees offer their work in return for the employer's promise of employment. Such a "contract" should be interpreted according to what the parties expect. And if the ex-employee and his coworkers expected to be fired only for just cause in such a situation, their expectation seemed legitimate. (*Woolley* v. *Hoffman-La Roche, Inc.,* 491 A.2d 1257, N.J., 1985)

## Relocation promises: A moving experience

The salesman at the large steel firm wasn't even looking for greener pastures. He was content tending his current fields. But the general manager of a small brass and aluminum company made him a godfatherlike offer. Head of sales, bigger salary, company car, country club membership, and other perks.

Still the salesman demurred. He was almost fifty, and would have to give up pension benefits accrued during nearly twenty years on the job. He'd have to move, sell the house he loved, and convince his wife to give up her job.

The green light flashed go, though, when he received this assurance from the general manager: "As long as your work is satisfactory, you can count on being with us until you retire."

So he packed up lock, stock, and barrel and moved. But a couple of years later, it was the general manager who retired. The sales manager was in line to replace him, but got bumped by another executive who got along with him like brass and aluminum. The upshot: A pink slip several months later for the sales manager. The reason: sour relationship with the new general manager.

The poor guy was now fifty. No mentor. No job. No prospects. No fulfillment of promise, which he charged in court. The appeals court ruled there was a contract. The sales manager had upheld his end of the bargain with satisfactory work. Now, the court ruled, the company was bound to honor its promise. (*Eklund* v. *Vincent Brass & Aluminum,* 351 N.W. 2d 371, Minn. App., 1984)

A female assistant manager for a finance company didn't let her relocation situation get to first base. When a new company policy took effect, she was given the option of relocating or accepting a promotion. She wanted neither. Her response: I was told by a former supervisor that I wouldn't be required to accept a promotion or relocate as a condition of employment. Response of new regime: Times change. We're going to have to reevaluate your continued employment.

The employee fainted dead away at the threat. Literally. Then she went home and sought professional help—physical, psychological, *and* legal. She heaped everything in her case: age, sex, breach of contract.

Her ace in the hole was a written document from five years earlier, signed by both her supervisor and his supervisor, which promised that if she accepted the promotion to assistant manager, she could not be requested to accept any more promotions or any relocations. The judge judged that she indeed did have a case. (*Crawford* v. *ITT Consumer Finance Corp.*, 653 F. Supp. 1184, 1986)

Another "jury should hear the case" case occurred in Pennsylvania when the headlines read NEWSPAPER FIRES NEWSMAKER. The circulation manager of a small paper was approached by a regional chain. It was a sweet offer: attractive career ladder, work with publisher who planned to retire in two years, become general manager of one of chain's largest papers. Sweeter still, that paper happened to be in the approachee's old home town.

It didn't take long for the manager to put his home up for sale and hightail it for his new assignment. It also didn't take long for him to get fired—three months, approximately.

He contended that the verbal promises of the "apprenticeship" to the publisher leading to future promotion to general manager amounted to a verbal employment contract which his new newspaper should honor. A trial court disagreed and dismissed. But an appeals court rewrote the story, just slightly. It didn't decide whether or not that promise of a promising career was binding. But it did rule that the claim had enough merit to be worthy of a trial. (*Marsh* v. *Western Pennsylvania Newspaper Co.*, 530 A.2d 491, Pa. Sup. Ct., 1987)

- *Employee Rights Alert:* Watch for promises that put specifics on your employment, in terms of time, or advancement, or responsibility, or a combination thereof. "Finish probation and you'll be considered a permanent employee." "Stay here two years and you'll be on the fast track to the director's slot." "Don't make waves in your first year and you'll be bumped up to the supervisor's level for sure." Those are the kinds of assurances that employees often hear, believe, and then see fall by the wayside.

## Reversing relocation

Relocation played an important part in an East Coast appeals court reversal of a reversal decision. A high-level executive in a big league financial firm met with a higher-level executive of a financial services company. What would it take to get you on our team, asked the president of the second firm. Security, replied the first executive. The job must be permanent because of my age. I don't want to have to go back in the marketplace job-hunting. I'd have to be there till I retired.

Done, exclaimed the president. Unluckily, that also described the job situation of the new employee just nine months after he pulled up stakes and moved his family to the city where his new employer was located. But the relationship was not done at all. It extended right into court, as the fired executive sued for violation of promise of employment and a jury handed him a $175,000 damages check.

Court number two overturned that ruling, claiming an oral contract wasn't enforceable. But court number three said add it all together: the promise, plus the decision to leave a perfectly good job, plus the necessity of relocating the whole family to another city. All that may be sufficient to establish that the parties intended to enter into a "permanent" employment contract. (*Hodge* v. *Evans Financial Corp.*, 823 F.2d 559, D.C. Cir., 1987)

On the other side of America, the word "permanent" became a pain in another promise case. In most circumstances, such an adjective applied to a job connotes steady or full-time, not a perpetual guarantee of employment. But when a Minnesota man transported his family to the West Coast after the promise of permanent employment, and then lost his job, a court ruled the employee relied on the promise and the employer should be held to it. (*Brawther* v. *H&R Block*, 124 Cal. Rptr. 845, 1982)

"Stay and grow" were the operative words in a relocation promise in Pennsylvania. An employee saw a job posting for a copywriter on the company bulletin board. She applied, received an offer, and accepted, even though it meant transferring to a different part of the country.

Tipping the scales in favor of the move was an assertion by the company personnel director that it was a job in which she could stay and grow. In less than six months, she had come and gone. Fired. She sued on the basis of that promise as a verbal contract that the job was practically permanent in duration. That claim was upheld by a federal court in the Keystone State in 1982. (*Forman* v. *BRI Corp.*, 532 F. Supp. 49, E.D. Pa., 1982)

## Hiring hype

Most employers are not into lies. Few consciously plan a bait-and-switch routine. It doesn't make good business sense. But *hiring hype* is not all that unusual. Glossing over the negative and focusing on the positive is standard operating procedure in trying to fill a position with a good candidate.

An accountant left her secure "numbers" job to become executive VP of a fledgling management consulting firm. Her promised new role: landing new business. Her interpretation: I'm a partner here. The reality: Instead of a partnership, she got the pits. Dreary administrative duties. Nothing like she had been led to believe. So she sued.

That was nothing compared to the East Coast manager who was lured into a new company with promises of big bucks, big title, big bonuses and stock options, big opportunities. Fired, he asked for big damages: $10.1 million to be exact, for fraud and breach of contract.

His story reads like a primer in promise problems. To lure him from his secure position he was allegedly promised a world of goodies. He'd be taking over a new operation for this huge multinational company. He would be in charge. He would make the decisions. His compensation would reach into seven figures. Sounded like a gold mine, but it didn't pan out. New business went sour and with it all his expectations. So he went for the gold in court instead.

In a more recent big bucks case, a food service supervisor handled a company's operations in two states. When hired, she allegedly received assurances, both written and oral, that her employment would be indefinite and that she wouldn't be fired except for good cause.

The company believed it had the good cause to go back on its promise. It accused her of falsifying expense account records of meals she supposedly shared with friends and charged to the business.

Pretext, rejoined the employee. You've breached my contract, broken your promises, caused me emotional stress, and upended the covenant of good faith and fair dealing. The jury unanimously agreed with that assessment and handed her $1.7 million (which naturally went to appeal by the defendant). (*Carillo* v. *R. H. Macy & Co., Inc.*, San Fran. Sup. Ct. No. 86-2543, 1988)

## Riffling your mind's files

If you think you've been the subject of hiring hype, it's likely it came from one of two directions. Dredging up dusty versions of past promises should focus on two targets, personnel people and operations individuals.

The personnel people are more likely to have made misrepresentations of specific job requirements and responsibilities. They're usually more careful in avoiding verboten words and impractical promises. But they aren't privy to the nitty-gritty details of jobs and so may lead you astray in terms of content and activity.

On the other hand, managers and supervisors know the jobs, warts and all. But they're not trained in "legalspeak." So they may have made unfulfilled promises about career opportunities, advancement, professional growth, etc., that give you a breach case of some sort.

Ask the following questions to get a handle on whether you may have a case against either group.

- Did they ask you to walk into a pedestrian job with the assurance that a superstar position was on the horizon? Which it wasn't!
- Do you know of any other individuals who suffered from the same sort of broken hiring promises as you?
- Did their job-related claims include golden specifics that never panned out? Salary increases? Sales bonuses? Number of people you'd supervise? Company expansion plans?
- Did they make any nonnumber promises that didn't come through? Responsibilities? Job focus? Performance requirements? Travel or lack thereof?
- Did they ever tell you that you could only be discharged for good cause or just cause, or does that pledge exist in any company document?
- Did they ever make sweeping statements about lifetime careers, employment until retirement, or any long-term assurances?

## Probation promises

One of the most volatile promise areas usually occurs just after the initial hiring: probation. It conjures up images of jail. And many employers have found themselves shackled by handcuffs because of probation promise snafus.

For example, one employer in California indicated that after successful completion of its probationary period an employee became "permanent," and was eligible for additional company benefits. That, said a court, constituted an implied promise of continued employment and termination only for cause. (*Walker* v. *Northern San Diego County Hospital District*, 135 Cal. App. 3d 896, 185 Cal. Rptr. 617, 1982)

Lack of a single word won the day in the case of a probationary fire fighter. During probation, employee termination could be kindled by any spark. He was fired after six months. Probation lasted, according to company's rule book, 180 days. That, of course, means working days, said the company, so the firing was legit. That, of course, is not necessarily so, said a court. The word *working* does not appear as a modifier of the word *days*. Award: almost $70,000.

It wasn't words, but reasons, that served as the crux of a probation case in Nevada. A new hiree at a real estate firm was on probation for thirty days. She was told that if she did a good job, she'd be hired full-time after probation, and then she could be fired only if her work was unsatisfactory.

Two weeks into probation, she was called in and told she was being laid off. Reason: sudden downturn in business. Her complaint: That wasn't one of the reasons given her on which her job loss could be based. Even her manager said she had done a good job in her short stint and that if business had allowed, he would have hired her full-time after probation. The Nevada Supreme Court agreed that the only condition for her continued employment was good work, not bad business.

## Promises: Money and time

A U.S. District Court of Appeals lobbed another grenade into the employer's camp without even making a final decision on a case that revolved around a promise of an annual salary review.

An employee worked for a year without any written agreement. When year two came up, a written agreement which would be reviewed one year hence called for a salary based on a four-day work week.

Five months later, the employee was shown the door. In the lawsuit that followed, the first court granted the company a summary judgment for dismissal of the dismissal case. Its reasoning: (*a*) the contract didn't state a definite term or say the relationship was not terminable-at-will; (*b*) stating the salary in annual terms does not by itself make the contract binding for a definite period; (*c*) other "promise" arguments of the employee (promise of salary review after one year, promise of quarterly cash bonus, promise of gross annual salary) didn't pass muster either.

But a higher court disputed that reasoning. The promise that salary will be reviewed is distinct from stating salary as an annual amount. That agreement to review *may* support a finding that the parties intended to establish an employment contract for a definite period, thereby limiting the employer's right to discharge. It's not definite, but it's possible. There being a question of fact, the summary judgment was tossed out, and the case sent back to trial. (*Hartman* v. *C.W.T. Travel, Inc.*, 792 F.2d 1179, D.C. Cir., 1986)

■ *Employee Rights Alert:* The big problem here, at least from the employer's viewpoint, was ambiguity. Many companies now include a phrase like "nothing in this agreement should be construed or interpreted to mean, promise, guarantee, or imply employment for any specific length of time." If such a disclaimer hasn't hit you yet, you might have a piece of a case with a salary review promise.

In a similar case, an employer's job offer mentioned three items: an annual salary, two weeks vacation in the first year, and a salary review after six months of employment. In the court case that followed discharge, the ruling was that the latter two, but not the first, created an inference that the parties had intended a minimum period of employment.

Time terms can go beyond inferring to interpretation. Under certain circumstances, for example, retaining an employee after a fixed term of employment has expired can be interpreted as an automatic renewal for another similar term.

## Promises of compensation and reference

An at-will employee in Tennessee was discharged. No problem there. But he had been promised a percentage of the company's stock. Problem there. Cough up the dough, ruled the state supreme court. (*Blasingame* v. *American Materials*, 654 S.W. 2d 659, Tenn., 1983)

A cashier at an insurance company was promised a favorable letter of recommendation if she resigned to pursue a job elsewhere. She never got the letter and sued for breach of contract. In court, it came out that the company never intended to give her that letter. The Montana Supreme Court decided she should prevail on the merits of the case. (*Gates* v. *Life of Montana*, 688 P.2d 213, Mont., 1983)

## When a promise—isn't

One person's promise is another person's poison, or something like that. Don't expect that everything you hear as a promise, is. Or that courts will always side with the employee when a broken promise is the issue.

One court suggested that the concept of promises could be negated by an employer by placing in its handbook, in a very prominent position, an appropriate statement that there is no promise of any kind by the employer contained in the manual; that regardless of what the manual says or provides, the employer promises nothing and remains free to change wages and all other working conditions without having to consult anyone and without anyone's agreement; and that the employer continues to have the absolute power to fire anyone with or without good cause.

Another employer ploy that can overcome claims of promises is to circumscribe all written and verbal statements about, for example, career opportunities with the phrase "if you qualify."

One new employee at a California hospital heard these words from a personnel representative: "We look forward to a long, pleasant, mutually satisfactory relationship." Turns out it was none of the three. But a court ruled that while the employee may have "heard" a promise, it was in reality merely an expressed hope.

On the other coast, an employment rep for a New York firm boasted about his company's record for job security. It was held to be just that, a boast of fact, not a promise.

Some companies have attempted to place limits on their "promises" by promising that only written statements represent the company's policy, not verbal ones made by any company employee, no matter whom. As you saw in several of the cases in this chapter, you may be able to overcome that defense if you can produce an opposing body of factors, such as contradictory documents, oral agreements, and an established group of practices and procedures that line up on your side.

Benefit statements, especially those with future references like retirement plans, are sometimes used by employees to bolster claims of promised continued employment. In the parry and thrust of employee rights, companies have turned to affirmations of employment-at-will status in their benefit statements to deflect such allegations of implied promises of continued employment.

Others drop in a statement early on in their benefits book that says something to this effect: Such benefits as contained herein do not constitute a promise of continued employment and don't restrict the company's ability to discharge.

## Personal promise audit

If you think you've been dealt a bad hand by broken promises, but you're not sure what cards to play in court, review your experiences in these areas. Remember, any "promises" may be verbal or written.

- Have you ever been promised continued employment subject only to good performance and behavior?
- Were you promised specific disciplinary steps or grievance procedures which were not followed?
- Did you ever hear any of these common, sometimes off-hand remarks, which you considered "promises":
  "As long as your work is up to snuff, you've got a job here."
  "We don't fire our people arbitrarily, only for good cause."
  "If you perform and behave acceptably, you can look forward to staying with us."
- Are there any contradictions in what was promised in, for example, your employment interview and what appears in the employee handbook? Or any discrepancies between what the personnel people told you and what the "operating" interviewer said?
- Did anyone in a position of authority with the company make any promises which were later reneged on? Did anyone ever imply you couldn't be laid off or fired?
- Is there any promise anywhere of termination only for just cause or good cause?
- Did you suffer any hardships because you acted on what you considered an employer promise?

- Can you point to a series of oral statements which may negate the effect of written ones?
- Do the facts and circumstances of your case lend credence to your claims of breached promises?
- Did you make a move based on a promise that backfired?
- Do any company policies—probation, promotion, pay—reinforce your contention that an employment promise was broken?

# CHAPTER 4

# Sexual Harassment: Throwing Off the Yoke of the Hands-On Employer

P ublic policy and promises provide good fodder for your efforts to lay claim to employment rights in the workplace. But another *P* word—privacy—has stirred up the most controversy and focused the spotlight of public interest on those rights. And the glare is nowhere more searing than in the area of sexual discrimination and harassment.

Privacy is the umbrella under which all kinds of employee rights and employer wrongs fall. It includes the drug-testing dilemma discussed in the next chapter and a laundry list of issues from record keeping to lie detectors that you'll see in chapter 6.

The Equal Employment Opportunity Commission is mandated to fight discrimination of just about any type, shape, or form. Discrimination based on sex has long been one of its prime targets, along with race, age, national origin, etc. The Title VII amendment to the Civil Rights Act is the main enforcement weapon in this particular area.

Sexual harassment is related to sexual discrimination, but often has a more subtle flavor to it. But bias by any other name is still bias. We'll give you a quick walk through the playground of sexual discrimination, then hit the most current problems, including pregnancy, maternity, and sexual harassment.

## Sexual discrimination—guidelines and decisions

The EEOC is outspoken on the subject of sexual discrimination. Its message to employers: Don't do it. Among its strictures:

- The principle of nondiscrimination requires that individuals be considered on the basis of individual capacities and not on the basis of any characteristics generally attributed to the group.
- An employer's rule which forbids or restricts the employment of married women and which is not applicable to married men is discrimination based on sex, prohibited by Title VII of the Civil Rights Act.
- Where it is necessary for the purpose of authenticity or genuineness, sex may be a bona fide occupational qualification (e.g., the sex of a charactor an actor would play).
- It is an unlawful employment practice to classify a job as "male" or "female" or to maintain separate lines of progression or separate seniority lists based on sex where this would adversely affect any employee, unless sex is a bona fide occupational qualification for that job.
- Sex as a bona fide occupational qualification must be justified in terms of the particular requirements of the particular job and not on the basis of a general principle, such as the desirability of spreading work.
- The bona fide occupational qualification exception related to sex should be interpreted narrowly. Labels—"Men's jobs" and "Women's jobs"—tend to deny employment opportunities unnecessarily to one sex or the other.
- The refusal to hire a woman because of her sex, based on assumptions of the comparative employment characteristics of women in general, is not a bona fide occupational qualification.
- It is a violation of Title VII for a help-wanted advertisement to indicate a preference, limitation, specification, or discrimination based on sex unless sex is a bona fide occupational qualification for the particular job involved.
- A preemployment inquiry may ask "Male, Female" or "Mr., Mrs., Miss," provided that the inquiry is made in good faith

for a nondiscriminatory purpose. Any preemployment inquiry in connection with prospective employment which expresses directly or indirectly any limitation, specification, or discrimination as to sex shall be unlawful unless based upon a bona fide occupational qualification.

■ It shall be an unlawful employment practice for an employer to discriminate between men and women with regard to fringe benefits.

## Sexual discrimination—a different perspective

You get the idea. Employment discrimination based on sex is out. Those EEOC guidelines are pretty stiff and formal. Just so you don't think sex is boring, here are a couple of sex-oriented cases that will get your discrimination juices flowing. Then you can plunge into one of the hottest controversies raging today, pregnancy and maternity leave.

Dirty toilets were judged the pits in a disparate impact sex discrimination case. A female carpenter apprentice working on a job site next to a main plant was in a quandary. She was disgusted by the available outdoor "johns," two of which at either end of the site were designated "janes." So she avoided going to the bathroom all day long.

Advised that such a strategy could cause bladder problems, she began using the main facility's restrooms, which were off-limits to construction workers. Nailed for breaking the rules, she hammered her way to court.

A trial court ruled that all employees were subject to the same rules and the same unsanitary conditions. An appeals court, however, objected to the trial court's suggestions that female employees, like the plaintiff, could have carried their own toilet paper, used a waterless cleaning device while using the toilets, or not sat down. That latter court contended that this employer had created an unacceptable discriminatory situation where its female construction workers were forced to choose between submitting to a discriminatory health hazard or risking termination for disobeying a company rule. (*Lynch* v. *Freeman*, No. 85-6020, 6th Cir., 1987)

A district sales manager in New Hampshire came up with a unique claim that combined handicap with sex. He had a sex change operation, became a woman, and was dismissed. His/her lawyer mounted a case based on the premise that he/she was a victim of discrimination against the mentally handicapped. That lawyer defined trans-sexualism as the mental conviction that the person is one sex while anatomically the body is another.

A twenty-five-year-old receptionist lost her job for an unusual reason. Poor typing? No. Inadequate filing? No. Insufficient telephone skills? No. Too big a bust? Yes. It seems her forty-inch measurement was too distracting to the office help. A Nebraska EEO agency agreed with the receptionist that she was discriminated against and awarded her $2,000 in back pay.

And the definition of sexual discrimination may very well depend on where you live. If the boss hired a girlfriend instead of you, is it sexual discrimination? In the District of Columbia, it's a good bet. In New York, it's probably not worth the wager.

A registered nurse in Washington, D.C., applied for a promotion and lost it to another nurse who was alleged to be in tight with the decision-maker doc. Evidence pointed to an intimate relationship, but there was no direct proof of sexual intimacy. A court of appeals ruled that the sex in Title VII sex discrimination meant more than merely gender and encompassed sexual relations, encounters, preferences, affiliations, and liaisons—like this one. Thus, the passed-over nurse won her case. (*King* v. *Palmer*, 598 F. Supp. 65 D.D.C. 1984, rev'd 778 F.2d 878, D.C. Cir., 1985)

But in New York, seven male respiratory therapists claimed they were jobbed when an administrator put in a promotion requirement that gave his girlfriend a big job edge. A trial court ruled for the seven, but an appeals court reversed. Sex means only gender and giving someone job preference on the basis of a romantic relationship may be unfair, but it doesn't violate Title VII. (*DeCintio* v. *Westchester County Medical Center*, 807 F.2d 304, 2d Cir., 1986)

## Sex discrimination and pregnancy

Basically the Pregnancy Discrimination Act (PDA) was added to Title VII to prohibit discrimination on the basis of pregnancy, childbirth, or related conditions. It fits in neatly with traditional sex discrimination strictures that have become the law of the land.

You'll get a better feel for what the PDA says and does by looking over figure 4, which is a fact sheet on the act, and figure 5, which answers some common questions about it.

The bottom line is the PDA makes it illegal to:

- Refuse to hire a woman because she is pregnant
- Fire a woman because she is pregnant
- Force a pregnant employee to leave work if she is ready, willing, and able to perform
- Stop the accrued seniority for an employee who has taken a leave to give birth or have an abortion, unless seniority doesn't accrue to other disabled workers under similar circumstances

That last point underlines an important consideration that runs through much of the pregnancy-related legislation and court decisions being promulgated today. Disability and pregnancy are often muttered in the same breath by judges and legislators.

If you're a woman affected by pregnancy and related conditions, you must be treated like other temporarily disabled employees for the purposes of employment. That means leave, benefits, seniority policies, the whole ball of wax must be applied to both types of "disabilities." It also means federal *and state* laws must be followed to the letter by your employers in these circumstances. California was the scene of a battle that involved pregnancy, leave, benefits, state and federal statutes, and, ultimately, the Supreme Court of the United States.

## The maternity leave/benefit brouhaha

In brief: A bank employee originally planned to be off the job for only a short period for her pregnancy. But complications developed and her doctor ordered a three-month respite. The bank filled the vacancy and had nothing to offer her when she came back. She reportedly hit the skids, couldn't pay the rent, was evicted from her home, and even lost custody of the child.

Hit by this landslide of problems, she vented her wrath on the bank, contending the California Fair Employment and Housing Act made it unlawful to refuse pregnancy leave for a reasonable amount of time, and gave her the right to reinstatement in the same or a similar job. The company contended that the California law con-

## Figure 4. Fact Sheet: The Pregnancy Discrimination Act

The Pregnancy Discrimination Act is an amendment to Title VII of the Civil Rights Act of 1964, which prohibits, among other things, discrimination in employment on the basis of sex. The act makes it clear that discrimination on the basis of pregnancy, childbirth, or related medical conditions constitutes unlawful sexual discrimination under Title VII.

The basic principle of the act is that women affected by pregnancy or related conditions must be treated in the same manner as other applicants and employees who are not so affected but who are similarly able or unable to work.

The Equal Employment Opportunity Commission has issued guidelines, including questions and answers, interpreting the act. These guidelines provide guidance as to what employment practices would be considered by the commission as violating the act.

### Hiring

The guidelines provide that an employer cannot refuse to hire a woman because of her pregnancy-related condition so long as she is able to perform the major functions necessary to the job. Further, an employer cannot refuse to hire her because of its prejudices against pregnant workers or the prejudices of co-workers, clients, or customers.

### Health Insurance

Any health insurance provided by an employer must cover expenses for pregnancy-related conditions on the same basis as expenses for other medical conditions. However, health insurance for expenses arising from abortion is not required except where the life of the mother would be endangered if the fetus were carried to term, or where medical complications have arisen from the abortion.

Pregnancy-related expenses should be reimbursed in the same manner as are expenses incurred for other medical conditions. Therefore, whether a plan reimburses the employees on a fixed basis, or on a percentage of reasonable and customary charge basis, the same basis should be used for reimbursement of expenses incurred for pregnancy-related conditions.

The amounts payable for the costs incurred for pregnancy-related conditions can be limited only to the same extent as are costs for other conditions. Neither an additional deductible, an increase in the usual deductible, nor a larger deductible can be imposed for coverage of pregnancy-related medical costs, whether as a condition for inclusion of pregnancy-related costs in the policy or for payment of the cost when incurred. Thus, if pregnancy-related costs are the first incurred under the policy, the employee is required to pay only the same deductible as would otherwise be required had other medical costs been first incurred. Once this deductible has been paid, no additional deductible can be required for other medical procedures.

If a health insurance plan excludes the payment of benefits for any conditions existing at the time the insured's coverage becomes effective (preexisting clause), benefits can be denied for medical costs arising from a pregnancy existing at the time the coverage became effective.

### Pregnancy and Maternity Leave

An employer may not single out pregnancy-related conditions for special procedures for determining an employee's ability to work. However, an employer may use any procedure used to determine the ability of all employees to work. For example, if an employer requires its employees to submit a doctor's statement concerning their inability to work before granting leave or paying sick benefits, the employer may require employees affected by pregnancy-related conditions to submit such statements.

An employer is required to treat an employee temporarily unable to perform the functions of her job because of her pregnancy-related condition in the same manner as it treats other temporarily disabled employees, whether by providing modified tasks, alternative assignments, disability leave, leave without pay, etc.

An employee must be permitted to work at all times during pregnancy when she is able to perform her job. If an employee has been absent from work as a result of a pregnancy-related condition and recovers, her employer may not require her to remain on leave until after her baby is born. Further, an employer may not have a rule which prohibits an employee from returning to work for a predetermined length of time after childbirth.

## Fringe Benefits

An employer may not limit benefits for pregnancy-related conditions to married employees. Further, if an employer has an all-female work force or job classification, the employer must provide benefits for pregnancy-related conditions if benefits are provided for other conditions.

If an employer provides benefits to employees on leave, such as installment purchase disability insurance, payment of premiums for health, life, or other insurance, continued payments into pension, saving, or profit-sharing plans, the employer must provide the same benefits for those on leave for pregnancy-related conditions.

Again, the principle that pregnancy-related disabilities should be treated the same as other temporary disabilities applies to the accrual and crediting of seniority, to the calculation of vacation and pay increases, and benefits for temporary disabilities.

## Right to Return to Work

Unless the employee on leave for pregnancy-related conditions has informed the employer that she does not intend to return to work, her job must be held open on the same basis as jobs are held open for employees on sick or disability leave for other reasons.

## Child Care

While leave for child-care purposes is not covered by the Pregnancy Discrimination Act, Title VII principles would require that leave for child-care purposes be granted on the same basis as leave which is granted to employees for other nonmedical reasons. For example, if an employer allows its employees to take leave without pay or accrued annual leave for travel or education which is not job-related, the same type of leave must be granted to those who wish to remain on leave for infant care, even though they are medically able to work.

## Figure 5. Questions and Answers on Pregnancy Discrimination

*Note:* When pregnancy discrimination was added to existing laws and regulations on sex discrimination, the Equal Employment Opportunity Commission published a series of questions and answers to help employers comply with the statute. As an employee, you should have the same information. Here are some selected Q & As.

*Q.* If, for pregnancy-related reasons, an employee is unable to perform the functions of her job, does the employer have to provide her an alternative job?

*A.* An employer is required to treat an employee temporarily unable to perform the functions of her job because of her pregnancy-related condition in the same manner as it treats other temporarily disabled employees, whether by providing modified tasks, alternative assignments, disability leave, leaves without pay, etc. For example, a woman's primary job function may be the operation of a machine, and, incidental to that function, she may carry materials to and from the machine. If other employees temporarily unable to lift are relieved of these functions, pregnant employees unable to lift also must be temporarily relieved of the function.

*Q.* What procedures may an employer use to determine whether to place on leave as unable to work a pregnant employee who claims she is able to work, or deny leave to a pregnant employee who claims that she is unable to work?

*A.* An employer may not single pregnancy-related conditions for special procedures for determining an employee's ability to work. However, an employer may use any procedure used to determine the ability of all employees to work. For example, if an employer requires its employees to submit a doctor's statement concerning their inability to work before granting leave or paying sick benefits, the employer may require employees affected by pregnancy-related conditions to submit such a statement. Similarly, if an employer allows its employees to obtain doctors' statements from their personal physicians for absences due to other disabilities or return dates from other disabilities, it must accept doctors' statements from personal physicians for absences and return dates connected with pregnancy-related disabilities.

*Q.* Can an employer have a rule which prohibits an employee from returning to work for a predetermined length of time after childbirth?

*A.* No.

*Q.* If an employee has been absent from work as a result of a pregnancy-related condition and recovers, may her employer require her to remain on leave until after her baby is born?

*A.* No. An employee must be permitted to work at all times during pregnancy when she is able to perform her job.

*Q.* Must an employer hold open the job of an employee who is absent on leave because she is temporarily disabled by pregnancy-related conditions?

*A.* Unless the employee on leave has informed the employer that she does not intend to return to work, her job must be held open for her return on the same basis as jobs are held open for employees on sick or disability leave or for other reasons.

*Q.* For the purposes of calculating such matters as vacations and pay increases, may an employer credit time spent on leave for pregnancy-related reasons differently than time spent on leave for other reasons?

*A.* No. An employer's policy with respect to crediting time for the purpose of calculating such matters as vacations and pay increases cannot treat employees on leave for pregnancy-related reasons less favorably than employees on leave for other reasons. For example, if employees on leave for medical reasons are credited with the time spent on leave when computing entitlement to vacation or pay raises, an employee on leave for pregnancy-related disability is entitled to the same kind of time credit.

*Q.* Must an employer hire a woman who is medically unable, because of her pregnancy-related condition, to perform a necessary function of a job?

*A.* An employer cannot refuse to hire a woman because of her pregnancy-related condition so long as she is able to perform the major functions necessary to the job. Nor can an employer refuse to hire her because of its preferences against pregnant workers or the preferences of coworkers, clients, or customers.

*Q.* Can an employer discharge, refuse to hire, or otherwise discriminate against a woman because she has had an abortion?

*A.* No. An employer cannot discriminate in its employment practices against a woman who has had an abortion.

*Q.* Is an employer required to provide fringe benefits for abortions if fringe benefits are provided for other medical conditions?

*A.* All fringe benefits other than health insurance, such as sick leave, which are provided for other medical conditions, must be provided for abortions. Health insurance, however, need be provided for abortions only where the life of the woman would be endangered if the fetus were carried to term or where medical complications arise from an abortion.

*Q.* If complications arise during the course of an abortion, as for instance excessive hemorrhaging, must an employer's health plan cover the additional cost due to the complications of the abortion?

*A.* Yes. The plan is required to pay those additional costs attributable to the complications of the abortion. However, the employer is not required to pay for the abortion itself, except where the life of the mother would be endangered if the fetus were carried to term.

*Q.* May an employer elect to provide insurance coverage for abortion?

*A.* The act specifically provides that an employer is not precluded from providing benefits for abortions whether directly or through a collective bargaining agreement, but if an employer decides to cover the costs of abortion, the employer must do so in the same manner and to the same degree as it covers other medical conditions.

flicted with the PDA and that it was discriminatory because it required *special benefits only for women.*

Doesn't do either, said the high court. Instead, it promotes equal employment opportunity by allowing women as well as men to have families and not lose their jobs. The decision, in effect, held that Title VII and the PDA do not preclude states from enacting laws requiring actions consistent with, but beyond federal statutes. Those federal efforts were aimed at instituting a floor under which pay benefits were not to drop—not a ceiling above which they couldn't rise. (*California Federal Savings & Loan Assoc.* v. *Guerra,* 55 U.S.L.W. 4077, 1986; 107 Sup. Ct. 683, 1987)

■ *Employee Rights Alert:* There's a good chance that the federales may very well insert their snoots into this area with some sort of mandatory parental leave bill requiring unpaid leave for both child care and temporary disability. Various members of Congress have been husbanding the idea through committees for a couple of years.

The general consensus is that the intent of Congress with the PDA was not to limit pregnancy-leave guarantees or benefits, but to extend to women the basic right to participate completely—and equally— in the work force, without denying them the same full participation in family life.

Health care coverage reflects that theory too. There's no mandatory law for providing health benefits (although again, certain legislators are pushing the idea). But if an employer does provide coverage, the rule of thumb is *similarity*. Pregnancy must be treated like other medical conditions. For example:

- If health care is provided for employees, maternity care must be included, and the coverage must be the same as for any other disability.
- If health care is provided for spouses of employees, that coverage must be the same for spouses of male and female employees. Therefore, if spouses of females are covered for temporary disabilities, spouses of male employees must be covered for maternity leave.
- Coverage must be the same for dependents of male and female employees. Employers may not offer optional dependent coverage, including major medical, which excludes or provides less coverage for pregnancy than for other disabilities, regardless of who pays the premiums.

## Everyone gets into the act

The EEOC and various states have also taken up the pregnancy/ maternity leave banner. The EEOC has issued guidelines on maternity leave spelling out what employers can and can't do under Title VII. Among them:

- Employers may specify a given amount of time for maternity leave provided that the time period can be modified, depending on the situation.
- Employers may only require a physical examination and doctor's certification of ability to return to work if such are required of all temporarily disabled employees.

- Employers may not require pregnant workers to exhaust their vacation benefits before receiving sick pay or disability benefits, unless all temporarily disabled employees are required to do the same.
- Employees who are on maternity leave are entitled to accrue seniority or vacation time on the same basis as other employees on medical leave.

Plus, employers may require that an employee give notice of her pregnancy, but only if the requirement has a *legitimate business purpose* and is not used to restrict the employee's job opportunities. (*Cleveland Board of Education* v. *LaFleur*, 414 U.S. 632, 1974)

The EEOC has also pursued a decade-long effort to prove the cumulative effects of a company's maternity leave policies were discriminatory. Many times expectant mothers were forced to take leave and were denied seniority or reinstatement rights. Those policies were not only judged to compare unfavorably with other company disability policies, but their ripple effect negatively affected women their entire careers.

By one count, at least nine states had laws specifically protecting pregnant workers, from California, Connecticut, Hawaii, Illinois, and Massachusetts, to Montana, New Hampshire, Ohio, and Washington. Connecticut's law barring pregnancy discrimination also guarantees pregnant workers reinstatement to the same job or an equivalent position, one that provides equal pay, seniority, and other benefits, unless the employer's circumstances have so changed as to make it impossible or unreasonable to do so.

Minnesota's Human Rights Act teamed up with Title VII in a pregnancy-pertinent case. In May, a receptionist asked for a six-week leave after the December due date of her child. It was all downhill after that request. She was hit with an unsatisfactory performance rating. Blasted with a warning about potential termination. Set back when a companywide raise didn't reach her paycheck 'til two months after everyone else was spending it.

In August she was told her job would be permanently filled while she was gone. The day she left for the hospital in November, she was fired. Eight days later her health insurance was terminated. A court decided all those experiences were pretextual, covering up disparate treatment. She got triple back pay damages, expenses for her sick child, and $10 thousand for pain and suffering. (*Gam-*

*mon* v. *Precision Engineering Co.*, No. 4-85-1217, U.S.D.C. Minn., 1987)

## Other pregnancy problems

Maternity/parental leave isn't the only sticking point in pregnancy-related cases. One female lost a job opportunity indirectly because of an impending birth. When she applied for the job training retarded adults, she was blissfully unaware that her bliss would be compounded by an impending birth. So was her employer.

She showed up for orientation almost two months later in maternity clothes. No problem so far. But she feared a mandatory tuberculosis test for new employees would hurt her baby, so she refused it. Problem. She offered the results of a different test as a replacement. Too outdated. No test, no job.

Then things got muddled. The potential employee investigated further and found the test couldn't hurt her baby. She offered to take it. She was stunned to find her position had already been filled. Two versions of the episode were rerun in the court. Conspiracy to discriminate against pregnant employee versus refusal to take a mandatory test.

The trial court judge believed the manager. A three-member panel of the federal appeals court found the employee version more credible. The full appeals court said go with the first judge and stop the second-guessing. (*Beatty* v. *Chesapeake Center*, No. 86-1176, 4th Cir., 1987)

Then there was the case where pregnancy and disability didn't go hand in holster. A female police officer was in the early weeks of pregnancy. Two months into her term, her doctor judged the rigors of street duty too rigorous for her unborn. She took sick leave expecting it to last seven months. But a police department investigation determined her in excellent health, well able to withstand the rigors of a desk assignment.

Her complaint: You don't make males on sick leave transfer to inside duties. Until her physician said she could perform all patrol duties, she wanted to be considered disabled. Her lawsuit dragged on so long it became a moot point. The child was a year old when an appeals court ruled the disability aspect of pregnancy involved inability to perform the job desired by the employer. She could still do the inside job. The court ruled against her. (*Wunning* v. *Johnson*, 114 A.D. 2d 269, 1986)

In fact, in one case, pregnancy discrimination was ruled justified. A young lady worked as an arts and crafts instructor for a girls club with members in the impressionable eight- to eighteen-year-old age range. One main mission of the club: to discourage teen-age pregnancy. So what does the single instructor do? She becomes pregnant.

That's a poor example we can't tolerate, said the employer in discharging her. You could make allowances, argued her lawyers. Find her another job on the payroll where she doesn't have direct contact with the girls, or grant her a leave, or transfer her. No such options available, retorted the employer. Such a move would negate our efforts at work force stability. The court: Policy is justified as a business necessity and bona fide occupational qualification. The mom-to-be loses. (*Chambers* v. *Omaha Girls Club*, No. 86-1447, 8th Cir., 1987)

■ *Employee Rights Alert:* Employers may claim a number of defenses in this area. You should know how to determine their validity. For example:

- Bona fide occupational qualification: Can they prove the pregnancy directly interferes with your ability to do the job?
- Business necessity: Did they explore alternatives, such as job transfer, that could have less serious negative effects on you?
- Neutral policy: Even if the policy applies to everyone indiscriminately, does it have a disproportionate discriminatory effect on expectant mothers?
- Similarity of procedures: Are all temporary disability requirements translated to pregnancy? Is a doctor's note required for both? Do both receive accommodation treatment, like modification of tasks or alternative assignments?

## Pregnancy and abortion

The Pregnancy Discrimination Act doesn't come right out and rule out discrimination against a woman who has an abortion. It does say that an employer doesn't have to pay health insurance benefits unless the life of the mother would be endangered or medical complications arise.

So what does the EEOC say in its guidelines? It flatly states an employer cannot discriminate against someone who's had an abortion. One big difference: The PDA is a legally binding statute; the guidelines aren't.

A midwestern case did little to settle the matter. A bank employee told her supervisor about her abortion. Eventually the employee was fired. In court, she pointed an accusing finger at her boss (a woman). The latter had railed against abortions in workplace discussions, she was Catholic and had gone to a well-known Catholic womens' college, and while there she had taken a course on sex and marriage.

Bank responded simply. The supervisor hadn't told anyone else about the abortion. And the termination decision had in fact been made by an entirely different manager. So the fired employee could not prove the four elements the court demanded for a legitimate prima facie case, those being:

- She was meeting the employer's legitimate job performance expectations
- She had an abortion
- She was terminated
- She could prove the person or persons responsible for termination possessed an animus toward abortions and knew of hers (*Doe* v. *First National Bank*, 45 F.E.P. Cases 711, N.D. Ill., 1987)

## Sex and pay or promotion discrimination

A woman wanted a promotion recommendation. Her superior wanted a dinner engagement. She didn't want to mix business with pleasure. He didn't want to hurry himself on the promotion move.

Six months elapsed. No promotion. No salary increase. She squawked and filed a sex discrimination charge. Magically, the promotion came through. Unmollified, she went through with the charge. The company defense: She didn't follow proper Title VII filing procedures and failed to show a causal connection between her losses and the actions of her supervisor. Come off it, said the court. Forget the technicalities. The relationship was established. She has a green light to seek compensatory and punitive damages. (*Blessing* v. *Lancaster County*, 609 F. Supp. 485, 1985)

Another woman worked for, of all things, an Equal Employment Opportunity official whom she claimed blocked her promotion and kept her from doing her job correctly because of her sex. That latter charge came front and center when she was fired for not accomplishing three objectives set out for her in a performance review.

It was an unusual case for another reason. She wasn't claiming to be a victim of sexual advances or suggestions. Rather, her contention was her supervisor's animosity toward her entire sex created a hostile environment. He not only made demeaning remarks about females in general (and not about males), but he blocked her access to records and information she needed to do her job. Said a judge: Yes, you *can* have sex discrimination and harassment without overt sexual advances. (*Delgado* v. *Lehman,* 665 F. Supp. 460, E.D. Va., 1987)

■ *Employee Rights Alert:* Getting ahead is tough enough without gender motivated roadblocks being thrown up in your path. One of the most potent vehicles for steamrolling those obstacles is the Equal Pay Act, which used to be enforced by the Department of Labor, but now falls in the employee rights bailiwick of the EEOC. If you think your pay rights are being denied because of your sex, check out the EPA.

Among other things, the Equal Pay Act:

■ Provides that fringe benefits, including pension and retirement plans, must not discriminate between men and women performing equal work. Differentials predicated on sex-based actuarial studies are not allowed. Spousal and family benefits available to employees of one gender must be extended to employees of the other. Cost of benefits is no defense for discrimination.

■ Will focus close scrutiny on situations when one sex is concentrated at lower levels of the wage scale and there is no historical relationship other than sex to account for wage differences.

■ Has blown two Equal Pay Act–violation defenses out of the water. One invalid defense is wage differential based on differences in the average cost of employing one sex group versus the other. The second is unequal rates of pay established by collective bargaining.

■ Has placed on thin ice two other defenses. Under the microscope of the Equal Pay Act will be higher pay for one sex group because of extra duties, and head of household preferred treatment that has no relation to individual job performance.

■ Continues to give its blessing to four standard defenses to alleged pay discrimination actions, those defenses being merit, seniority, quantity or quality of production, and any factor other than sex.

## Sexual discrimination and stereotyping

So she used a little profanity now and then. Didn't everyone? So she was pushy and sometimes a little overbearing. Didn't a lot of partners display those aggressive characteristics? So what did they want already?

"They" were partners in the big accounting firm who were to vote on her ascension into those hallowed ranks. And they wanted her, according to their comments, to:

- Take a course in charm school
- Act more feminine
- Walk, talk, and look like a lady
- Wear more makeup and jewelry

Turned down for the partnership, she turned up the heat in court. Sex stereotyping was her battle cry. Several courts pitched their tents on her side. The partnership application was tainted by stereotyping in performance appraisal. The system allowed negative comments that were clearly discriminatory. She was judged as a female, not as an employee. The company failed to alert partners to the possibility their judgments could reflect bias, failed to discourage stereotyping, and failed to investigate and correct allegations that a double standard was being applied. In sum, the partnership selection process was impermissably affected by gender bias. The case has all the earmarks of a Supreme Court target. (*Hopkins* v. *Price Waterhouse*, 618 F. Supp. 1109, D.D.C. 1985; Nos. 85-6052, 85-6097, 1987; 825 F.2d 458, D.C. Cir., 1987)

In another case, minimum height and weight requirements in the Alabama State prison system were found to have an adverse impact on women. They were based on stereotype and tradition, not job-related performance standards.

Dress codes often fall more heavily on women because of traditional stereotyped expectations. A pregnant desk clerk looked kind of wan and her complexion was broken out. Wear lipstick and makeup, ordered her manager. Company policy. The clerk refused, was fired, and ended up in court. The judge found no business necessity in the policy, the rule was specifically aimed at one employee (a pregnant woman to boot), and the other reasons for dismissal were pretexts. A circuit court affirmed. (*Tamimi* v. *Howard Johnson Co., Inc.*, F.2d F.E.P. Cases 1289, 11th Cir., 1987, CA11, No. 85-7300)

Another female worker wore shorts to work one day. The dress code called for suitable attire and common sense. She was ordered home to change and docked twenty minutes. Can't do that, ruled an arbitrator. The dress code was merely the supervisor's notion of propriety for women—not a business or safety concern. Plus it was a working condition that came under the bargaining agreement the employee worked under.

On the lighter side are a couple of reverse discrimination cases where male stereotypes were attacked. One occurred up in Canada according to a report out of Winnipeg. A Saskatchewan man wanted to be a tree counter. But a commercial nursery told him he was barking up the wrong tree. Company officials believed women were superior tree tabulators because they had greater dexterity, were more adaptable to repetitive jobs, and paid greater attention to small details. A human rights commission went out on the limb for the guy and ruled prejudicial assumptions about sexual differences led to job denial. He got $1,308 for damages, lost wages, and loss of dignity.

Speaking of dignity, a male nudist in one of LA's canyons didn't like the way a camp set its fees. A practice started back in the sixties to make up for decades of sexual discrimination against women gave the fairer sex a fairer deal when it came to dues. The male nudist squawked. The camp told him to keep his shirt on, that it would stop stereotyping women as the target of discrimination and start charging similar fees.

## State and local sexual discrimination and harassment regs

Lots of states, and even municipalities, have statutes or regulations that in some way affect sexual discrimination or harassment cases. The axiom here is the same as throughout the employee rights field: Always check every available option, especially state and local considerations.

Here's a taste:

- New York State Human Rights Law prohibits employment discrimination by employers with four or more workers on the basis of pregnancy, childbirth, or related conditions. New York State employers can't compel a pregnant employee to take a leave of absence unless the pregnancy prevents satisfactory job performance. New York has a mandatory disability law, so employees on pregnancy leave are entitled to disability benefits.
- The Philadelphia Fair Practices Ordinance and the Wisconsin Fair Employment Act protect homosexuals from employment discrimination by making it unlawful to discriminate because of "sexual orientation."
- The Alabama Human Rights Law prohibits discrimination based on "parenthood" and the District of Columbia Human Rights Act prohibits discrimination based on "family responsibilities."

## Sexual harassment in the workplace

So what about sexual harassment? What exactly is it? Is it really in the eyes of the beholder? Is it:

- When a group of men in a broker's office paste nude photos from *Playboy* magazine on the bios of new female employees?
- When an executive spices up a business slide-show with photos of naked women and some suggestive comments?
- When administrators in a health center tell a businesswoman that they're showing an educational film and then reel off the porn classic *Deep Throat*?
- When a superintendent fondles female clerks and exposes himself to them, claiming it's all part of the traditional office "give and take."

It used to be so much easier to judge, when quid pro quo (basically, give something to get something) was the standard. Then the supervisor, usually male, demanded some sexual favor from the subordinate, usually female, in return for some economic or job consideration—a promotion or merely keeping a job. Most successful claims emerged from situations where a woman was fired or denied a job after resisting her supervisor's advances.

Then came the second generation of sexual harassment suits, where black and white were replaced with shades of gray, where quid pro quo was replaced by hostile environment. And here's the case that ushered in that second coming.

## The environment becomes hostile

It had all the earmarks of kismet. She needed a job. He needed a teller trainee. They met. He hired. She advanced. Within four years, she was an assistant branch manager. Then came an indefinite sick leave. Within two months, she was canned. Then came the lawsuit. Sexual harassment.

Flashback in court: While she was still a trainee, the bank manager who had hired her had behaved in a fatherly manner. After her first promotion came the change. He invited her to dinner and then a motel. At first she refused, but then acquiesced, fearing for her job. He made repeated demands for sexual favors. They had intercourse forty to fifty times over the next few years, he embarrassed her several times in front of coworkers, and in fact forcibly raped her a couple of times.

The accused manager denied all charges and claimed she was retaliating for another workplace-related dispute. A trial court ruled that if a sexual relationship did exist, it was voluntary on the woman's part. It had nothing to do with continued employment or advancement. And even if it had been sexual harassment, the company had a policy against it and had received no complaints about it, so it wasn't liable.

A federal appeals court reversed. One need not fear for job or advancement opportunities to be the subject of sexual harassment. Forget the voluntary aspect and the testimony that she dressed and behaved provocatively. She suffered sexual harassment through a hostile environment, and the employer is liable as well.

That's when the Supreme Court waded in with its precedent-setting pronouncement. Here are some of the points the Court made:

- Title VII prohibits discrimination with respect to terms, conditions, or privileges of employment. That phrase extends beyond economic matters to encompass the entire spectrum of disparate treatment of men and women. The EEOC guidelines follow a similar route, thus laying waste to the argument that a quid pro quo situation is necessary to prove sexual harassment.
- Sexual harassment also stamps as guilty conduct that interferes

with performance or creates an intimidating, hostile, or offensive working environment.
- To be actionable, the offensive conduct must be severe and pervasive and alter conditions of employment.
- Whether an employer is liable depends on traditional common law principles and the total circumstances of each individual case.
- Evidence of voluntary participation is indeed relevant. (*Meritor Savings Bank* v. *Vinson*, 106 S.C. 2399, 1986)

## Laying out the "unwelcome" mat

That last is an often overlooked point in this case which has become a sticking point in a number of other sexual harassment cases. In the EEOC definition of sexual harassment, the key word is "unwelcome." The Supreme Court indicated that evidence of sexual attitudes, activity, and behavior may be introduced in a sexual harassment case if it's relevant to prove a defendant's advances were not "unwelcome."

That, of course, opens up a whole 'nother can of worms regarding privacy and off-the-job relevance. In a Utah case, the defendant tried to get depositions from the female plaintiffs' boyfriends, fathers of their children, paramours, and even a photographer who allegedly took suggestive shots of some of them. He was denied access to all but the photographer. But a Michigan court of appeals held that testimony about a female plaintiff's conduct outside the work setting was relevant to dispute her claim that she was a moral, religious woman especially sensitive to explicit jokes.

Sexual overtures that are "unwelcome" may not be considered to be unlawful. The Supreme Court held in *Vinson* that evidence of an employee's promiscuity on the job is relevant to determining whether the employee deemed sexual overtures or conduct "unwelcome." The Supreme Court, however, warned that such overtures may be unwelcome harassment even though the party's participation appeared "voluntary" because no threat of adverse job action was made.

The EEOC and a number of federal courts have held that an employee's voluntary participation in sexually related conduct rebuts any claim that the individual was the victim of unwelcome sexual harassment. The EEOC has gone so far as to impose an affirmative duty on an employee who is involved in sexually related jokes, touching, comments, or other conduct to clearly indicate to the alleged harasser that continuation of the conduct is unwelcome. Otherwise the conduct does not constitute sexual harassment.

Let's ask again: What constitutes sexual harassment?

Said one harried executive: It's harassment when something starts bothering someone. The EEOC is a little more specific. It defines sexual harassment.

> Unwelcome sexual advances, requests for sexual favors, and other verbal or physical conduct of a sexual nature constitute sexual harassment when (1) submission to such conduct is made either explicitly or implicitly a term or condition of an individual's employment, (2) submission to or rejection of such conduct by an individual is used as the basis for employment decisions affecting such individual, or (3) such conduct has the purpose or effect of unreasonably interfering with an individual's work performance or creating an intimidating, hostile, or offensive working environment.

See figure 6 for a portion of the EEOC's fact sheet on sexual harassment.

## When sex gets complicated

Sounds neat and simple, but of course it isn't. And the mere fact of sexual harassment is often colored by other practical and legal circumstances. For example, *public good* was invoked in a case where a female machine operator applied for a higher paying position. Boss: Be nice to me and it's yours. Operator: I'm married with three kids. She got the promotion, but refused the nice part. Within months she was demoted and fired. A New Hampshire court ruled that a termination motivated by bad faith or malice or based on retaliation is not in the best interest of the public good. (*Monge* v. *Beebe Rubber Co.,* 114 N.H. 130, 1974)

*Pretext and EEOC activities* can also be stirred in with sexual harassment. A female janitor in Arkansas was the apple of her supervisor's eye. He told coworkers to leave so they could be alone, touched and grabbed her, and made suggestive remarks. She also caught him peering over a restroom stall door at her and listened as he threatened her recent marriage.

## Figure 6. Fact Sheet: Sexual Harassment

The Equal Employment Opportunity Commission has long recognized that sexual harassment, like harassment in an employment context resulting from discrimination on a prohibited basis, is an unlawful employment practice in violation of the Civil Rights Act of 1964, as amended. To reaffirm its position that sexual harassment is sexual discrimination, the commission amended the existing "Guidelines on Discrimination Because of Sex" to deal specifically with sexual harassment.

### Patterns of Harassment on the Basis of Sex

Sexual harassment can occur in a variety of circumstances and encompass many variables. Although the most widely recognized pattern is that in which a male supervisor sexually harasses a female employee, this form of harassment is not the only one recognized by the EEOC. The commission's view of sexual harassment includes, but is not limited to, the following considerations:

■ A man as well as a woman may be the victim of sexual harassment, and a woman as well as a man may be the harasser.

■ The harasser does not have to be the victim's supervisor. (S)he may also be an agent of the employer, a supervisory employee who does not supervise the victim, a nonsupervisory employee (coworker), or, in some circumstances, even a nonemployee.

■ The victim does not have to be of the opposite sex from the harasser. Since sexual harassment is a form of sexual discrimination, the crucial inquiry is whether the harasser treats a member or members of one sex differently from members of the other sex. The victim and the harasser may be of the same sex where, for instance, the sexual harassment is based on the victim's sex (not on the victim's sexual preference) and the harasser does not treat employees of the opposite sex in the same way.

■ The victim does not have to be the person at whom the unwelcome sexual conduct is directed. (S)he may also be someone who is affected by such conduct when it is directed toward another person. For example, the sexual harassment of one female employee may create an intimidating, hostile, or offensive working environment for another female (or male) coworker.

■ A finding of unlawful sexual harassment does not depend on the victim's having suffered a concrete economic injury as a result of the harasser's conduct. For example, improper sexual advances which do not result in the loss of a promotion by the victim or the discharge of the victim may, nonetheless, constitute sexual harassment where they unreasonably interfere with the victim's work or create a harmful or offensive working environment.

■ There is no requirement that the victim complain to the harasser or report the sexual harassment to his or her supervisor or employer. However, the employer will not be held responsible for harassment by a coworker or nonemployee unless the employer knew or should have known of the conduct and failed to take immediate and appropriate corrective action. Similarly, the employer will not be held responsible for sexual harassment by a supervisor which does not result in economic or tangible harm unless the employer knew or should have known of the conduct and failed to take immediate and appropriate corrective action. But if the employer fails to communicate to employees an explicit policy against sexual harassment, and if it provides no available means by which employees can make their complaints known to officials in a position to correct the problem, then lack of knowledge will not shield the employer from liability.

### Case-by-Case Basis

The commission will look at the record as a whole and at the totality of the circumstances, such as the nature of the sexual advances and the context in which the alleged incidents occurred. The determination of the legality of a particular action will be made from the facts, on a case-by-case basis.

When she filed a complaint with the EEOC, he started acting rotten to the core. He wrote memos to himself on her alleged poor performance and then fired her based on them. A circuit court affirmed that she was discharged in retaliation for pursuing an EEOC claim. (*Mays* v. *Williamson & Sons, Inc.*, No. 84-2418, U.S. Ct. App. 8th Cir., 1985)

In some cases, *individual liability* can be dragged into sexual harassment cases. No sexual favors or economic considerations were involved when some coworkers made life miserable for a female employee. They shot rubber bands at her, engaged in boisterous speculation about her virginity, and sketched obscene cartoons with her as the main target. A company supervisor swept aside her complaints, but the court trashed the offending employees with individual punitive damages. (*Kyriazi* v. *Western Electric Co.*, 461 F. Supp. 894, D.N.J. 1978; aff'd 647 F.2d 388, 3d Cir., 1981)

And even when *an offending action isn't sexual*, it can fall in the realm of sexual harassment. A company claimed that only conduct of a sexual nature can be considered sexual harassment. Not so, said a circuit court. When the harassment and unequal treatment would not have occurred except for the fact that the offendees were women, that's the bottom line. Title VII reflects Congressional intent to throw out the widest possible dragnet in the definition of discriminatory practices. (*Hall* v. *Gus Construction Co., Inc.*, 842 F.2d 1010, 8th Cir., 1988)

## When sex harassment—isn't

A radio station advertising sales rep was tops at her job, numero uno in the sales force. She also captured the top slot on the owner's love chart. He invited her to lunch, revealed another affair he had had with a station employee, and told the startled rep he liked relationships with women who could keep their mouths shut.

He asked her to drive him to the airport, where she had to fend off his attempts at a good-bye kiss. When he returned, she later testified in court, he gave her a look you don't see everyday in the office. He also asked to speak to her alone in the conference room and again suggested a liaison. Plus there were numerous suggestive looks and little innuendoes.

All these details came up in court after the station manager discharged the rep, and she sued for invasion of privacy and emotional distress.

The Alabama judicial system, notoriously conservative in its judgments, rebuffed her on both counts. It ruled an invasion of privacy claim based on this type of sexual harassment must cause mental suffering, shame, or humiliation to a person of ordinary sensibilities. Apparently this one didn't. And as far as emotional distress went, mere insults, indignities, threats, or annoyances, such as those in this case, don't qualify as outrageous, extreme, outside all possible bounds of decency, utterly intolerable in a civilized society. (*McIsaac v. WZEW-FM Corp.*, 495 S.2d 649, Ala. Sup. Ct., 1986)

■ *Employee Rights Alert:* The point is made over and over in all kinds of employee rights cases. Where you live and work is often as important to your case as its actual merits. Not only do statutes and regulations vary from state to state, but court decisions and precedents do too. Alabama, by the way, is not the state of choice for employees and their rights cases.

## Differences make the difference

While other courts may be more liberal in their interpretations of what constitutes sexual harassment, two qualities often receive the most focus, *persistence and language.*

There's a big difference between sexual slurs, insults, and innuendoes, and a female supervisor commenting on a male subordinate's "good looks" or a male supervisor's commenting on a female worker's "stunning figure." Neither of these qualified as sexual harassment in court.

In fact, in a workplace where vulgar language was common, and was employed by the plaintiff herself, a court decided her Title VII claim didn't make the grade. You see, she became upset when a coworker made some sexually offensive remarks. So she kicked him in the family jewels and then got booted from her job. But she lost in court.

There's also a big difference between an *isolated incident* and a *pattern* of continued harassment. Who draws the line where is what makes sexual harassment claims so dicey. A supervisor twice introduced an employee as the "Dolly Parton of the office." Even combined with a few similar remarks, that wasn't enough to establish a pattern of harassment.

A department store employee claimed some mechanics flirted with her, asked her on dates, and made some suggestive comments and one particularly lewd remark. A judge contended that these were isolated incidents that didn't create a hostile environment. The remarks could have been interpreted in a variety of ways, but none of the comments reached the level of harassment or subjected her to vulgarity, demeaning comments, improper inquiries about her private behavior, or explicit propositions. Thus, in these instances, no sexual harassment.

## Sexual harassment—close but no cigar

You would expect a plaintiff and defendant to disagree over what constitutes sexual harassment. But even within the judiciary itself, conflicting opinions often go bump in the judges' chambers.

An executive secretary had a rather checkered business background. Her career path spiraled upward—administrative assistant to credit and office manager duties—but her interpersonal relations were the dregs. Coworkers found her abrasive, willful, and difficult to stomach. She was rude to customers and yelled at colleagues.

Eventually she locked horns with a supervisor with whom she only occasionally dealt. Even the judge who heard the case described this man as crude and vulgar. He made obscene comments about women in general and the difficult supervisor in particular, but only in their infrequent dealings. Other women complained about the crude fellow too. So his supervisor took him aside and gave him some fatherly advice on shaping up. Other than that, the company didn't move to curb his vulgarities.

The troublesome female latched onto the crude behavior, added a pinch of nude and semi-nude posters in the workplace, and came up with a sexual harassment stew. A court turned off the heat. The vulgar supervisor didn't often deal with the defendant, so his behavior wasn't persistent enough to kick in a Title VII claim on her behalf. And those posters weren't so drastic or shocking or severe as to affect the psyches of women. The EEOC guidelines on sexual harassment specify conduct that unreasonably interferes with an individual's work performance or creates a hostile working environment. This was not the case here, ruled the court.

In fact, the sexual mores of "modern America" were dragged into this case with the court comment that "shopping centers, candy stores, and prime-time television regularly display pictures of naked bodies and erotic real or simulated sex acts. Living in this milieu, the average American should not be legally offended by sexually explicit posters."

The whole business drew the ire of a dissenting judge who wanted that *reasonable person* rule replaced by a *reasonable victim* or *reasonable woman* rule. His ideas are the kind all sexual harassment claimants would love to see held by the courts hearing their cases. In not so many words, his views were:

- No woman should be subjected to an environment where her sexual dignity and reasonable sensibilities are visually, verbally, or physically assaulted as a matter of prevailing male prerogative.
- Reasonable women don't condone the pervasive degradation and exploitation of female sexuality perpetuated in American culture.
- The presence of pinups and misogynous language in the workplace can only invoke and confirm the debilitating norms by which women are primarily and contemptuously valued as objects of male sexual fantasy.
- Sexual language can seriously affect the psychological well-being of the reasonable woman and interfere with her ability to perform her job.
- Majority tolerance of occasional and isolated offensive acts and conduct in the workplace shields and condones behavior which Title VII would have the courts redress. (*Rabidue* v. *Osceola Refining Co.*, 805 F.2d 611, 6th Cir., 42 F.E.P. Cases 631, 584 F. Supp. 419, 1986)

## Speedy sex—how prompt is prompt?

Is twenty-four hours fast enough? Is eighteen months too long?

Courts are very sensitive to two characteristics of sexual harassment charges, the speed with which they're addressed and the effectiveness with which they're dealt. A lack of speed adds much greater credence to your case. But the reverse is true too.

A female had been on the job for only a couple of days when she ran smack dab into sexual harassment. She was on a company trip with a group of coworkers and an outside company consultant. It was the latter whose conduct she found objectionable. She complained to her supervisor, a female, who went to the company president. Just hang in there another day and you'll never have to deal with him again, promised the prez.

Not timely enough, said the woman, who packed her bags and went home. A district court agreed to the tune of $25,000. Hold on, chided an appeals court. That resolution was pretty darn prompt. In fact, said the court, since the demise of the institution of dueling, society has seldom provided instantaneous redress for dishonorable conduct. (*Dornhecker* v. *Malibu Grand Prix Corp.*, 828 F.2d 307, 5th Cir., 1987)

But investigating and providing a resolution to sexual harassment charges must be both *prompt and adequate*. Two secretaries found themselves the target of a supervisor's amorous advances, persistent and personal.

With secretary number one, he constantly asked her to drinks, lunch, and dinner and even invited himself to her house. She made it clear she wasn't interested in having a relationship with a married boss. With secretary number two, he passed lewd remarks about her body, told her she was on his mistress hit list, and when she rebuffed him, he stiffed her with more work than she could handle.

Both secretaries began to suffer severe bouts of trembling and crying. One was hospitalized twice and forced to take an extended sick leave. When their complaints reached the personnel manager, an investigation ensued. But in the meantime they were asked not to go to the EEOC. They were refused transcripts of investigatory interviews. They didn't get any written assurance of job security, nor was there any reinstatement of sick leave. And to top it off, the offending supervisor was not immediately removed as their direct supervisor.

Later that unworthy worthy was demoted and received a pay cut. Unimpressed with the company's handling of their charges, the secretaries sued. Both trial and appellate courts agreed that sexual harassment did exist, and while the company had a policy against it, it was ineffectual and deficient. (*Yates* v. *Avco Corp.*, 819 F.2d 630, 43 F.E.P. Cases 1595, 6th Cir., 1987)

■ *Employee Rights Alert:* The *appropriateness* of an investigation often tilts the scales one way or the other in a sexual harassment charge. One company president conducted his own version of a sexual harassment investigation. He went right to the accused supervisor and asked whether the charges were true. Only one flaw in the process. The supervisor happened to be his brother.

## Way too little, way too late

If you'd like a Grade *A* example of both lack of celerity and ineffectuality, take a gander at this Sun Belt case.

After seven years of struggle, a women had risen through the ranks from secretary to senior buyer. She reported to the purchasing manager at a company plant, who invited her out for a business dinner. When she rose to go after eating, he began to give her the business.

He ordered her to sit back down and indicated he expected dessert to involve spending the night together. When she threw cold water on that plan, he got hot under the collar and told her she'd regret her rebuff. She did.

While she didn't report the incident, their relationship soured. The company picnic provided the setting for the next confrontation. The purchasing manager started with a couple of indecent suggestions, progressed to grabbing and fondling the buyer, and topped it with some juicy obscene remarks.

After extricating herself from that sticky situation with the help of a coworker, she went to the comptroller about the problem. Both went to personnel, where the charges were discussed by various staffers. Two months went by. Again she went to personnel, claiming she was now afraid of the purchasing manager. Personnel said it would check with headquarters back east.

About that time the buyer heard tales of a trouble-shooter back at company headquarters with a good reputation. Eight months after the fateful dinner and six months after the picnic report, she met the trouble-shooter, who reported the incident to her own superior and indicated the employee was becoming ill because of the problem.

The response: Solve the situation at the local level. Another month brought nothing but new harassment techniques on the part of the purchasing manager. One favorite: He'd call the buyer into his office, insist she remain standing, and stare at her for long periods. He also threatened to "destroy" her and halt all career advancement.

The next month brought two new developments. First the trouble-shooter told the buyer her case was "too hot to handle." Then the buyer contacted an equal employment opportunity specialist, who promised to get back to her, but never did. Then the doctor visits began: high blood pressure, nervous tic in one eye, chest pains, rapid breathing, other signs of emotional distress.

The senior buyer finally filed for a transfer. The next day she was placed on probation for poor performance. Now, eleven months after her first report, came a meeting in which she introduced a written note accusing her boss of sexual harassment and asking for protection from him. Said she: "I am collapsing emotionally and physically and can't go on."

The purchasing manager was confronted with the accusations. They were investigated. He was censured—thirteen months after the damaging dinner and dessert demands.

Five months later he was gone. But so—almost—was she. He was fired. She attempted suicide. After her recovery, she sued the purchasing manager and the company for assault and intentional infliction of emotional distress.

The courts had a field day with the case. The first one found the manager guilty of assault and battery, but not intentional infliction of emotional distress. It found the company guilty—and not guilty—of just the opposite charges. An appeals court reversed the company part of the decision. But the state supreme court saw it differently. The company inaction was an offense in itself. Plus it had a laundry list of policies that the employee had come to depend on, none of which worked.

In this particular case, the court broke the emotional distress offense into three parts: (1) the behavior must be extreme or outrageous; (2) the company must deliberately ignore or recklessly disregard the likelihood the sexual harassment could occur; (3) the employee must truly be emotionally distressed. In this case it was three strikes and the company was out. (*Ford* v. *Revlon, Inc.*, No. CV-86-148-PR, 1 Indiv. Empl. Rts. Cases 1571, Ariz. Sup. Ct., 1987)

■ *Employee Rights Alert:* The question of employer liability for individual managers' actions is often raised in sexual harassment claims. As you saw, even the U.S. Supreme Court avoided making a blanket statement on the subject. In this Arizona case, the company tried to wash its hands of a manager's guilt, but the court accused it of being lax in its own right on its employee's rights.

The Supreme Judicial Court of Massachusetts cast its vote on the side of "vicarious liability" in one employer responsibility case. A supervisor began making suggestive remarks to a worker. She complained to the director of manufacturing, who sent her to personnel. Contacted about the charge, the supervisor not only denied it, but turned the tables on the worker and accused her of sexually suggestive remarks. He then called a meeting of all female employees except the alleged victim and explained the allegations. But no one was questioned about any incidents.

The situation simmered. No more actions. No warnings. No discipline. Just tension. Then the complaining party was given a transfer. She refused, got pink slipped, and sought solace in the judicial system. Said a court: Sexual harassment by a supervisor stigmatizes an employee and implicitly carries the threat of job-related retaliation. Plus the company's investigation was deferential and inadequate.

(*College Town* v. *Massachusetts Commission Against Discrimination*, 400 Mass. 156, 1987)

------

## Sexual harassment and ménage à trois

Three's definitely not company when it comes to sexual harassment claims. Usually the "third person in" is the one who's called upon to solve the problem. As in hockey fights, it's often that individual who bears the brunt of the battle. Sometimes they battle back.

A salesman commiserated with his new female coworker. She was upset because the branch manager was hitting on her. She confided that he wanted to set her up in an apartment and had indicated her job was on the line if she didn't cooperate. The salesman got his dander up and went for the branch manager's scalp by going over his head to the district manager.

The district manager warned the branch manager to back off. The latter agreed. But soon after the female of the first part resigned, after learning she was targeted for dumping on the unemployment heap. Then the sympathetic salesman had the screws put to him. He was on the receiving end of his first corrective interview in four years of employment. Within a month, despite an improved performance and a gain in sales, he was terminated.

A district court reviewed his record: high performance marks, company honors, no discipline problems. He had held a good faith belief that the female employee's complaint was genuine and warranted investigation under Title VII. Conclusion: He was involved in statutorily protected opposition to an alleged unlawful employment practice and suffered an adverse action because of that. That spells retaliation and adds up to $22,000 in back pay plus attorney's fees. (*Jenkins* v. *Orkin Exterminating Co., Inc.*, 646 F. Supp. 1274, 1986)

A personnel director in Boise suffered a similar fate, with multiplied results. His assistant complained of sexual harassment perpetrated upon her by the biggest of the big guys, the company president. During a thirteen-month investigation, the director determined that his assistant was being unfairly isolated and was the object of retaliation. He spoke up. He was knocked down, and out of his job.

He bounced up and counterpunched with a suit based on Idaho common law and the state human rights act. A jury found the prez guilty of retaliatory discharge, breach of contract based on company personnel policies, and intentional infliction of emotional distress. The initial award certainly wasn't small potatoes: almost half-a-million for loss of past and future wages and benefits, and a million bucks in punitive damages. (*O'Dell* v. *Besabe,* No. 88574, 4th Dist. Ct., 1987)

Parties of the third part can become enmeshed in sexual harassment cases in other ways as well. Some courts have held that employers who promoted employees who granted them sexual favors discriminated against those who refused.

You saw earlier in this chapter how a nurse claimed she lost a promotion to another Florence Nightingale who happened to be involved in a sexual relationship with the doctor who made the promotion decision. The evidence was indirect: long lunches, kissing, physical contact in front of coworkers. That's enough, said an appeals court. The complaining nurse did not have to provide direct evidence of intentional discrimination or explicit evidence of a sexual relationship. (*King* v. *Palmer,* 598 F. Supp. 65 D.D.C., 1984; rev'd 778 F.2d 878, D.C. Cir., 1985)

A New York court has widened the lasso of third party sexual harassment. It held an employer liable for the conduct of a polygraph examiner who was giving tests (and more!!) to female company employees and was accused of sexual harassment. And the Washington Supreme Court ruled a trio of two supervisors and one worker were responsible for a hostile environment surrounding a female employee —the latter for creating it and the former two for not taking prompt and corrective action to stamp it out.

## Sexual harassment or discrimination audit

We've combined a number of questions on sexual discrimination and sexual harassment. These are by no means exhaustive, but will put you on the right track if you're caught in such a case.

- How long has harassment been going on and when did you first report it?
- Just how serious is the transgression? Was it merely boorish and unprofessional, or downright coercive or stressful?
- How fast did the company act on your complaint? Was the speed appropriate to the size of the organization and reporting lines involved?

- Were job transfer or temporary reassignment offered as alternatives?
- Was the compliance to a sexual suggestion a condition of employment or promotion?
- Does your company have policies that conform to federal, state, and local regulations on sexual harassment, maternity leave, etc?
- Did anyone in authority, even an indirect superior, engage in sexual harassment toward you? Does the company have an anti–sexual harassment training program for supervisors? A meaningful dispute resolution program?
- Does your company have a firm policy that it won't tolerate sexual harassment? Provide a workable means to investigate and resolve complaints? Investigate complaints fully and fairly? Impose swift and appropriate discipline on offenders? Protect victims from reprisal?
- Does the company have posted notices and widely disseminated proscriptions against sexual harassment?
- Does the company maintain investigatory files for sexual harassment claims? Keep personnel information out of them to avoid retaliation?
- Did the company conduct a swift and appropriate investigation that included:

    Censure or leave or some type of separation for the accused harasser

    Turning over transcripts of witnesses

    Offering some type of separation, such as leave, for the victim, plus assurance of job protection

    Corrections and amendments for personnel records when appropriate?

- Does the company policy about sexual harassment require the employee to report to an immediate supervisor, thus discouraging reporting and diminishing faith in the employer's good faith and fair dealing? Does the policy outline how to go to higher authorities in case your immediate superior is involved in the harassment?
- Did anyone connected with the company ever tell you not to go to an outside agency, such as the EEOC or a state human rights commission, with a sexual harassment complaint?
- Can you prove the harassment significantly altered the conditions under which you had to work?

- Can you prove that any advances made to you were not encouraged or welcomed, and very definitely rebuffed?
- Are company hiring practices sexually discriminatory? Rule of thumb in hiring: equal treatment. If a company refuses to hire mothers of school-age children, does it also refuse to hire fathers? Married women, and married men? How about wives of current employees, and husbands?
- What about attitudes toward morality? Another rule of thumb is, if it doesn't affect the job or the business, it's none of their business. Does your company have sanctions against divorce or extramarital affairs?
- If you think your discharge is tied to your pregnancy, do you have the timing to prove it? Did the company act precipitously? Has it documented unsatisfactory behavior or just vague opinions? Were any work deficiencies pointed out, and were you given a reasonable opportunity to improve? Were you warned of specific disciplinary consequences? Were superiors consulted on your discharge? Were you offered alternatives, or a chance to appeal?

# CHAPTER 5

# "Jar Wars" Sparks Courtroom Battles

R ight behind sexual harassment as a prime progenitor of privacy problems is the question of substance-abuse testing. Mostly that substance is drugs other than alcohol. We'll use drug testing as the umbrella phrase since it's most common.

Amidst all the charges and counteries flying back and forth in the heated controversy over drug and alcohol testing, one simple principle is gaining momentum: Testing—without good reason to suspect that the individual employee has a job-performance-impacting substance-abuse problem—is usually a legal no-no.

It doesn't speak to all the problems. But the cry is getting louder. And a long-drawn-out California case has turned up the volume. A transportation company ordered all 489 people in its engineering department to sign medical consent forms and be subject to urine tests. Only 488 agreed. The lone dissenter refused and was fired for failing to obey proper authority. Her lawyer claimed violation of employment contract, subjection to extreme emotional distress, and invasion of privacy.

The company's position was made even more precarious by the fact that its involvement in the transportation industry subjected certain of its employees to federally mandated drug tests under certain circumstances. At the same time it was requiring routine drug tests, the government was okaying such tests only when reasonable suspicion existed of work impairment by drugs or alcohol.

The specific situation of the programmer in question was almost as complicated. After her refusal, the company first said there would be a hearing. Then it abruptly fired her. The court faced three legal questions:

- Was it wrongful discharge based on the reasoning that a dismissal in retaliation for refusing a potentially unnecessary test given without prior notice is against public policy? Answer: Yes.
- Since California courts hold that the employment relationship involves the covenant of good faith and fair dealing, was the concept breached? Answer: Yes.
- Was there intentional infliction of emotional distress for the summary method of acting? Answer: Yes.

Added up, the monetary damages went like this: $272,000 punitive, $180,000 lost wages, $32,000 for distress. Total: Almost half a million dollars. (*Luck* v. *Southern Pacific Transportation Co.*, No. 843230, Cal. Sup. Ct., 1987)

- *Employee Rights Alert:* This case is a good reflection of the number one commandment in all privacy cases. An employer's authority extends only as far as performance and behavior on the job. Unless a problem surfaces that impacts on-the-job results, deters satisfactory performance, or threatens the well-being of individuals or the company, it's usually not in the employer's bailiwick of control.

There are aspects of this case to note that go beyond the particular to the generic. If you're involved in any court case, but especially a privacy one like drug testing, factor these questions into your case preparation:

- Was the defense presentation made by a single individual? Any signs of personal bias?
- Is there a case to be made for second-hand information and hearsay versus personal direct witnesses?
- Was there arbitrary or capricious use of employer authority or power?
- Are there any claims that were not precisely accurate or were

downright false? Even if unimportant, does that throw a negative light on the opposition's important contentions?
- Are there any contradictions between supervisors and others testifying for management?
- Did management try to cast aspersions on employee records without having actual records backing the aspersions?
- Is there a David versus Goliath syndrome that can be emphasized to advantage?

## Federal laws, drugs, and privacy

Privacy issues in drug testing and handicaps are tied together by the federal Rehabilitation Act of 1973. Many drug testing cases in the public sector are filed under that act, and state statutes that affect private sector employees often run along similar lines and reflect principles of the Rehabilitation Act.

The act itself mandates that no one should be excluded from job opportunities or denied job benefits because of handicaps, and that employers should reasonably accommodate legitimate handicaps as long as it doesn't cause undue hardship.

A landmark Philadelphia case in 1978 set the stage for alcoholics, drug addicts, and recoverees to be protected by the handicap law. The city police department had a policy of not hiring anyone with a drug history. The three plaintiffs in the case were rehabilitated drug users, whose final medical checks had turned up their previous usage and turned the hiring personnel against them. Their contention: The city treats drug users as if they were handicapped but then discriminates against them. It shouldn't jump to conclusions but base its decisions on hearings about performance. The courts agreed. (*Davis* v. *Bucher,* 451 F. Supp. 791, E.D. Pa., 1978)

Note that the Rehabilitation Act does contain this exclusion:

> . . . the term "individual with handicaps" *does not* include any individual who is an alcoholic or drug abuser whose current use of alcohol or drugs prevents such individual from performing the duties of the job in question . . . or creates a situation in which their employment would constitute a direct threat to the property or safety of others.

Here is a quick scan of some other drug or alcohol use cases tied to handicaps:

- Occasional use of drugs or alcohol is not a handicap because it doesn't constitute substantial impairment of a major life activity. (*McCleod* v. *City of Detroit*, 39 F.E.P. Cases 225, E.D. Mich., 1985)
- Former addicts and rehabilitated drug users are almost certainly handicapped and can't be discriminated against. (*Johnson* v. *Smith*, 39 F.E.P. Cases 1106, D. Minn., 1985)
- An employer covered by the Rehabilitation Act is only required to make reasonable accommodation in these cases. (*Southeastern County College* v. *Davis*, 442 U.S. 397, 1979, 41 C.F.R. section 560-1.3)

## State substance abuse testing

While federal statutes and constitutional guarantees apply to public employers and federally connected contractors, many states have enlisted on the side of the private sector employee in the privacy war over drug and alcohol testing. Some have general prohibitions against testing or provide parameters in which it must be done. Others have civil remedies for those who have been aggrieved, or make violations a misdemeanor offense.

That's why if your privacy invasion claim involves substance abuse testing, your first move should be to check state rules and regulations. Here, in brief, are a few examples from different states. Note especially the italicized passages.

*Connecticut:* Law sets guidelines for preemployment urinalysis. Prospective employees must be informed in writing at the time they apply that they'll be tested for drugs. That testing must conform to certain requirements, including *triple testing for positives,* a copy of test results given to the subject, and confidentiality. *Specifically prohibited is the presence of a monitor or observer during the process of producing a urine sample.*

*Iowa:* An employer may not condition employment on successful completion of a drug test . . . but *a drug screen can be performed as part of a preemployment physical.* Probable cause is required for testing current employees.

*Minnesota:* Employers must have a written drug policy that contains information on who will be tested, when the testing will be requested or required, the consequences of refusing to be tested, and the rights of job applicants who refuse to undergo testing. Job applicants may be tested only after a job offer has been made and only if that test is required of all applicants offered the position.

*Vermont: Testing may be conducted only on probable cause that the employee is using drugs or alcohol on the job,* and is permitted only if an Employee Assistance Program is provided.

*Utah: No reasonable suspicion is demanded.* Employers are protected from being sued for mistakenly firing a nondrug user as long as they reasonably relied on two tests. The regulation offers protection against defamation suits. Utah has fewer due process requirements than many states.

*Montana:* May not require job applicants to submit to drug testing unless employment is in *hazardous work environments* or jobs that involve security, public safety, or fiduciary responsibility.

Some states (e.g., California) even have privacy protection guarantees written into their constitutions. Says Massachusetts: "A person shall have a right against unreasonable, substantial, or serious interference with his privacy."

In fact, that Massachusetts statute was part of a 1982 case in which three salesmen were fired for refusing to answer a questionnaire. The company wanted to find out why its sales force was performing so poorly. Among the questions it came up with were ones dealing with drinking, as well as other off-the-job problems.

Highly personal, offensive, and not related to performance, cried the salesmen. Goodbye, cried the company. Split decision, cried the court. Based on the statute protecting privacy rights, it was a bad faith firing. But there was no privacy invasion, because the salesmen really had not answered the questions. (*Cort* v. *Bristol-Myers Co.*, 385 Mass. 300, 431 N.E. 2d 908, 1982)

Then there are local drug testing rules as well. For example, a San Francisco ordinance prohibits most public and all private employers from random or companywide drug testing of employees. Testing can occur only if reasonable grounds exist to believe the employee is so impaired that he or she poses a clear and present danger to themselves or others. An employee can challenge the results and the law doesn't include preemployment tests.

Despite all the state specifics, gray areas persist. There are no court decisions holding that state (or federal) constitutions directly limit a private employer's right to test or impose test-related discipline. And what of the question of discipline or termination for substance abuse away from work? Must there be specific evidence of on-the-job impairment? How tolerant will courts be of testing for sensitive positions? Of random testing? Of instituting testing without any "bargaining" with the work force?

No one knows the answers, which is why substance abuse testing is one of the most volatile of all privacy issues. As a start, ask yourself if your company: has a policy on grounds for testing, lists actions that might result from positive results, guarantees confidentiality, offers information on whom to contact if there is a problem, names types of samples required, has a method of reporting prescription medicine, tells the type of facility used, and requires second test opinions.

---

## Drugs outside of wrongful discharge

Drug testing has many ramifications outside of wrongful discharge. Disability benefits are affected, for example. In a Pennsylvania case, a federal judge and an arbitrator agreed: An employer can't make drug testing a condition of receiving continued benefits, especially when there was no reason to believe the disability was caused by drugs.

An off-the-job injury had kept a worker off the job for two weeks. A company physician gave him the green light and pronounced him fit for work. His personal system still flashed a yellow caution. That made his employer see red and another examination was scheduled. The worker was a no-show. He claimed he overslept as a result of prescription pain medication. Further exams will include drug tests, decided the company. Not for me they won't, decided the worker, who eventually became an ex-benefits receiver and then an ex-worker.

The standard company policy said that if disability were the result of drug or alcohol abuse, no benefits would be paid. The court: That doesn't give the company the right to test unless there is more than a remote likelihood that the employee will be impaired on the job or when independent evidence of that abuse exists. The level of suspicion in this case just wasn't high enough to justify the benefits denial. (*Equitable Gas Co.* v. *United Steelworkers of America*, No. 87-0940, W.D. Pa., 1987)

Oregon has taken a hard-line stance in the unemployment benefits–drug testing arena. The State Employment Division adopted a policy that denies benefits to job applicants who refuse to take tests mandated by prospective employers. The policy also denies benefits to employees fired for refusing tests if the employer had reasonable cause to order the test. Benefits aren't denied if the employee is fired after refusing to take a random test.

Defamation jumped in bed with drugs in two cases thousands of miles apart. Down in the Southwest, a worker was tested for drugs after he fainted on the job. Result: Traces of what could be methadone. The company's safety director wrote up an accident report that the employee tested positive. To an external inquiry, the company labor director said in effect that the worker was discharged for drug use.

During a lawsuit for defamation, an independent pathologist assessed the drug found in the employee's system as similar to, but not, methadone. The jury weighed in with $150,000 in compensatory damages and $250,000 in punitive for the employee. (*Houston Belt & Terminal Railway Co.* v. *Wherry*, 548 S.W. 2d 743, Ct. Civ. App., Tex., 1977)

Up in the Northeast, a restaurant-chain manager was accused of drug use and ordered to take a polygraph. Dishonesty was added to the charges when the test went against him, and he was fired. When extenuating circumstances turned the jury in his favor, he was awarded $50,000 for defamation and almost $400,000 for invasion of privacy. An appeals court affirmed the decision. (*O'Brien* v. *Papa Gino's of America*, 780 F.2d 1067, 1st Cir., 1986)

## Practical aspects of drug testing

If you're involved in a drug or alcohol testing privacy case, you should not only know your rights, but also what courts look for in the way of company policies and practices that lead to *defensible* positions on this issue. Most employees should have no quarrel with a company that boasts these twelve court-friendly substance abuse testing strategies:

- Makes testing a condition of employment for all applicants
- Limits testing of current employees to those in special situations, such as workers whose jobs pose significant impact on other workers or the public (e.g., drivers)

- Tests only when there is strong evidence of suspected abuse, such as obviously impaired on-the-job conduct
- Emphasizes the voluntary aspects, the purpose and the justification
- Announces tests beforehand, lets employees know they are being specifically tested for certain substances, and limits the intrusiveness of the tests
- Keeps all results confidential
- Confirms all positive results through alternative tests
- Stresses drug rehabilitation as part of its program
- Has a high-level review of any drug-based termination decision
- Has a well–spelled out and disseminated policy that is consistently applied and focuses on standards that depend on performance and behavior
- Has a policy and grievance avenues for employees who refuse testing
- Insures a solid chain of custody to protect the integrity of the testing

## One step forward, two steps back

New techniques have given drug-testing proponents added ammunition. One of the latest weapons in jar wars is obtained with scissors. It is claimed that long after traces of cocaine and marijuana disappear from the urine, the residue remains trapped in users' hair.

While the procedure is still in the development stage, the claim is that just five or six strands of hair will indicate what a person ingested, when, and how much. Either body or facial hair will do, since the roots absorb drug residue from the bloodstream.

On the other hand, you have the antitesting forces pointing out that common medications and products can trigger false positives. Among the reports in media ranging from *Newsweek* to the *Personnel Journal:* Vicks inhaler contains a substance that registers as an amphetamine; the painkiller ibuprofen, found in Advil, can generate a positive for marijuana; and poppy seed bagels can produce cocaine indications.

In fact it's reported that false positives for amphetamines can be triggered by synthetic compounds like phenylpropanolamine, contained in 151 drugs sold over the counter, including Contac.

Other commonly ingested over-the-counter medications reported to have prompted drug positives are Alka-Seltzer Plus, Allerest, and Nyquil. There's even been chemical confusion between the skin pigment melanin and THC, the active ingredient in marijuana.

So confusion reigns in the crazy world of drugs and alcohol. And some stranger-than-true incidents have merely kept the brew at a boil. Consider:

- A new phrase entered the lexicon of the world of job descriptions when the National Collegiate Athletic Association (NCAA) introduced the "urine validator," an individual who monitors the process of taking urine samples for drug testing.
- Not only are there new job descriptions, but there's a whole new industry: producing, marketing, and selling drug-free urine. A Texas entrepreneur labels its product for experimentation purposes only and touts itself as "your urine specialists." At fifty bucks a pop, it'd have to be awful special!
- A woman in the human services field for the state of North Dakota claimed her civil rights were violated. She was fired for using a hallucinogenic substance—peyote. As a member of the Native American Church, though, such usage was part of her religion, so she sued for a million bucks. Oh yes, her occupation: drug and alcohol counselor.
- The widow of a brewery worker in Detroit complained that there was no such thing as a free lunch. Her husband died of alcohol-induced liver disease. Her lawyer pinpointed the cause: a company policy of offering free beer before work, at breaks, and during lunch.
- A Massachusetts man was reported to be cooking up a million dollar lawsuit. Seems he was pulled over and accused of driving under the influence. He failed a breathalyzer test and pleaded guilty. But he blamed his local bakery: The owner sold him a rum cake, which our driver claimed caused him to fail the test. And so it goes.

To further analyze whether you have a general case, ask yourself:

- Did your employers conduct themselves according to the twelve commandments listed earlier in this chapter?
- Did they commit an act or disclose information offensive to an ordinary person?

- Did they abuse the right of qualified privilege in discussing your case?
- Did they communicate false information or go beyond the bounds of need to know?
- Did they initiate emotional distress with inadequate notice or unreasonable search and seizure?
- Did they verge on assault and battery with a nonconsensual taking of blood or urine?
- Did they insure accuracy of tests, use labs with high quality standards, double-check by including control samples with real ones?

# CHAPTER 6

# Privacy Rights in the Workplace: It's a Whole New Ball Game

P rivacy in the workplace pulls together a host of problems. You've already seen how sexual harassment and substance abuse testing fall into that embrace. Some others are straightforward categories: polygraphs, search and seizure, handicaps. Then there are those with fancier monikers: intrusion upon seclusion, record-keeping negligence. . . . The list is almost endless.

In general, your employer's right to have any control over your private life extends only to the boundaries of its legitimate business interests. Determining that fine line sometimes requires fancy footwork. Courts in many cases are using the "reasonable person" approach. That is, if there were such an ideal individual, how would he or she react to the specific evidence?

## Some background on privacy

Before we get into the swing of the privacy ball game, it might help to set the stage with some pregame warmups.

Privacy in the American workplace has been around a long time, but only recently has the pendulum swung in the direction of the employee. Back in the old days, companies not only controlled their own businesses, but sometimes the entire towns in which they operated. Employee rights, as you may suspect, were not a paramount concern.

It's reported that Henry Ford's workers were promised their "lucrative" $5-a-day salaries only after his "sociologists" visited their houses and deemed them morally qualified to work for him.

Basically privacy through the years has involved a collision of two equal and opposing rights. On the one hand you have employers' rights to hire and retain employees who do their jobs conscientiously, safely, and honestly, with proper behavior and acceptable performance. On the other hand, you have employees' rights to be treated fairly, to not be discriminated against, and to not have their private lives mixed with their workplace existences.

## Privacy law of the land

In reality, there isn't any. Oh, there's the federal Privacy Act. But it applies only to government agencies. And there's the Fair Credit Reporting Act. It sets standards for all kinds of "consumer" reporting and defines consumers so broadly as to include employees and job applicants. That means investigative reports about employees' financial backgrounds may require notification and disclosure of employer activities on request. Also, if adverse actions are taken against you on the basis of such reports, you can demand an explanation.

There's also the Omnibus Crime Control and Safe Streets Act of 1968 that includes provisions that cover hidden surveillance, and has been interpreted to restrict employer eavesdropping on private conversations. And there's a provision in the National Labor Relations Act which forbids surveillance if it interferes with the right to organize.

Even the Family Education Rights and Privacy Act of 1974 can hold a smidgen of employee privacy rights within its boundaries. Basically it protects student records in public schools. But it can be expanded to affect educational material in personnel records, requiring written consent for any information release.

## States ride to the rescue

But there's no all-encompassing federal legislation that directly deals with the overall issue of employee privacy rights. So naturally the states have jumped into the vacuum with a checkerboard of different laws and regulations.

Many are based on the federal Privacy Act which deals mainly with employee records: what can be kept and what can't, rights of examination, and restrictions on dissemination. About two dozen states have adopted specific laws on privacy, like Michigan whose detailed statutes include most requirements of the federal Privacy Act. Then there are other states with privacy protection in their state constitutions, notably California, which specifically protects the privacy of communications made under a promise that they will be held in confidence.

Several states have adopted their own versions of the Fair Credit Reporting Act. Others have laws against giving false derogatory employment references. Still others forbid the use of arrest records rather than convictions in employment decisions.

Another twenty some states have statutes that prohibit blacklisting of former employees, usually involving the prohibition of false statements on job applications.

State laws generally prevent release of information to third parties without consent and enable employees to inspect their records. The strictest states on disclosure are California, Connecticut, Maine, Michigan, Oregon, and Pennsylvania.

There are also so-called service letter laws, although they appear on their way out of the workplace playground. They require that an employer release certain information, on request, about an employee. For example, Indiana, Missouri, and Nevada demand that the "true reason" for termination be given. Other states have more limited laws, which focus on specific employers, like Nebraska's which affect government contractors.

You'll find a number of state privacy issue charts throughout this chapter. View them with a shaker of salt. Changes are occurring every day.

## State by state by state

As you've seen time-and-again in the employee rights scene, where you live is almost as important as the facts of the case in determining just what kind of case you have. With no federal privacy laws that apply to private employers, each state goes its own way in specific laws, their application, and their interpretation. And the courtroom results can fall all over the legal spectrum. Want us to bounce a few cases off you?

A 1984 New Jersey court decision ruled that a UPS driver could not be fired for having an adulterous affair. That case tossed sex and company policy into the privacy stew. It heated up when the employee claimed he was discharged under a company policy forbidding married men from engaging in extramarital affairs. It said nothing about unmarried men similarly engaged, he said, and so violated a state law that forbade discrimination on the basis of marital status.

The company's rebuttal: Termination was based on antinepotism policy. Employee's rebuttal to the rebuttal: I was fired in retaliation for exercising my natural rights to privacy. Trial judge ruled for company, but appeals court sent it back for review: The trial judge should consider not only the alleged company policy itself, but whether that policy entailed extended inquiry by the employer or any surveillance by the employer of the extramarital sexual activities of its married employees. (*Slohoda* v. *UPS*, 475 A.2d 618, N.J. App., 1984)

In Michigan, a vehicle rental employee lost a court case when she challenged her termination which was based on dating a coworker. But another Michigan court ruled that a part-time cop's rights were violated when he was canned for living with a woman whose divorce from her husband wasn't final.

A federal judge in Missouri ruled an employee did have grounds for a record-keeping negligence suit because he claimed his employer had put false information into his personnel file. But a D.C. judge refused to acknowledge a negligence claim when an employer neglected to put an employee's promotion notice in his file.

Some states require that a privacy invasion be physical, like trespassing. In others, it can be mental, like sexual harassment. In one case, a supervisor's coercive demands were judged to involve a privacy intrusion. (*Philips* v. *Smalley Maintenance Service*, 711 F.2d, 1524 11th Cir., 1983)

As with all employee rights issues, privacy cases overlap. We've chosen the following categories to be part of this privacy ball game. We've tried to cover most of the important bases. Here's the scoreboard. See if you recognize any personal hits.

---

## First inning: Stepping on employee toes off the job

Technically, it may be referred to as intrusion upon seclusion. One court summed it up this way: "One who intentionally intrudes, physically or otherwise, upon the solitude or seclusion of another or his private affairs or concerns, is subject to liability to the other for invasion of privacy, if the intrusion would be highly offensive to a reasonable person." (There's that reasonable person again.)

Mostly intrusion into seclusion or tramping on toes occurs when an employer interferes—or tries to—with personal decisions or private lives. Among the most famous, or infamous, of the privacy cases in the annals of American business involved a romance between a marketing manager and a sales coworker.

The manager was on the fast track to executive excellence before being derailed by a shoot-from-the-hip superior. An outstanding performer by many measures, she constantly exceeded her designated quotas, received top ratings in the company's incentive and evaluation programs, racked up marketing prizes and awards, and was accepted into the firm's accelerated career development program for employees who showed exceptional managerial potential.

Two catches: She was in love; and the object of her affection defected to a competitor. At first, no one above her on the management totem pole objected. In fact, after her promotion she rang up another $4,000 merit increase twelve months down the line. But a short time later she was called on the carpet and had the rug pulled out from under her career.

First, it was suggested that her continued dating of the competitor's salesman was a conflict of interest, or at least had all the earmarks of one. Her response: You've known all along of the relationship. Their reply: That was then, this is now. Either stop dating or you're out of the management position.

She was taken aback by the turn of events, but also told to take a few days to choose. The very next work day, the decision was made for her. She was out as a manager. Violation of company practices and procedures, she cried. The company went ahead and transferred her to a nonmanagement position in another division. Her lament changed: You've effectively—and wrongfully—terminated me.

A jury agreed. Key point: A memo from the chairman of the firm which underlined the company policy of recognizing employee privacy, leading to the expectation that her job would be protected under that policy. When the protection failed to materialize, she collected a cool $300,000.

■ *Employee Rights Alert:* This case emphasizes two points you should keep in mind if you think your privacy has been invaded. One, your employer may not impose his or her personal code of ethics or morality on your job situation. Two, the company must adhere to its policies just as closely as you must. In this case, not only was there a policy against privacy intrusion, but the definition of conflict of interest was spelled out in the personnel manual. And it didn't apply! (*Rulon-Miller* v. *IBM,* 162 Cal. App. 3d, 208 Cal. Rptr. 524, Cal. App., 1984)

Romantic misadventures have been known to trip up employers even when there was no direct management involvement in the privacy invasion. When a white woman became the manager of an apartment complex in a Midwestern state, her black boyfriend became a regular visitor. That didn't set well with a pair of racist maintenance men.

They tossed a host of racial insults and threats at the woman, who reported their conduct to management. A top executive wrote back: I'm not sure we can keep our staff from saying those things. Things went from bad to worse as the apartment manager began to catch flack from her superior about her performance. Eventually she lost her job but won her day in court as a judge decided management may be held responsible for its workers' actions. Not only can't an employer cross the line into controlling off-the-job romance, but as this case demonstrates, it must also be aware when off-the-job dalliances generate on-the-job privacy invasions. (*Moffit* v. *Glick,* 604 F. Supp. 229, N.D. Ind., 1984)

## Social mores and sex

Relationships outside the "traditional" and the "accepted" have managed to stir up hot feelings and hotter court battles when managers applied their standards to the conduct of others.

An insurance agent attended his company's "Honor" convention in what management thought was less than an honorable fashion. He showed up with a woman who wasn't his wife, with whom he was found to be conducting an extramarital affair. And he had the audacity to introduce her around as his spouse.

Terminated, he blasted back with a slew of condemning contentions, among them:

- The company had no written policy forbidding extramarital affairs
- The company never indicated an employee could be terminated for such actions
- The conduct of company officers fostered an atmosphere of permissiveness
- His rights of free expression and free association were being squashed
- The real reason he was fired was because he was such a good agent and was out-earning top company officers

Court decision: His public policy claims are all wet. The firing stands.

- *Employee Rights Alert:* Any time a personal situation like this arises, ask yourself: Is the company legislating morality or regulating purely private conduct? Is there a course of conduct or past practice of the employer on which conclusions or intentions can be drawn? Is there a company policy that openly engaging in a certain type of activity can be grounds for corporate divorce? (*Staats* v. *Ohio National Life Insurance Co.,* 620 F. Supp. 118, W.D. Pa., 1985)

Speaking of divorce, that modern by-product of marriage has also caused the judicial fur to fly. A public school system was in an uproar. Phone calls were pouring in from the community wanting to know what kind of example a system with three divorcees in its ranks sets for its children.

Seeing his system's image heading down the drain and losing ground to the local private school, the superintendent decided to pull the plug on a divorced teacher up for rehire. She sued for violation of constitutional rights of privacy and liberty.

A district court failed her case. Untenured. But an appeals court sent her to the head of the courtroom: Matters relating to marriage and family relationships involve privacy rights that are constitutionally protected against unwarranted government interference. (*Littlejohn* v. *Rose*, 768 F.2d 765, 1985)

The privacy zone for personal invasion and toe trampling has been extended by some courts to include the home. An employee and his supervisor got in a verbal tiff that culminated in the latter making a snide remark about the former's wife's sexual proclivities. He rubbed the dig in with "and everybody knows it" as many of the employee's coworkers looked on.

Both the employee and his wife sued for defamation, invasion of privacy, and intentional infliction of emotional distress. Turns out the employee had been engaged in a long-standing feud with the company. He heard through the grapevine that management had a hit list of complainees, and he was on it. According to rumors, supervisors were to provoke targeted employees into committing acts for which they could be discharged.

All this came out in court, although the company denied the plot charges. Instead, it placed blame for the fight on the employee's shoulders, contending the supervisor's remarks erupted strictly in the heat of battle.

A jury disagreed and awarded damages to both husband and wife (though not defamation for the wife). An appeals court affirmed. The offending remark was a calculated attempt to cause distress. It was clearly an outrageous intrusion into the wife's personal life. (*Keehr* v. *Consolidated Freightways*, No. 86-2126, 7th Cir., 1987)

## Second inning: Publicizing information that's best kept quiet

An example of this breach of privacy would be one where you got a memo listing the reasons you were fired and then saw the same memo tacked up on the company bulletin board for all the world to see.

A California man suffered just such ignominy. The memo sent to him listed unauthorized absences, failing to observe departmental rules, and dishonesty as his termination crimes. Suddenly he felt like a common criminal with his poster on the local post office wall.

He had a case for invasion of privacy. (*Payton* v. *City of Santa Clara*, 183 Cal. Rptr. 17, 1987)

But you can't always have your cake and eat it too. A Georgia woman hollered privacy invasion when a construction company supervisor was heard bragging that she had been just another notch on his sexual gunbelt. But a judge pointed out she had already let the cat out of the bag in detailing the liaison in a sexual harassment complaint that was on public record.

Record keeping contains the most quicksand in the information publicity and protection area. The battle over employee records privacy has raged on a number of fronts for a number of years. The basic question revolves around who gets access to what information in personnel records. The issue has expanded to include arguments over what information is allowed to be collected in the first place, and what obligations an employer is under to protect the valid material collected.

Role reversal may occur in this area, with employers lining up with employees. Back in the seventies, a landmark Michigan case pitted a union request for an employee's psychological test scores against an employer's refusal to disclose private employee information. The United States Supreme Court upheld the employer's protection contention. (*Detroit Edison* v. *N.L.R.B.*, 440 U.S. 301, 1979)

Of course, employers and employees are not always—or often—on the same side in record-keeping snafu suits. Negligence or lack of due care is often the knife that clefts the relationship.

In New Jersey, a manufacturer was faced with a raw materials shortage. It was forced to lay off a sales rep. The parting seemed amicable enough. The company even gave the rep a written recommendation and a positive letter of introduction for potential employers.

A few months later, however, the former salesman heard a different tune being crooned by a local credit reporting bureau. Seems a company report indicated he left by mutual agreement because of a poor sales record. The rep popped a cork and sued, claiming company negligence in keeping personnel files. The next cork that popped was from his champagne bottle when a court agreed with him. (*Bulkin* v. *Western Kraft East*, 422 F. Supp. 437, 1976)

## Practical record keeping

If you think you're in a position to record a privacy invasion in the record-keeping area, ask yourself:

- What state laws apply in your case (e.g., personnel file inspection, records retention)? Did the company adhere to them? (See Appendix)
- Are there signs any company authorities kept inappropriate material, especially outside the personnel files (e.g., supervisor's personal records)?
- Are there appropriate safeguards in place to protect files and restrict access to them? Are those limits spelled out in company policy?
- Are internal and external disclosure rules spelled out and followed?
- Did management communicate rules on record keeping to all employees, including yourself?
- Are record collection techniques consistent and focused on reliable sources? Are actual needs matched against material collected? Do they only collect and keep information that is job-related?
- Is there a company system to weed out dated material? Do they conduct periodic audits to purge files of irrelevant or illegal material?
- Do they allow you to inspect your records, copy, amend, correct, and disagree?

## Setting the record straight on medical records

One of the most sensitive areas in records involves those of the medical variety. One well-known case bounced from court to court. A computer company employee had made a real brat of himself, complaining long and loud about his lack of promotions, mishandled evaluations, ignored suggestions. He even complained about the way the company handled his complaints.

Finally, after running through a litany of physical ills including frayed nerves, splitting headaches, and sleepless nights, he was encouraged to see a private physician retained by the company. After the exam, the doc called the man's supervisor and suggested a shrink would be more in order, since paranoia seemed to be prevalent.

When that diagnosis was reported in a memo to other company managers, an invasion of privacy suit ensued. The first court agreed that mental health was certainly a highly personal matter. But it also felt that the managers had a legitimate reason to discuss the diagnosis; the publication was limited; and the internal disclosures were reasonable and didn't overstep any privacy bounds.

Another court disagreed. The company did have a policy requiring the medical staff to get employee authorization for any informational disclosures. Since the plaintiff's expectations of privacy were raised by that policy, the appeals court lowered the boom and ordered a jury trial to decide the fate of the potentially paranoid person. (*Bratt* v. *IBM*, 785 F.2d 352, 1st Cir., 1986)

A telephone company in New England was disconnected for telegraphing too much medical information to too many people. The problem here was AIDS-Related Complex (ARC). A company worker missed a number of days, but had legitimate, though vague, notes from his doctor. 'Fess up, said his supervisor. How come you're out so much?

After extracting a pledge of confidentiality, the employee explained his dilemma. In no time, the company wires were humming. The supervisor told his superiors, who then blabbed to a group of employees. Some of the latter were a trifle upset and offered to get together a bow-tie party and lynch the sick employee.

The employee chalked up initial victories in two courts. Here is the unappetizing way one court summed up the case: The state of a person's gastrointestinal tract is as much entitled to privacy from unauthorized public or bureaucratic snooping as is that person's bank account, the contents of his library, or his membership in the NAACP. (*Cronan* v. *New England Telephone*, 1 Indiv. Empl. Rts. Cases, 651 Mass. Sup. Ct. 658, D.C. Mass., 1986)

Medical records privacy has become a high priority on both the federal and state levels. Even the Secretary of Labor was stymied by medical disclosure rules. A company which kept OSHA illness and injury records denied access to that information without a subpoena. A court said that refusal was within the company's rights; that the government needed to describe the documents to be inspected and the scope and purpose of the search, in order to prevent "arbitrary invasion of privacy."

On the state front, Montana became the first to adopt the Uniform Health Care Information Act developed by the National Conference of Commissioners on Uniform State Law. While not a direct reaction to the workplace medical records controversy, it does reflect the emerging trend: written permission of patient before dissemination, accessibility by patient, ability to amend, confidentiality.

In some states you can't be discharged for failing to furnish information about admissions to a psychiatric hospital. In others, when applying for a job, you don't have to answer questions about physical, psychological, or psychiatric conditions unless they are related to job capability.

If medical records appear to be the root of your pain, check to see if:

- The company collects and retains only medical information that is required for business or regulatory reasons
- You have complete access to all medical data on yourself
- You are offered the option of amending or correcting information you consider inaccurate
- The company has policies that limit disclosure of medical facts to those with a legitimate business need to know, and that company personnel abide by those policies
- No disclosures are made without your consent except to satisfy legitimate investigatory or business needs

## Third inning: Intruding into the private living space or personal domain of an employee, as in search and seizure

Sometimes the intrusion is strictly physical, like several of the cases that follow. Some states even *require* the invasion to be physical, like trespassing, to trigger a solid privacy invasion case. A tragic case in this area involved a man who believed his wife was having an affair. He snooped into her attendance record on the night shift, and was told by her supervisor that she had been absent a number of nights. Believing his paramour suspicions confirmed, he committed suicide. The wife sued. A tragedy, but not a physical intrusion, so no privacy misconduct on the part of her employer, ruled a court. (*Kobeck* v. *Nabisco,* 305 S.E. 2d 183, Ga. App., 1983)

Sexual harassment sometimes gets special treatment in this regard. It may be viewed as an intrusion, even when the state law normally requires physical conflict. An Alabama statute required such physical "touch" for its enforcement. But a federal appeals court in that state ruled that when the act was one of a highly personal nature, such as a supervisor's coercive demands, it could be considered an intrusion into privacy.

## Search and seizure: The wrong side of the law

It's a given that drug use and internal theft are costing U.S. businesses billions of dollars annually. That's why the search and seizure aspect of privacy intrusions in the workplace has employers searching for answers.

A well-known case involved a Texas department store which allowed its employees to use company lockers. It even supplied locks—usually. It seems, though, that they were in short supply at one point, so an employee supplied her own—with management's full knowledge.

You can probably guess the rest. Missing merchandise. Store manager breaks padlock and rummages through purse and locker. Employee cries foul. Management first denies culpability, then claims it was within its rights as the store owned the locker; there was a business necessity of finding the culprit responsible for the theft; and company policy allowed search both of employees' persons and lockers.

Several courts volleyed this one around. The original decision backed the employee's contention that with her own padlock and the company's permission to use it, there was a clear invasion of privacy.

The court: The employer deliberately intruded upon an area where employee had a legitimate expectation of privacy . . . managers also intruded on her personal property . . . with neither the employee's permission, nor justifiable suspicion that she had stolen any store inventory. Judgment: $8,000 for anguish and $100,000 in exemplary damages, sort of like a fine imposed to set an example.

An appeals court ruled on several procedural points and ordered a new trial. It also knocked out the smaller award because the reasonable person rule was not proven. But it kept the bigger one because an unwarranted intrusion itself can be wrong. The opinion: The company deliberately intruded on an area where there was a *legitimate expectation of privacy* and it wrongfully intruded on her personal property. (*Trotti* v. *K-Mart*, 677 S.W. 2d 632, Tex. App., 1984; *K-Mart* v. *Trotti*, 686 S.W. 2d 593, Tex., 1985)

■ *Employee Rights Alert:* An employer's words, actions, and/or policies can create areas in the workplace where you can legitimately and reasonably expect a measure of privacy. But the reverse can hold true too. In one case, an executive had papers stored in a locked credenza. He claimed that restricted his employer's ability to call them into play in court. Not so, said the court. Apparently the executive had given his secretary a key to the credenza as well as free access to all its contents. The papers were judged fair game. (*O'Donnell* v. *CBS*, 1st. Cir., 1986)

## *High court searches for the lowdown*

The U.S. Supreme Court searched for a solution to a 1987 seizure case that made the headlines. A psychiatrist at a state-owned hospital in California held sway over residents and allegedly used his power for personal aggrandizement. Two sexual harassment complaints had been filed against him and other questions about his influence had arisen.

When a new computer appeared in the psychiatrist-administrator's office, the hospital director became suspicious. Donation from a supporter, the administrator claimed. Better take an administrative leave, while we investigate, said the director. I'll take vacation instead, responded the administrator, as he packed up his computer and went home.

The vacation lapsed into suspension and then termination. A committee searched the doctor's office. It was hospital policy to separate "state" property and safeguard it in such situations. The shrink claimed the committee grabbed his personal items. Two courts disagreed on whether he had a case. The high court said the case should indeed be tried. The right to search an employee's place of work should be determined by individual circumstances.

Because this was a public sector case, the constitutional protection against unreasonable searches by government was a consideration. But there are several lessons here for private sector employees you should be aware of.

For one, the expectation of privacy may be reduced by actual office practices or procedures, or by legitimate rules. For another, privacy must be judged in a business context, not just a theoretical absolute. Your office, for example, may be a Grand Central Station for subordinates, managers, executives, secretaries. How much privacy do you actually enjoy?

Then there's the question of what's a *reasonable* expectation of privacy. In this case, the court agreed that the psychiatrist did have a right to expect privacy and that the hospital did take personal belongings (which were in fact returned to him). But what constitutes *unreasonable* search and seizure, especially in a private sector work environment? That's your concern.

The court's concern, in this case, was that a search would normally be justified when there are reasonable grounds to suspect evidence of misconduct will turn up. Legitimate work-related purposes, such as retrieving a file, can also justify an office intrusion. But that intrusion must be as nonintrusive as possible, and should be confined to the specific objective of the initial incursion.

It's tough to sort out what standards apply to the reasonable/ unreasonable controversy and where employer/employee privacy boundaries exist in such cases. As the Supreme Court said, circumstances dictate. But you may get a better idea of privacy parameters from this explanation which rose from the hospital case:

> At a hospital, the hallways, cafeteria, offices, desks, and file cabinets, among other areas, are all part of the workplace. These areas remain part of the workplace context even if the employee has placed personal items in them, such as a photograph placed on a desk or a letter posted on an employee bulletin board.
>
> Not everything that passes through the confines of the business address can be considered part of the workplace context, however. An employee may bring closed luggage to the office prior to leaving on a trip, or a handbag or briefcase each work day. While whatever expectation of privacy the employee has in the existence and outward appearance of the luggage is affected by its presence in the workplace, the employee's expectation of privacy in the *contents* of the luggage is not affected in the same way. The appropriate standard for a workplace search does not necessarily apply to a piece of closed personal luggage, a handbag, or a briefcase that happens to be within the employer's business address. (*O'Connor* v. *Ortega*, No. 85-530, 1986)

## Search and seizure: Let's get physical

That office intrusion was nothing compared to the physical intrusion that kicked up a storm back in the early seventies in Louisiana. A telephone company employee failed to report to work or answer his phone, so two supervisors went to his trailer home—twice. Worried about his welfare, said the company.

Balderdash, retorted the employee, who had been found asleep inside surrounded by empty liquor and wine bottles. They were out to get me, he said, as evidenced by the fact they had brought a locksmith to break in and a witness to testify against me.

The company case was indeed weakened by the fact that the supervisors made those two trips, and took notes and a witness. The court agreed with the employee that the employer was more interested in proving wrongdoing than in helping. The tort of intrusion upon seclusion may be applicable even if evidence justifies discharge. (*Love* v. *Southern Bell*, 263 S.2d 460, La. App., 1972)

Speaking of drinking, a purchasing agent for a public agency in Florida hit the bottle pretty good. His thirst was sated by a pint of gin a day. One result: He missed 389 days on the job in three years. Fired, he claimed job discrimination based on a law requiring counseling for handicapped federal workers. The court ruling judged him legally crippled by alcoholism and entitled to a whopping six-figure back pay award.

■ *Employee Rights Alert:* The physical aspects of search and seizure extend to workplace encounters when push comes to shove. An employer may not restrain your individual freedom to move. That's false imprisonment. If your employer claims legal authority to do so, you could have a false arrest claim. And if the employer deliberately makes a false report to authorities, you could charge malicious prosecution.

That physical aspect has been emphasized over and over. A seventeen-year-old cashier in New Jersey was accused of falsely ringing up refunds and pocketing the cash. The store manager kept her in his office for four hours until she "confessed." A jury turned that confession into $100,300 in compensatory and punitive damages. (*DeAngeles* v. *Jamesway Department Stores*, N.J. Sup. Ct. App. Div., 1985)

In a similar case, three company managers triple-teamed a supervisor for three hours until the individual finally signed a resignation notice and "admitted" guilt concerning certain money given him for his driving duties. The company didn't even challenge the claim of unlawful imprisonment. An appeals court said the facts may even support a tort claim of intentional infliction of emotional distress. (*Kaminsky* v. *UPS*, N.Y. Law Journal, p. 16, col. 1, 1986)

## *Search and seizure audit*

Here are some cans/can'ts and shoulds/shouldn'ts in the search and seizure privacy area:

- Your employer can't demand that you remain in, say, a meeting room to answer questions. You can leave at any time unless they are prepared to make a citizen's arrest and suffer the consequences if it is judged wrongful.
- Your employer should announce any search and seizure plans in advance and provide a mechanism for you and other employees to discuss them. Management should also disseminate a precise policy and offer the reasons behind it.
- You should be told the specific procedures that apply, how they will be carried out, and what will happen to you if you don't cooperate. Employers cannot just make up the rules—and sanctions—as they go along.
- Your employer cannot chew you out in front of other employees or stigmatize you in other ways with a public show of force. Your defamation or privacy invasion case is bolstered dramatically by such staged drama.
- Your employer, in most cases, can't use undercover agents, secret surveillance, or entrapment. You can probably use any of them to improve your case.

## Fourth inning: Appropriating an employee's name or likeness for advertising or similar purposes

Actually, this is only a half-inning, because it's so rare. In such instances, very few companies fail to cover themselves with releases of some sort. But there was one interesting report in a national business magazine in the mid-eighties.

You may recall that in the 1981 NFL National Conference Championship game, Everson Walls of the Dallas Cowboys had the unenviable task of covering San Francisco's superstar receiver Dwight Clark. With the game on the line, Clark hauled in a pass from quarterback Joe Montana that made him the hero of the 28–27 49er victory.

Unluckily, that also made Walls, at least in part, the goat. And even more unluckily, a picture of the play, identifying Walls as the ultimate victim, by name, received widespread publicity. In fact, a camera company used it in its ads for color film.

Not pleased, Walls indicated he planned to toss a prevent defense at the company, asking for unspecified damages, on the basis that: "Such publication constitutes an unwarranted invasion of plaintiff's privacy—his right to be left alone, to have a life of seclusion free from intrusion, and unwarranted publicity."

Another half-inning involves placing an employee in a false light. This can be done by spreading erroneous information, which most employers are careful not to do, or by creating a misconception, which is more likely, though not all that common.

Still, there have been cases. One was the big airline bust in late '87. A national flyer rounded up ten of its baggage handlers on suspicion of drug use. It paraded them through the Miami airport along a guard-lined path to a waiting van. After questioning, they were herded into buses in front of other employees.

Their lawyers had a field day. They charged their clients were treated like terrorists, right in front of passengers and workers alike. They claimed defamation, invasion of privacy, intentional infliction of emotional distress.

Across the continent in Oregon, a supervisor fired a subordinate when he received an anonymous letter that the latter had been drunk in public. Then he repeated the allegation in front of over one hundred employees. An appeals court gave a green light to the false light claim and upheld a $350,000 defamation judgment.

"Complete denial of her dignity as a person." That was how a Maryland court described a company's behavior in forcing a woman to resign after she refused to take a lie detector test. A state appeals court lent emphasis to that description by affirming a $1.3 million judgment against the company.

## Fifth inning: Handicapping the problem of handicaps as a privacy health issue

The main federal law governing handicaps is the federal Rehabilitation Act of 1973. While it applies only to federally connected employers, it also serves as the model on which many states' regulations are based. In some cases, the states' regulations are stricter than the national mandate, and reach right into the private sector.

The specifics of the legal end of federal handicap discriminations are spelled out clearly. A handicapped person is anyone who meets any of these conditions:

- Has a physical or mental impairment which limits one or more major life activity
- Has had such an impairment in the past
- Is regarded by others as having such an impairment

With such broad parameters, it's no wonder the definition of handicapped has opened wide to embrace a host of ailments, from AIDS to drug or alcohol abuse to lots of less well known problems. No longer does the notion of handicaps conjure up visions of wheelchairs or Seeing Eye dogs.

Some courts have ruled that a mental disorder can be treated as a handicap. Others include the perceptual problem of dyslexia and chronic diseases like diabetes. The general theory is that a life activity is significantly impaired, but the employee is still able to perform his or her job acceptably and without creating a hazardous situation.

Here's how a court in Maryland explained it from an applicant's perspective: "If the evidence shows that the applicant has the present ability to physically accomplish the job," said the court, "the employer must establish a reasonable probability that . . . employment in the position sought would be hazardous to the health and safety of the [employee] or to other employees or frequenters of the place of employment."

### Defining a definite handicap

But the gap between theory and reality keeps the handicaps issue in the news. What is, and isn't, a handicap? An important correlation:

How far must an employer go to accommodate the handicapped employee?

The list of handicap "claims" is a long one. Some have succeeded. Some haven't. Many are unusual, to say the least. Or as in this well-known New York case, the most.

A stout woman was rejected as a job applicant because she was dangerously overweight. The company's doctor made it plain: Her physical condition would cost the company higher insurance premiums, put it at greater risk if something happened to her at work, and bring on the likelihood of more sick days and absenteeism than the normal employee. The court which heard the case was just as plain. The company was guilty of handicap discrimination. (*Division of Human Rights* v. *Xerox*, 478 N.Y.S. 2d 982, N.Y. App., 1984; aff'd 65 N.Y. 2d 213, 1985)

In another fat-related fiasco, a female surgeon in Detroit was reported to have "scalpeled" her employer to the tune of $600,000. First she claimed sexual discrimination when her hospital privileges were rescinded. But a judge agreed with her employer that the real reason for the action was her verbal abuse of nurses and patients. So she switched tactics at a later trial and doctored her discrimination claim to read handicap, on the basis of obesity and narcolepsy (a condition the hospital said caused her to fall asleep at the operating table). The jury at that trial salved her wounds with the big-bucks award.

■ *Employee Rights Alert:* If you're "pleasantly plump" and think you may have a case, don't plan a victory feast yet. Courts in Pennsylvania and Wisconsin, for example, have carved up the notion of obesity as a legal handicap.

The postal department seems to have more than its share of unorthodox handicap cases. In one, a cross-eyed postal worker couldn't operate a letter-sorting machine at an acceptable pace. He claimed his discharge was discrimination because he was handicapped. Crossed eyes don't impair a major life activity, said the court. Another postal employee tried to kill his wife. He claimed alcohol made him do it, so he was handicapped and shouldn't be discharged. The court ruled he was actually fired for criminal behavior. A left-handed letter carrier claimed he was slow at his job because of his port-sided nature. The court gave him the back of its hand when he disputed his discharge on the basis of left-handedness being a handicap. The court: Major life activities include only those functions necessary to maintain physical independence, like seeing and walking.

An epileptic butcher suffered a seizure at work and was offered a transfer. He rejected it and the company cut him loose. In the first court, the company was exonerated because the problem was work-related and affected safety, a doctor said the employee was under only fair control, and the company had offered an accommodation. Plus two other epileptics were on the company payroll, so a claim of blanket discrimination against this particular type of handicap was null and void. A later court, however, overruled and found in favor of the butcher. (*Jansen* v. *Food Circus Supermarkets, Inc.*, N.J. Sup. Ct. App. Div. No. A-5386-84TI, 1988)

For eight years, a male homosexual went to work in a government office dressed as a woman. He lost his job in a reduction in force. When he heard of another low-level government job opening up, he marched in dressed to the nines and applied. The job position shortly thereafter disappeared. He claimed officials eliminated the job because they thought he was mentally ill and handicapped. In fact, the American Psychiatric Association has recognized transvestism as a handicap. But because the condition isn't "automatically apparent" (whatever that means), the complaint was dismissed. (*Blackwell* v. *U.S. Department of Treasury*, 656 F. Supp. 713, D.D.C., 1986; aff'd No. 86-5690, D.C. Cir., 1987)

By no means are all physical or mental handicap cases so unusual, nor do they all get chalked up in the employee victory column. They also don't always generate the accommodation demanded. Everything depends on the circumstances of the specific case. Some examples:

- After a coronary bypass, a job was judged too strenuous for a worker to handle
- A hearing impairment disqualified a worker as an aerial photographer
- A bodybuilder muscled his way out of his airline attendant job
- A psychiatric social worker's suicidal tendencies precluded her from working with patients
- Blind workers could be qualified for reading jobs if the cost of hiring readers to help them was reasonable

## AIDS and privacy

No health privacy issue has generated more controversy recently than Acquired Immune Deficiency Syndrome, the dreaded AIDS.

Confusion reigns as federal, state, and local courts and governments tackle this deadly disease in its relationship to employee rights and handicap discrimination.

Precedents are few and far between. A few years ago, a West Hollywood judge ruled that a nail salon could refuse to give an AIDS victim a pedicure because there was no conclusive evidence on how the disease is spread.

But the West Virginia Human Rights Commission came down hard on a restaurant which fired an employee who was diagnosed as testing positive for HIV (Human Immunodeficiency Virus), but had not contracted the disease. The company claimed the flagrant flaunting of his homosexual proclivity soured business and sparked his discharge. But there were no warnings about his behavior, no counseling, no reprimands or discipline. In the end, the restaurant had to fork over about fifty grand for humiliation, embarrassment, and emotional and mental distress.

The one anchor in this stormy sea seems to be a landmark case involving a Florida teacher with tuberculosis. She was judged legally handicapped but still able to do the job. Plus her disease wasn't classroom contagious. Experts believe AIDS plaintiffs will hold this case up as precedent for their own.

In particular, they point to the way the appeals court approached the question of trade-off in the tuberculosis case: "whether the defendant's justifications reflect a well-informed judgment grounded in a careful and open-minded weighing of the risks and alternatives, or whether they are simply conclusory statements that are being used to justify reflexive actions grounded in ignorance or capitulation to public prejudice." (*Arline* v. *School Board*, 772 F.2d 759, 11th Cir., 1985; *School Board of Nassau County, Fla.* v. *Arline*, No. 85-1277, 107 Sup. Ct. 1123, 1987)

Some AIDS cases have made their way into courts, most notably in Florida and California. An appeals court in the Sunshine State ruled disclosure that a person has AIDS can make that individual subject to social censure, embarrassment, and discrimination. (*South Florida Blood Service* v. *Rasmussen*, 467 S.2d. 798, Fla. App., 1985)

The Florida Commission on Human Relations ruled that an employee who contracted AIDS was covered by the state's antidiscrimination regulations affecting handicaps. (*Shuttleworth* v. *Broward Co.*, F.C.H.R. No. 85-0624, Daily Labor Rptr. No. 242, 1985)

In California, the State Fair Employment and Housing Commission struggled with the case of a quality control analyst who was taken off the job after being diagnosed as having AIDS. The company continued his benefits to the tune of some $70,000 before he eventually died. But his estate contended the company should have isolated him from his coworkers and let him stay on the job. In another California case, an appeals court accepted the fact that AIDS is a handicap and ordered a teacher could return to the classroom despite his ailment as long as he was otherwise qualified.

And in Maryland, the Human Rights Commission issued discrimination guidelines which define HIV seropositivity as a handicap. Check out figure 7 for a quick look at state trends in this area. (*Chalk v. U.S. District Court*, 45 F.E.P. Cases 517, 9th Cir., 1987)

Even some cities are getting in on the act, including Los Angeles, San Francisco, Denver, Cincinnati, Austin, and Philadelphia. They've adopted laws forbidding AIDS-based discrimination in, among other things, employment.

Complications in the AIDS privacy issue may spread. As the financial impact of covering AIDS victims through benefits plans hits employers, ERISA may enter the picture. That act prohibits discrimination or discharge for the purpose of removing an individual from a company's employee benefits plan.

Employment screening may also be affected. Since AIDS appears to be on its way to becoming generally accepted as a handicap, testing for HIV is likely to be considered illegal, since it can't be shown to be job-related. In fact, some states already directly prohibit pre-employment testing for AIDS.

## Sixth inning: Smoke gets in your eyes and wafts into the courtroom

Like other privacy issues, the smoking controversy is no Johnny-come-lately. In 1914, Thomas Edison is quoted as having written to Henry Ford that he employed no person who smoked cigarettes. In fact, tradition has it that cigarette smoking only came on the scene as a replacement for chewing tobacco and spitting, as a result of the public hue and cry over that disgusting habit. The more things change, the more they remain the same.

Although smoking doesn't generally get to the discharge stage, it

**Figure 7. State Trends and Administrative Actions on AIDS as a Handicap**

*Legend:* Y = AIDS is officially treated as a handicap on the basis of a court decision or formal policy.

I = AIDS is informally treated as a handicap on the basis of general agency practices or public statements.

N = Aids is not treated as a handicap.

U = Policy is uncertain.

| State | Status | Comment |
|---|---|---|
| Alabama | I | |
| Alaska | U | |
| Arizona | Y | |
| Arkansas | I | |
| California | Y | |
| Colorado | I | |
| Connecticut | I | |
| Delaware | I | |
| District of Columbia | Y | |
| Florida | Y | |
| Georgia | I | |
| Hawaii | I | |
| Idaho | I | |
| Illinois | Y | |
| Indiana | I | |
| Iowa | I | |
| Kansas | I | A formal policy prohibits AIDS-based discrimination by state agencies. |
| Kentucky | I | |
| Louisiana | I | |
| Maine | I | |
| Maryland | I | |
| Massachusetts | Y | The state also restricts AIDS testing. |
| Michigan | Y | |
| Minnesota | I | State employees are protected against AIDS-based discrimination by executive order of the governor. |

| | | |
|---|---|---|
| Mississippi | I | |
| Missouri | Y | |
| Montana | I | |
| Nebraska | Y | |
| Nevada | I | |
| New Hampshire | I | |
| New Jersey | Y | AIDS testing by employers is heavily restricted. |
| New Mexico | I | |
| New York | Y | |
| North Carolina | I | |
| North Dakota | I | |
| Ohio | Y | |
| Oklahoma | Y | |
| Oregon | Y | |
| Pennsylvania | Y | A Philadelphia ordinance bans employment discrimination on the basis of AIDS. |
| Rhode Island | Y | |
| South Carolina | I | |
| South Dakota | I | |
| Tennessee | I | |
| Texas | Y | |
| Utah | I | |
| Vermont | I | |
| Virginia | I | |
| Washington | Y | |
| West Virginia | I | |
| Wisconsin | Y | The state also restricts AIDS testing. |
| Wyoming | I | |

has become a smoldering issue in employee rights which has burned more than one employer's ash.

In a case when discharge did enter the picture, an Oklahoma City smoke eater (a.k.a. fire fighter) snuck out behind the figurative barn for a couple of puffs. Caught brown-fingered, he was fired on the basis of his employer's regulations against smoking.

His being a public employee, the fire fighter protested his constitutional rights to privacy were being violated. Not so, said the court.

Smoking is not related to the fundamental and intrinsic human function protected by the constitutional right to privacy.

The judges also applied a balancing test which may clear up some of your own confusion on this issue. Question: Is the limit on individual liberty justified by a rational purpose? In this case, the health and safety of the public, closely tied to the health of the fire fighter, indicated the limit was. (*Gruesendorf* v. *Oklahoma City*, No. 85-1807, 10th Cir., 1987)

That constitutional aspect, of course, doesn't apply to private employers. But they have suffered their share of smokey times.

A Missouri office worker suffered a laundry list of problems he blamed on coworkers' smoking, including sore throats, dizziness, headaches, blackouts, memory loss, and inability to concentrate. A physician confirmed that his was a reaction to tobacco smoke. He used the company grievance system to request moves, but they didn't help and he ran out of options.

Two years later the National Institute for Occupational Safety and Health (NIOSH) recommended employers adopt smoking regulations. The Missouri employee's company did, making a reasonable effort to segregate smokers from nonsmokers. The employee filed a series of new complaints that his supervisors failed to segregate him, thus aggravating what he was now calling his handicap.

Exasperated, company management offered two choices: work in the computer room with no smoke, but a pay cut, or use a respirator. The employee chose the latter. It didn't work. A court injunction was next on the agenda.

His two points: Prevent the employer from exposing me to tobacco smoke at work and prevent the company from letting my individual reaction to smoke affect my pay and working conditions.

The first judge dismissed on the basis that there was no basis for an injunction to be issued. In fact, argued the employee's lawyer, there were two bases. One was that the employer had a general obligation to provide a reasonably safe workplace. The other was the employee was suffering immediate and irreparable harm. Only he himself believes that, ruled the judge in dismissing the case. (*Smith* v. *Western Electric*, 643 S.W. 2d 10, Mo. App., 1982; *Smith* v. *AT&T Technologies*, No. 44-6121, Cir. Ct. St. Louis Co., 1985)

## Smokers' rights upheld

The prototype winning case from the employee's point of view involved a New Jersey secretary who filed suit against her telephone company employer to stop all smoking in her office.

She was armed to the teeth for the hand-to-hand combat in court. Statements from her doctor that just passively inhaling tobacco smoke and its by-products harmed her health and well-being. Proof that one lone smoker near her could trigger allergic reactions of nose bleeds, eye irritations, headaches, nausea, and vomiting. Plus scientific studies on the harmful effects of second-hand smoke.

She found a sympathetic ear for her teary dilemma. Said the court: "The evidence is clear and overwhelming . . . cigarette smoke contaminates and pollutes the air . . . creating a health hazard for the smoker and for all those around him or her. . . . [The] right of the individual to risk his/her own health does not include the right to jeopardize the health of others."

■ *Employee Rights Alert:* The court in this case even went so far as to include this "irony" in its judgment. The company had a no smoking rule around its equipment to protect it. A company that demonstrates as much concern for machines should be equally sensitive to human beings. Besides any concrete "evidence" that you can unearth to back an employee rights claim you make, don't overlook color—ironies, oddities, idiosyncrasies—in your case. Courts are only human, you know. (*Shimp* v. *New Jersey Bell*, 368 A.2d 408, N.J. Sup. Ct. Ch. Div., 1976)

Benefits and unemployment compensation claims have also swirled around the smoking dilemma. One man quit his job due to the fear that second-hand smoke in a poorly ventilated area threatened his health and safety. The court: The employee held that fear honestly and in good faith, so his resignation was for good cause and he is eligible for unemployment benefits. (*McCrocklin* v. *Employment Development Department*, 156 Cal. App. 3d 1067, 205 Cal. Rptr. 156, 1984)

Another employee was also judged eligible for benefits, even though after she left her job she looked for work only with employers who didn't allow smoking in the workplace. Since the woman was sensitive to smoke, employment where smoking was allowed would not be suitable, said a court. (*Alexander* v. *Unemployment Insurance Appeals Board,* 104 C.A. 3d 97, 1980)

A worker's comp claim for disability was approved after the employee collapsed at work due to an allergic reaction to tobacco smoke. The court: Such a problem met the requirement that the ailment be job-related. (*Schober* v. *Mountain Bell*, 630 P.2d 1231, N.M. Ct. App., 1981)

And in a nationally watched case, an employee filed for industrial insurance benefits for lung disease, claiming her ailment was caused by exposure to coworkers' smoke. Claim denied. Okay, said the woman, I'll file for company negligence in failing to provide a safe and healthful workplace. Case denied. Failure to state a cause of action. Decision overruled. The appellate court: Let her have her day in court. (*McCarthy* v. *State of Washington, Department of Social and Health Services*, No. 7667-5-11, Wash. Ct. App., 1986)

## Feds, states, municipalities

In ascending order of impact, those three legal entities have jumped feet first into the smoking fray. Many cases include the general duty clause of the federal Occupational Safety and Health Act which requires employers to provide a workplace free from unsafe conditions. That's been a tenuous argument at best in the smoke fight. There are no Occupational Safety and Health Administration (OSHA) standards for tobacco smoke levels in the workplace, nor has the agency determined that tobacco smoke is a recognized liability that an employer must control.

Also on the federal list is the Rehabilitation Act, which involves handicaps and accommodation. It also, of course, only involves federal employees. One well-known case resulted in a sort of split decision. A court deemed an individual to be so sensitive to smoke as to fall under the handicap definition. But it also decided the employer had made all reasonable accommodations, as required by the act. (*Vickers* v. *Veteran's Administration*, 549 F. Supp. 85, W.D. Wash., 1982)

Statewise, the regulatory trend is growing. By some counts, over 80 percent of the states have some type of smoking restrictions, and about a quarter specifically include the workplace. Figure 8 gives you a brief overview of just that.

Some state smoking specifics:

- A new hire who lies about smoking can be fired in many states. If it is made clear beforehand that the company doesn't hire

## Figure 8. Roundup of Smoking Trends

| State | Status |
|---|---|
| Arizona | Banned in state-owned buildings. |
| Arkansas | Banned in some public buildings or in any place of employment where owner or other person in charge posts notice saying smoking is banned by law. |
| California | San Francisco, Palo Alto, and Los Angeles have ordinances on smoking in the workplace. |
| Colorado | Restricts smoking in public places and encourages offices and commercial establishments to designate nonsmoking areas. |
| Connecticut | Smoking regulations for public and private employers. |
| Florida | Regulations for public places, including place of employment. |
| Hawaii | Regulations for public places (including banks, theaters, etc.) and public employers. |
| Maine | Regulations for all employers. |
| Michigan | Regulations for public employers and some public places, even ones owned by private businesses (like Hawaii). |
| Minnesota | Public places, including businesses frequented by the public. |
| Montana | Public employment. |
| New Hampshire | Regulations for all employers. |
| New Jersey | Regulations for places of employment and some public places. |
| New Mexico | Regulations for public employees with fifteen or more workers. |
| New York | The state had regulations but a court struck them down; New York City has regulations for public places and places of employment; Suffolk County also has smoking regulations for places of employment and public places. |
| Oregon | Regulations for places of state employment. |
| Rhode Island | Regulations for all employers. |

| South Dakota | Smoking banned in some public places. |
| Utah | Regulations for all public places, including all places of employment. |
| Vermont | Regulations for employers of ten or more employees. |
| Wisconsin | Regulations for public places and publicly owned buildings. |

*Smoking restrictions: Connecticut* requires employers of fifty or more workers to provide smoke-free areas. *New York City* requires the same for businesses with fifteen or more workers. *Massachusetts* actually bars the hiring of smokers as public officers, fire fighters, motor vehicle investigators or examiners, and crash crew at Logan airport.

smokers, the EEOC has declared, a no-smoker policy is OK since it reduces health hazards and other employee costs—as long as the policy is applied in a nondiscriminatory manner.

- In 1988, Minnesota prohibited smoking in public places, including places of employment frequented by the general public. In places not frequented, restrictions or prohibitions kick in when there is close proximity or poor ventilation that causes smoke pollution detrimental to the health and comfort of nonsmokers.

- Florida reverses the usual procedure and requires employers to post areas where smoking *is permitted*, not those where it is prohibited. All other areas are considered nonsmoking.

- A New Jersey statute calls for, among other things, the rights of the nonsmoker to prevail over those of a smoker in any conflict. An employer who adopts an acceptable smoking policy is protected from many kinds of lawsuits by nonsmoking employees.

- A California employer fired a worker who actively protested smoke in the workplace. Retaliation and intentional infliction of emotional distress, bawled the employee. The court: Grounds for suit exist under California's long-established policy which protects the rights of employees who complain about unsafe or unhealthy working conditions. (*Hentzel* v. *Singer Co.*, 138 Cal. App. 3d 290, 188 Cal. Rptr. 159, 1982)

## *Smoking close to home*

It's on the local scene, though, where smoking restrictions have become most prevalent. Hundreds, maybe thousands, of cities, towns, and municipalities have enacted laws that rein in smoking, mostly in public places, but even in workplaces. New York City possesses some of the more stringent regulations. Here are some nonsmokers' rights in the Big Apple.

- You can designate your workplace as a nonsmoking area, at least eight feet from a smoking space.
- If designating a nonsmoking area doesn't reduce the effects of smoke on you, your employer must take reasonable steps to separate or ventilate better to reduce smoke levels.
- Smoking should be banned in auditoriums, elevators, halls, restrooms, and the like.
- Cafeterias, lunch rooms, and lounges must have 50 percent of their capacity or floor space designated nonsmoking.
- You are protected against retaliation for exerting your rights, and a grievance procedure should be available to you.

## Seventh inning: Stretching the truth about lie detectors

The roller-coaster ride of lie detector use over the years appears to have been smoothed out somewhat by the 1988 federal legislation placing severe restrictions on the use of polygraphs in the workplace.

Even employers may breathe a sigh of relief that there are finally some ground rules to the game. It used to be you couldn't tell who could do what, when. As recently as 1986, a Maryland appellate court was reported to have affirmed a Baltimore court's award of $1.3 million to a drugstore employee who was fired after refusing to take a polygraph test.

The history of lie detectors is littered with such results. More recently, it's also suffered the slings and arrows of politicians, one of whom likened it to "twentieth century witchcraft," while another exclaimed: "Some 320,000 honest Americans are branded as liars every single year. That's a stigma they have to wear every day the rest of their lives and careers."

With such strong antipolygraph feelings, it's no wonder a restrictive national regulation finally made it through Congress and to the desk of the president.

In brief, here are the main points of public law 100-347, Employee Polygraph Protection Act of 1988.

■ The law was designed to take effect at the end of 1988, with detailed regulations due out in the fall of that year.

■ All private sector employers (except those too small or too local to be in interstate commerce) are covered by the new law. Federal, state, and local government agencies are not covered.

■ The overall effect is to ban the use of lie detectors (a broad term including polygraph and other kinds of electrical or mechanical detectors) to screen job applicants, or to screen employees.

■ The law makes it unlawful directly or indirectly to require, request, suggest, or cause any employee or prospective employee to take or submit to any lie detector test (except in situations that the law itself permits).

■ The law also prohibits disclosure of the results of a polygraph examination by an examiner, or an employer, except as permitted in the law. The examiner may disclose results to the employee examined, or the employee's lawyer or other agent if requested in writing; to the employer; or to a court or government agency if properly ordered. The same goes for the employer.

■ The new law does not ban all testing. A polygraph test can be requested of an employee if (1) there has been a theft or other loss or damage; (2) there is an ongoing investigation that has already produced enough evidence that the employer has a reasonable suspicion that a particular employee was involved; and (3) the suspected employee had access to the stolen property or damaged area.

■ If an employer has a *reasonable suspicion* that an employee is guilty, and if the employer has evidence that the employee had access to the property in question, then the employer can request a polygraph exam, and failure to take the exam or failure to pass it can lawfully be listed as a reason for termination or other action. But the law warns that termination or other adverse action cannot be based on the test results alone.

A reasonable suspicion means that there is enough evidence that the *average person* would *suspect* that the particular employee was involved. The employer doesn't have to have *knowledge* that the employee was involved before requesting a polygraph exam, nor does it have to have *proof*.

■ There are exceptions. An employer offering guard and other security services can give a polygraph test to job applicants on a routine basis *if* the job applicants are going to work at locations where the public health and safety could be threatened, or where money and valuables are handled, or proprietary information is kept. Airports, public utilities, power plants, banks, and computer facilities would be examples.

A drug manufacturer who is licensed to handle or produce controlled substances can test a prospective employee who is going to be working where he or she will have access to controlled substances; and it can test a current employee if (1) the employee had access to the property, controlled substance, or *person* that is the subject of an investigation, and (2) there is a reasonable basis for suspecting the employee—the same two requirements that must exist for an employer in any industry to give a polygraph test, except that a drug manufacturer need only show *potential* loss or damage to itself.

This is what the law requires if a test is going to be given:

- The employee to be tested can refuse or terminate the testing process at any point.
- The polygraph examiner cannot ask questions in a manner designed to degrade, or needlessly intrude on an individual's privacy.
- The employee (or examinee) cannot be asked any questions concerning his or her religious beliefs or affiliations, beliefs or opinions on racial matters, political beliefs or affiliations, sexual preferences or behavior, or beliefs, affiliations, opinions, or lawful activities regarding unions or labor organizations.

In the pretest phase, the law says, the person being tested will be given the following in writing:

- Notice of the date, time, and location of the test, and a statement that legal counsel can be consulted before each phase of the testing process.
- A statement of the nature and characteristics of the tests and instruments involved.
- A statement that the testing area does or does not contain a two-way mirror, camera, or other observation devices. The employee will be told that either she or he or the employer can, with the other's knowledge, make a tape recording of the testing process.

Next, the employer must read aloud, and must have the employee sign, a written notice informing him or her:

- That the employee cannot be required to take the test as a condition of employment.
- That any statement made during the test can become additional supporting evidence that, together with the test results, can be used as a reason for termination or other adverse employment action.
- Of the limitations of the law (such as the ban on questions touching on religion, etc.).
- Of the employee's legal rights and remedies if the test is not conducted properly, and of the employee's rights and remedies under the law.

## Beyond polygraphs

There are a slew of other types of tests that may also infringe on employee rights at work, including psychological, physical, mechanical skills, aptitude, etc.

Where most employers get in dutch with the law in this area is when the tests screen out an inordinate number of persons of a protected group, (e.g., women or blacks). The EEOC has guidelines and policies calling for stringent programs of test validation to wipe out discriminatory effects. In fact, the Supreme Court in 1971 ordered employers to cleanse their selection processes of even unintentional discrimination which occurred when cultural bias was inherent in the tests.

Most employers have tailored their tests to fall within legal guidelines for accuracy, validity, reliability, consistency, and so forth. To get a handle on whether some aspects of testing in your case may not have been kosher, ask:

- Has it been validated?
- Does it screen out a high percentage of any group?
- Does it effectively predict job performance?
- Is it geared to predict company specific job performance as opposed to general industry standards?
- Is it given under objective and consistent circumstances?

## Eighth inning: Technology troubles in privacy problems

Modern technology sometimes plays a role in privacy invasion claims, and courts are not often well-disposed to such activities.

A Birmingham woman who worked for a telemarketing firm one day got an incoming call. During the course of the conversation, her invitation to apply for a position at another company came up. She was plenty miffed a short time later when her manager referred to that offer.

In fact, tempers flared so hot she was fired. She went straight to a lawyer without passing *go* or going home. And she did collect an out-of-court settlement after a court of appeals heard her case. She knew that the company policy was to occasionally monitor telemarketing calls to ensure proper sales procedures were being followed. But she also knew it was against company policy to listen to personal conversations. She even threw federal wiretapping laws into the brew. The court swallowed her argument: The employer could only monitor calls that were clearly related to business. (*Watkins* v. *L. M. Berry & Co.*, 704 F.2d 577, 11th Cir., 1983)

That was the gist of a finding in a case that went the employer's way when a federal appeals court ruled the employer *could listen* on an extension phone *in the course of business*. (*Briggs* v. *American Air Filter Co.*, 630 F.2d 414, 5th Cir., 1980)

A telephone was the instrument of choice in a sexual harassment case. The manager of a restaurant was hitting on his assistant with mash notes left in her menus and suggestive remarks slipped into her hand at opportune times.

Eventually he graduated to a series of suggestive telephone calls. Even the manager's wife got into the wireless act by calling the assistant manager and lambasting her with abusive language based on the mistaken impression that she was indeed having an affair with the insistent husband.

When the assistant's complaints fell on deaf management ears, and "be patient" was the only solace she got, she marched into court. The ruling: If the content of the phone calls was abusive, they may be invasions of privacy. And if the language in the notes was suggestive, that also may add up to invasion. (*Rogers* v. *Loews l'Enfant Plaza*, 526 F. Supp. 523, D.D.C., 1981)

The court in the telemarketing case set out these principles: First, even if you've accepted employment with the knowledge the company has a monitoring policy, that doesn't mean you consent to all call interruption. Second, the "course of business" exception applies only to that—business—not personal communications. Third, the employer who monitors calls should make every effort to minimize the intrusion of that act.

Computer privacy is also a hot issue. A black female computer operator became plenty bugged when she found her machine had been. She had earlier complained about her performance appraisal results and company pay policies. She went so far as to file charges with the EEOC. Its finding: Her case had merit. Some time later her computer began to act up. The cause: Her company had placed an electronic security trace on the line to monitor her work. Then she acted up and her angry explosion detonated her discharge. In her suit, the employee claimed the trace was a retaliatory act. Since it prompted the behavior that got her fired, and it wouldn't have come about except for her earlier complaints, she was the victim of a discriminatory act. The court agreed. (*Reeder-Baker* v. *Lincoln National Corp.*, No. 87-1287, 7th Cir., 1987)

## Ninth inning: Back at the beginning—hiring

"Employee" privacy rights start before you become an employee. (Check out the "promises" in chapter 3.) As the concept of equal employment opportunity has expanded, so has the list of no-no areas for prospective employee probes.

In general, the discrimination areas include the usual race, sex, age, national origin, color, handicap, etc. But there are several nuances to the questionable questioning issue that you should keep in mind.

For one, it's not necessarily the questions themselves that are illegal, but their discriminatory use. Strictly speaking, for example, the EEOC may not forbid a gray area question. But it views these with "extreme disfavor" because they could be the improper basis of a hiring decision. The EEOC position: If an employer isn't going to use an answer, then why ask the question.

For another, bona fide occupational qualification is generally a legitimate employer excuse for an otherwise questionable question.

For a third, timing is important. Take the question of whom to contact in case of emergency. The answer isn't needed to judge the applicant, but it is needed after the candidate becomes an employee. Same with the question of dependents for insurance purposes after the hiring.

For a fourth, a questionable question may raise your hackles, but you don't want a snippy "you can't ask that" to lower your chances of getting the job. It's a tough call when an irrelevant or potentially discriminatory question comes up, whether to stand up for your rights and risk the wrath of a potential employer. About the best you can do is ask politely: "Could you tell me how that question relates to position $X$ that I'm applying for?"

Here is a list of topics that *could be* discriminatory if they were asked during the course of your hiring interview:

- Age or date of birth
- Place of birth, parents' place of birth
- Individual to be notified in case of emergency
- Native language, how you acquired capability in foreign language
- Disabilities, defects in sight, speech, hearing
- Height and weight
- Marital status, number of children or dependents, family plans, child care
- Home ownership, previous residences
- Arrest or conviction records
- Overdue bills, outstanding loans, previous wage garnishments, or bankruptcies
- Armed forces service of any country and type of discharge
- Education levels (unless justified by position)
- Clubs, social organizations, church group, religious or political affiliations
- Credit and bank records
- Private morality issues like divorce, abortion
- Spouse career
- Union membership
- Previous filings for worker's compensation
- Maiden or family name

# Age Discrimination: You're Not Getting Older... You're Just Getting More Rights!

A woman who had been hired in 1952 as a bank teller and had worked her way up the ladder to become an assistant loan counselor over the course of twenty-eight years was told in 1980 that her position was being phased out. She could continue to work for the bank, she was informed, if she wanted to go back to being a teller again.

The woman, faced with no real options, swallowed her pride and took the demotion. But a month later, she was fired without any notice whatsoever.

The woman took the bank to court, claiming that she had been a victim of age discrimination. "Nonsense," the bank said, "we fired her solely because of her lousy work performance. It had nothing to do with her age."

But as the court case pressed on, the woman's attorneys were able to provide direct evidence that the bank president himself often referred to older employers as "deadwood" and "ballast."

As a result, the judge ruled that the poor performance ratings were nothing more than a cover-up provided by the bank to defend its actions. As far as the court saw it, the bank president had decided that he just didn't want to pay this woman based upon her twenty-eight years of seniority plus the benefits she had accrued over the years.

The price tag on this one? The woman was awarded $1.3 million in punitive damages based upon age discrimination, plus $94,000 in actual damages, and another $100,000 for emotional distress. (*Flanigan* v. *Prudential Federal Savings & Loan Assn.*, No. 85-380, Sup. Ct. Mont., 1986)

## The law of the ages

One thing is very clear about getting older and holding down a job.

If you're over the age of forty and your boss, supervisor, or company tries to fire you, they had better have lots and lots and lots of evidence with which to document why you're over the hill.

In fact, ever since the passage of the Age Discrimination in Employment Act (ADEA) in 1978, very few areas of employee rights have affected management so strongly and so directly. According to the EEOC, there were eleven thousand age discrimination suits filed nationwide in 1982. Three years later, that number jumped to over sixteen thousand, and by 1990, legal experts are predicting that the age claims will number over thirty thousand—that's a threefold jump in just eight years.

Looked at from another perspective, it cost companies over $20 million in age discrimination awards to disgruntled employees in 1982. And that number went over the $30 million mark in 1985. At that rate, angry employees who have seen their fortieth birthday—and their jobs—come and go will collect over $60 million in legal damages in 1990.

Why the sudden jump? Two main reasons. One, the baby boom generation is now entering its forties. As the manager crunch at the higher corporate levels continues in this country, as cutbacks come, more and more fairly well-paid employees who happen to be over the age of forty are being let go. Younger—and cheaper—employees are hired to take their place. In retaliation (and not surprisingly) many of the over-forty crowd are filing age discrimination lawsuits.

Second, of all the recent legal actions regarding employee rights, the ADEA stands alone as the only federal statute that firmly forbids age discrimination in all fifty states. Any employee over the age of forty is covered by this encompassing law, and with all the age-case headlines, people are becoming increasingly aware of the clout that the ADEA carries. In many states, the laws regarding age discrimination are even stricter (see figure 9).

The Age Discrimination in Employment Act is fairly clear as to what your boss can—and can't—do when it comes to firing workers over the age of forty. More specifically, the law states:

- That all employees over the age of forty are to be considered in the eyes of the law as a "protected group."
- That all individuals who qualify as members of this protected group cannot be denied employment opportunities, cannot be fired, cannot be shortchanged when it comes to wages or salary simply because of their age.

In other words, if you're forty-plus and you're turned down for a job because "you're too old" or because "we were looking for someone a bit younger" or because "we're not sure you're going to fit into our youth movement too well," then you've probably got a real good case of age discrimination.

- *Employee Rights Alert:* By the way, you should also be aware that the courts around the country as well as the EEOC have no problem with extending the limits of the ADEA. It's clear that age discrimination claims definitely include an entire range of personnel actions such as hirings, promotions, demotions, discharges, transfers, denials of jobs, and downgrading of positions. But in addition, more and more courts are finding claims regarding denial of pension funds, ERISA, and other aspects of retirement coming increasingly under the realm of age discrimination.

## For every rule, an exception

Yes, of course, there are certain situations under the ADEA in which age becomes a legally pertinent factor. Those situations, known as bona fide occupational qualifications, come into play in unique positions where age, physical ability, and the personal safety of yourself or others become intertwined.

Here's a quick rundown on the few exceptions to the ADEA:

- The bona fide occupational qualification, as mentioned above, occurs when an employer can legally limit a job to workers of a certain age if the employer can prove that age is a critical factor in the performance of that job.

## Figure 9. Highlights of the Age Discrimination in Employment Act

### What It Does

It protects workers over the age of forty from arbitrary and capricious discrimination in hiring, firing, pay, promotions, fringe benefits, retirement, and other aspects of general employment.

The law was specifically designed to promote the employment of older people on the basis of ability rather than age, and to help employers and workers find meaningful ways in which to cope with on-the-job problems arising from the impact of age on employment.

### Coverage

All private employers of twenty or more workers are covered by the law, as well as all federal, state, and local governments and employment agencies. Labor organizations with twenty-five or more members or which operate hiring offices that recruit potential employees or obtain job opportunities are also affected by the law.

### Exemptions

Until December 31, 1993, state and local governments may make age-based hiring decisions for fire fighters and law enforcement officers if the particular age limitation was in effect on March 3, 1983, and the action taken is pursuant to a bona fide hiring or retirement plan that is not a subterfuge to evade the purposes of ADEA.

Institutions of higher learning—until December 31, 1993—may involuntarily retire an employee at age seventy who is serving under a contract of unlimited tenure.

The law does not apply where age is a bona fide occupational qualification. It also does not bar employers from differentiating among employees based upon reasonable factors other than age, or from observing the terms of a bona fide seniority system or any bona fide employee benefits plan (e.g., retirement, pension, or insurance plan), except that no such seniority system or employee benefits plan will excuse mandatory retirement and/ or refusal to hire.

### Filing a Charge

A charge of unlawful discrimination must be filed with the EEOC within two years (three years in the case of willful violations) of the alleged violation. To preserve the right to file a private lawsuit, the charge must be filed within 180 days. In states having age discrimination laws, this is extended to 300 days of the alleged violation or 30 days after termination of proceedings by the state enforcement agency, whichever is earlier.

### Where to File a Charge

At any EEOC field office. If there is not an EEOC office in your vicinity, call toll free 1-800-USA-EEOC for information or to file a charge.

### Confidentiality

The identity of a complainant, confidential witness, or aggrieved person on whose behalf a charge is filed ordinarily will not be disclosed without prior written consent. The filing of a charge protects your right to file a private suit. If you file a charge, your name will be given to your employer.

### Filing Suit

Your lawsuit may be brought by the EEOC. Damages may be recovered for a period of two years prior to the filing of the suit, except in the case of willful violation where three-year damages may be recovered.

### Private Lawsuits

Individuals may file a lawsuit on their own behalf but not until sixty days after filing their charge of unlawful discrimination with the EEOC and, where there is a state age discrimination law, with the state agency. Should EEOC take legal action, however, the individual may not file a private suit.

### Health Insurance Benefits

Employers must offer all employees and employees' spouses sixty-five years of age and older the same health coverage under the same conditions that are offered to employees under age sixty-five.

### Pension Coverage

Generally, after January 1, 1988, pension benefits accruals or allocations must be continued by all employers for persons who work beyond a plan's normal retirement age. Plan limitations on the amount of benefits, years of service, or years of participation are permissible if imposed without regard to age.

### Penalties for Employer Violations

Penalties for violating ADEA include payment of damages, interest, liquidated damages, attorneys' fees, and court costs.

Recognizing the need for flexibility in fashioning conciliation agreements, the EEOC's policy is to seek full and effective relief for each and every victim of employment discrimination, whether it is sought in court or in conciliation agreements reached before litigation.

### Retaliatory Measures

Employers, employment agencies, and labor organizations are prohibited from retaliating against any person who files a charge, participates in an investigation, or opposes an unlawful practice.

- Reasonable factors other than age occur when a younger worker is selected over an older worker for reasons other than age or cost efficiency. "Reasonable factors" is most often cited when a company has to make cutbacks in its staff or is reorganizing.
- Bona fide seniority systems, based upon length of service. Such seniority plans, to be legal or bona fide, usually grant the most rights to those employees who have the longest service to the company. And of course, the plan must be applied uniformly to all employees of all ages.
- Bona fide employee benefit plans. Like seniority plans, these plans must provide the greatest benefits to those who have served the company longest, and such a plan must not discriminate against older employees.

The key here to remember is that in all instances, the company must have a bona fide plan in all of its moves. Your boss can't use any exceptions as a subterfuge to get around ADEA requirements, even though some bosses try.

## Some examples of bona fide occupational qualifications

A bona fide occupational qualification situation might include a company-anointed age limit of fifty-five for, say, airline pilots or bus drivers. The airline or bus company might have some very serious concerns about pilots or drivers whose reflexes, strength, or eyesight has normally deteriorated by age fifty. And in some situations, the EEOC has allowed these qualifications. But—and this is important —that airline or bus company better have some solid and convincing evidence that the cutoff point should be fifty. (Remember, up until 1989, the United States had a president who was in his mid-seventies.)

When it comes to establishing a bona fide occupational qualification, most courts look upon two main criteria: (1) that nearly everyone over the age in question is unable to perform the duties of that job safely or efficiently, and (2) that some older workers have traits that keep them from doing the job safely and efficiently, and age is the only available way to effectively screen for these characteristics.

Of course, as pointed out, this can become a little tricky. In a case in Wisconsin a few years ago, a county governing board passed a law that required all its police officers to retire at age fifty-five. The reasoning of the board? Simply that police work is too strenuous and too dangerous to allow cops over fifty-five to continue to work.

Unfortunately for the county, several of the affected police officers disagreed with this blanket indictment of their capabilities and fought back on the grounds of age discrimination. What about experience on the job, they asked. Doesn't that count for something in police work?

In its response, the county claimed that youth, or at least something short of old age, was a bona fide occupational qualification for police work. The court didn't see it that way. What the county was really trying to say, the judge explained, was that police work required a certain amount of physical ability which just happens to be associated with youth. But to say that any officer over the age of fifty-five can't handle the job any more is wrong. The court decided in favor of the cops and struck down the law as age discriminatory. (*EEOC* v. *Marathon County*, 26 F.E.P. 1736, 1981)

Cases centering on bona fide occupational qualifications crop up all the time, and while a few such qualifications are respected by the law, many are struck down as being artificial and discriminatory.

The EEOC has brought cases against a number of companies as well as state agencies in this area. In one instance, in a suit brought against the Baltimore and Ohio Railroad by 221 former railroad workers who felt they had been unjustly forced to retire because of a mandatory age limit, a settlement of $8.5 million was agreed upon by the railroad and the former railroad workers.

The same thing happened in a case by the EEOC against the Hampton Institute, which had tried to force employees to retire by a certain age. That cost the institute $56,000 in settlement costs.

In another suit brought against the Oregon State Department of Corrections. a policy calling for the retirement of all personnel over the age of sixty resulted in a settlement of $150,000 for six victims of this age discrimination.

There are literally dozens of cases like these in which an arbitrary upper age limit has been set by a governing body which is always defended as a bona fide occupational qualification. These days, however, the courts are asking companies and agencies alike to explain why this age limit policy is so essential. And unless that company or agency can come up with a pretty good reason, not only is that age limit knocked down, but invariably big cash damage awards are handed down as well.

## "Reasonable factors other than age" at work

Here's an example of a case involving reasonable factors other than age.

A department store that was faced with declining business decided it needed a bold new strategy to effect a turnabout in its business. To accomplish this strategy, thought the bosses, they would have to attract a whole new, younger crowd to the store.

To do that, the company introduced a brand new image—an image that was geared mainly to a younger audience. These changes also meant the hiring of a younger work force in order to attract younger buyers.

These changes, of course, gravely concerned the older, well-established employees, and when six of the older workers lost their jobs, the charges began to fly back and forth.

When the case got to court, the company claimed that this new campaign was absolutely essential because business was so poor in its former shape that the company faced a total shutdown. Now, at least, the department store was still viable. As a defense then, the department store owners claimed that the moves they made were not based upon age but rather upon reasonable factors other than age.

As it turned out, the court understood the department store's concerns and had sympathy for its moves. But it also felt that when a business decision directly affects workers in a protected age group—even if that impact was unintentional—then it still becomes a case of age discrimination. The court held in favor of the affected older workers. (*Bishop* v. *Jelleff Associates*, 398 F. Supp. 579, 1974)

■ *Employee Rights Alert:* What's the main difference between *bona fide occupational qualification* and *reasonable factors other than age?* Certainly they are close cousins under the scope of ADEA, but in a nutshell they break down like this:

With a bona fide qualification, a company has taken an action which is normally seen as illegal, but then the company has to defend its action as a realistic exception to the rules.

With reasonable factors, a company is in essence saying that it has not violated any part of the ADEA at all, that its actions are based solely on business reasons and have nothing to do with age discrimination.

## Can anybody over the age of forty be fired?

Oh, don't be misled. Yes, the ADEA is a formidable beast, but people over the age of forty are fired every day. And it's perfectly legitimate.

If your boss has kept a well-documented record on you regarding chronically poor work habits, tardiness, excessive problems on the job, and so on, then you can be fired and the courts will most likely be tempted to agree with your boss and not you.

For example, when a new chief executive officer took over an insurance company, the first thing he wanted to do was clean house of all the unproductive employees. And as it turned out, many of those employees were over the age of forty. We have nothing to worry about, the over-forty crowd rationalized. If he fires us, we'll slap him with a discrimination suit so fast it'll make his head spin.

Well, the boss did just that, but he did his homework before giving certain employees the boot. For starters, he fired only those employees who had lousy productivity sheets or had histories of being troublemakers. In one case, he fired an executive whose general business management philosophy ran totally counter to his own.

And yes, all these dismissed managers were over the age of forty and all filed suit. But the court in this case held in favor of the new boss because he had enough evidence to show that he had fired these people based upon—yes—reasonable factors other than age. That is, their age had nothing to do with their being dismissed; there was too much evidence of them being poor workers. (*Pirone* v. *Home Insurance Co.*, 673 F. Supp. 306, 1983)

## ADEA on the job

To get a better feel for how the ADEA works, here's a small sampling of some important cases where age discrimination was the major factor.

In 1982, three corporate executives who happened to be in their late forties were fired by a department store because management wanted some "young, fresh blood" on the job. Nobody disputed that the three executives were doing a good job; it was just that the boss wanted some new, younger faces on the scene. The three dismissed executives sued on the grounds of age discrimination and the courts awarded them a cool $2.3 million in damages. (*Cancellier* v. *Federated Department Stores*, 21 F.E.P. 1151, 1982)

A fifty-two-year-old woman who worked for the state of Delaware also made the critical mistake of getting older. The woman, a statistical planner, had worked for the state for eight years when she was let go in 1982.

"New reorganization of the department," was the reason she was given, "and we're afraid your job has been eliminated." But when the state department hired a man who happened to be thirty-two and who was given most of the ex-employee's job duties, it didn't take the former statistical planner much time to figure out what was going on. In a nutshell, she was making $36,000 a year, and the thirty-two-year-old man had been hired for about half of that.

She took the state to court on a claim of age discrimination and won her case to the tune of $325,000 in back pay, pension, health benefits, and lost interest. (*Gelof* v. *Papineau*, No. 83-210, U.S.D.C. Del., 1986)

Then there was the case of the golden oldie disc jockey, who was let go from a radio station in Illinois where he worked for nine years. At the age of fifty-one, the deejay was stunned when he walked in one morning and found out that his on-air services were no longer needed. "We're changing our format," trumpeted the station's general manager. "We're going from our 'beautiful music' style to a more upbeat adult contemporary, and we're afraid you just don't fit in." Even worse, the station had just hired a twenty-nine-year-old program director and within the last few months, it no longer had any employees over the age of forty.

It didn't take long for the court to figure out what was going on here and a jury awarded the deejay $200,000 in age discrimination damages. That amount was later affirmed by the U.S. Court of Appeals for the Seventh Circuit.

As mentioned above, it hasn't taken the courts much time to extend the impact of the ADEA. A city in Pennsylvania came up with a reduction in force policy that would lay off those fire fighters who were eligible for pensions first. In other words, the oldest guys would get hosed. The courts ruled, of course, that such a policy directly violated the spirit of the ADEA and the policy was struck down. (*EEOC* v. *City of New Castle*, 32 F.E.P. 1409, 1983)

The ADEA theory was at work in a major class action suit in which the Equitable Life Assurance Company tried to cut back its employee payroll by laying off workers who just happened to be over the age of forty.

A crowd of 363 angry former life insurance employees saw this as blatantly discriminatory and took Equitable to task. The result? In April of 1985, the major insurance carrier was ordered to pay a total of $12.5 million to those workers. Ouch!

## Watching the movement build

It should be clear from cases like these that more and more older employees are beginning to fight back when they think they've been held back or lost a job because of their age. And the courts are right there to back these older employees all the way. Even if there is the slightest hint of age discrimination, the courts will step in and straighten the matter out—usually in favor of the employee. Even written documents don't stand in the way.

In a case in Pennsylvania, an employee who was over the age of forty and therefore covered by the ADEA lost his job in a reduction in force. When the dismissed employee took his former employer to court on the grounds of age discrimination, the company claimed that the worker had, in fact, signed a waiver form in which he gave up his right to sue the company if and when he was ever let go. "And even more importantly," argued the attorneys for the company, "he signed this waiver form voluntarily."

"Unfair!" cried the worker, "I had to sign that waiver form. Otherwise you would have never hired me. You can hardly call that 'voluntary'."

The court volunteered its agreement with the fired worker. It ruled that the waiver form was certainly not voluntary at all, and as a result it awarded the fired employee a total of $305,000 in damages. (*Valenti v. International Mill Services, Inc.*, F.2d 3d Cir., 1987)

---

## The ol' reduction in force ploy

A reduction in force, if not handled properly, can always ignite a flurry of age-related lawsuits. A fifty-four-year-old manager of a concrete plant was called in by the president of the firm and told very simply, "Joe, we gotta cut back on personnel and payroll, and the truth is that we can no longer afford to pay your salary." The reason: "Because you're one of the highest paid guys on the staff, that's why."

"But how you can say that?" countered Joe. "After all, just a few months ago you gave me a raise in pay."

"I gave everyone here a raise in pay. But now I have to cut costs—and the first thing I did was to let you go and replace you with a guy who will earn only half your salary."

Not satisfied with this explanation, the dismissed manager went to the EEOC and complained that just because the company was performing poorly was no reason to replace him with a younger, less expensive employee.

In listening to the evidence, the seventh circuit of the U.S. Court of Appeals ruled that the company had missed the boat three times here. One, when it comes to drastic cutbacks on payroll, the company has to be able to prove that such cutbacks are essential. In this case, the company hadn't done that. Two, there's an obligation on the part of the company to find and pursue other, less detrimental alternatives to firing an experienced worker, such as finding another position for him within the company or merely cutting his salary back a bit. And three, a company just can't fire a worker who's over forty and replace him or her with another employee who's considerably younger (under forty) and less expensive to keep on the payroll.

On all three criteria the company had not complied and as a result, the court found in favor of the dismissed fifty-four-year-old manager. (*Metz* v. *Transit Mix, Inc.*, 828 F.2d 1202, 7th Cir., 1987)

## On the horizon: Age harassment

And just in case the ADEA doesn't cover enough ground, there's a new extension of the age discrimination law out there. It's known as "age harassment." In a policy announcement from the EEOC, the commission said that the harassment of older workers by coworkers and/or supervisory personnel must be treated in the same legal manner as sexual harassment.

In other words, an employer will be held liable on the grounds of age discrimination if older workers are harassed on the job, supervisors know about this harassment or should have known about it, and these same supervisors do nothing to stop or prevent the harassment.

In a sense, this is similar to the extension by the U.S. Supreme Court on sexual harassment and the so-called hostile environment policy which was explained in chapter 4. An employer can be held liable for sexual harassment if the victim is subject to a hostile working environment and the employer does nothing to correct the problem. The same is now true of age harassment.

For example, suppose your supervisor refers to either you or a coworker of yours as "being a little more accident prone these days because of age." Or remarks that he's not going to bother teaching you about the firm's new computer system because, "Let's face it —it's tough teaching an old dog new tricks." Or suppose one of your coworkers likes to start the day by poking fun at you and your advancing age. Even if the cracks are meant in jest, if they bother you—and your supervisor is aware of this joking and knows that it bothers you—then you have every right to have your boss step in and stop it.

Comments like these—even if meant innocently and nonmaliciously—can and will be interpreted by a court of law as inherently discriminatory based on age.

That's what happened in a case where a forty-nine-year-old employee claimed he lost his job because, among other items, he was harassed in the office by his bosses who would say that "guys forty years old are too old to work here" and that he was described as being "just too old for the job."

His bosses claimed that all these comments were made in jest and with no maliciousness. Too bad, the court said, as it ruled in favor of the dismissed worker. (*Cooper* v. *Asplundh*, Nos. 85-2316, 85-2369, 10th Cir., 1988)

## Other forms of age harassment

Sometimes this kind of harassment can be subtler and crueler. Suppose, for example, that your boss wants you to retire but you've resisted. All of a sudden, you find yourself handling all the physically demanding tasks on the job, such as having to lift heavy boxes and move large crates around. You get the very distinct feeling that your boss is deliberately making your job tougher for you, hoping to break your spirit by giving you physically demanding jobs.

This, too, is a form of age harassment, and if you took your employer to court, you'd probably have a solid case.

## Look for the warning signs

Age discrimination can be easy to spot, and it can also be well camouflaged. Many times, you won't even know it's hit you until it's too late. That's why it's important to know the warning signs of age discrimination.

To start with, there are three basic criteria regarding age discrimination cases for an ADEA claim to prevail in court: (1) you must prove that you are over the age of forty; (2) you must provide prima facie evidence of being discriminated against in your work because of your age; (3) you must provide enough evidence that if it weren't for your age then you wouldn't have been discriminated against. In other words, you must be prepared to show that your work performance was acceptable and that the only criterion working against you was your age.

To illustrate these three elements of an age discrimination suit, consider the following case.

An over-forty employee who worked for a water company was fired by his supervisor, who was in his late twenties. The reason for the dismissal? The older worker had loused up some recent water meter readings.

"That's not the real reason, your honor!" countered the dismissed employee. "They just wanted to get rid of me because I was older than they were. Even called me an 'old goat' on occasion."

Sure enough, as the evidence was presented in court, it became clear that the older worker had an outstanding performance record over the years, that the recent mistakes over some meter readings were minor at best, and that indeed he had been the victim of age harassment.

Thus the court, in looking for the three criteria of age discrimination under ADEA, found all three satisfied: (1) the affected employee was over forty; (2) he had been fired from his job because of his age; and (3) if it weren't for his age and his age alone, then he wouldn't have lost his job. The company's accusations of his lousing up the meter readings were just a trumped-up charge in an attempt to mask the real reason for dismissal, the employee's age. (*Smith* v. *Consolidated Mutual Water Co.*, 787 F.2d 1441, 1986)

## Other ways employers get into trouble

Don't think for a moment that employers have an easy time in avoiding age discrimination traps. In fact, employers are constantly making mistakes when it comes to age discrimination, even if it is accidental or unintentional. For example, have you ever heard a manager or supervisor in your firm say, "What we need around here are some young, fresh employees who really want to work"? If you have ever heard that kind of comment, that's a good first element for an age discrimination lawsuit.

Or perhaps because of a falling off in business, company management has decided to lay off those workers who happen to make the most money on the job. Seems fair, doesn't it? And democratic too. After all, all the boss is saying is that he wants to lay off the highest paid employees, case closed.

Except that in most cases, the employees who make the most money on the job are those employees who have been with the firm for the longest period of time and are also the oldest workers on the payroll. As a result, the boss' move to cut back on payroll may have started out as a seemingly fair and democratic method of getting rid of overhead, but it has graduated into the reality of becoming age discriminatory.

Once again, the courts have made it clear that it makes no difference what the company's original motives were when it comes to discrimination. All that matters is the end result, and if the bottom line is that a new policy results in age discrimination, then the company and its policy can be held liable.

Indeed, this is a problem that employers often trip over—that the result of management action can be discriminatory even though that was the last thing that management had in mind.

## Advertising age traps

Again, the octopus arms of the ADEA are very far reaching. Ever read a newspaper advertisement that lists the following headlines under help wanted: BRIGHT COLLEGE GRADUATE, YOUNG AMBITIOUS WORKER, RECENT GRAD WANTED.

You can probably scan your local newspaper and see these headlines every day. The fact of the matter is, they're potentially discriminatory. Trigger words like "young" or "college graduate" or "recent grad" start the alarm bells ringing at the EEOC because the obvious conclusion to be drawn here is that the hiring company wants only applicants in their early twenties.

Suppose an older woman in her sixties—a grandmother who went back to finish college after her family had grown up—applied for one of those jobs. After all, wouldn't she fit the criteria of "recent college grad" if she just obtained her diploma a few months ago? How do you think the hiring officer of the company would react if a woman in her sixties showed up to apply for the job as a recent college graduate? If that hiring officer says something like, "Gee, Granny, we were looking for someone, you know, about forty years younger," then he's looking down the barrel of a first class age discrimination suit. (*Hodgson* v. *First Federal Savings & Loan Assn.*, 455 F.2d 818, 1972)

The same reasoning applies to those situations where a long-time employee is let go, laid off, or simply fired from a job just a few months before obtaining his or her pension. Courts really dislike seeing an older individual lose out on a pension only a year or two shy of vesting.

As with everything else in life, timing is critical when it comes to dismissal and age discrimination. Firing an employee just before a pension vests or just before retirement sends a loud and clear signal to the court that something is amiss.

Consider the case we mentioned back in chapter 1 of the employee who worked for a department store for thirteen years. He'd been a top flight employee, getting salary raises and promotions in his long tenure with the company, when one day, just two years before his pension was to vest, he was given his walking papers. When he questioned his supervisor, he was told he had been fired simply because the store didn't want him to collect a pension. In court, the department store openly admitted that this was the reason why it had let the veteran employee go. After all, the department store argued, a pension is just another benefit which is not guaranteed under law and, besides, the department store had the right under the doctrine of employment-at-will to fire any employee at any time and for any reason.

Not only did the court rule that such a practice was dishonest, but that it was also a direct violation of the public's best interest in denying a worker his pension. And of course, age discrimination was certainly at work in this case. The employee got his job and his pension back. (*Savodnik* v. *Korvette's, Inc.*, 488 F. Supp. 822, E.D. N.Y., 1980)

## Employee rights in benefits and ERISA

As mentioned earlier, the scope of the ADEA has been extended by court decisions to cover most situations where there's a strong suspicion that a company has denied employee benefits or a pension to older workers.

Can a company make changes in its pension or benefits plan? Yes, it can, but the EEOC will very carefully scrutinize any changes to make sure that no workers end up losing any benefits they had before the new plans were put into effect. And as the cases above show clearly, the EEOC takes a very dim view of older workers who get fired just before their pension vests or before they're eligible for benefits based upon years of service to the company.

In the view of the ADEA, if a company is forced to make significant changes in its pension or benefit program, there had better be some real solid reasons why. In altering pension and benefits programs, a company's changes had better be legitimate and equally fair to all employees regardless of age. However, the laws are very tricky in this murky area of employee rights.

For example, under federal law and enforced by the EEOC, if your employer offers health insurance coverage for the families of younger employees, then the company must also provide the same kind of coverage for those employees over the age of sixty-five. And as you might suspect, in most cases, the older the worker, the older his or her spouse, and usually, the more expensive their medical bills are.

On the other hand, in other situations under the ADEA, the basic rule when it comes to an employer's investment in an employee's benefit package is this: The employer only has to provide an equal amount of investment for each employee—regardless of the employee's age. That means that an equal investment by a company may not buy an equal amount of benefits for each employee, but that's the current extent of the law.

For example, a company may have a policy in force that allows for so much term insurance per employee, and to that end, the company may pay a $20 monthly premium for each employee. That's fine, but of course, a $20 monthly premium will buy a lot more coverage for a worker who's, say, twenty-five than for the worker who's sixty-five. But under the ADEA, the company has made the same monetary investment for each worker, regardless of age, and that's all it's obligated to do.

## ERISA's scope

The Employee Retirement Income Security Act, better known as ERISA, works very closely with the Age Discrimination in Employment Act. Curiously, most personnel managers whose job it is to know and understand the provisions of ERISA think that it deals primarily with just employee pension plans. That's true but there's more. ERISA deals with all the benefits you receive at work, of which your pension happens to be one example.

In other words, if you think you've been shortchanged on some benefits due you at work, you would have your attorney check out the recent court cases in which the scope of ERISA has come up.

The courts have made it very clear that ERISA covers everything from pensions (retirement income and deferred benefits) to current employee benefits, including medical, surgical, hospital care, unemployment, vacation, and severance pay.

## *How it works*

ERISA doesn't necessarily dictate to your employer what kinds of benefits the company must provide, but ERISA does make it clear from various court interpretations that if your company does provide certain benefits, then the administration of those benefits had better be straight on the money. Furthermore, the courts don't even care if there's nothing in writing regarding a company's benefits plan; that is, the courts go by what is in practice, not whether or not it's written down somewhere in a company handbook.

If you don't think you're getting everything that's owed you at work as a benefit, make certain you check it out with your personnel director. Tell 'em that ERISA sent you.

## A note regarding this area of the law

Keep in mind that the laws regarding pension plans, employee benefits, ERISA, and the like are extremely complicated. If you have specific questions about your company's coverage (and policies vary greatly from company to company), be sure to check with your company's personnel office first, and then with the EEOC or your attorney if you aren't satisfied with the answers you're getting.

Check out the summary plan description and any other documents regarding employee benefits your company has given to you over the years. These must be clearly written and in plain English. They should be complete, and spell out the company's obligations to you as an employee.

You should also check out any exceptions to the plan and find out how other employees qualify for those special exceptions. It might be worth your while to find out, to see if you can qualify.

What's the bottom line regarding age discrimination cases and employees' rights? That the entire area is expanding rapidly, especially as the work force in general gets older, and that all employees, from the assembly line to the mid-level managers, are beginning to assert their rights when age is the critical factor in their career.

If you have questions or concerns about your rights in the state in which you work, be certain to check the particular laws regarding age discrimination in that state. As mentioned earlier, the federal ADEA only goes so far; in some states, the laws regarding age discrimination are even tougher.

# CHAPTER 8

# Performance Appraisals: If They Didn't Do Them Right, Then Your Rights May Have Been Wronged

I f you work for a company, no matter whether it's a small twenty-person shop or a member of the *Fortune* 500, you've probably become familiar with a yearly boss-to-employee confrontation called the performance appraisal or performance review.

You know the scene: You mark the date on your calendar, you mentally map out your strategy as to how you can highlight your achievements in the past year and skirt around any setbacks, you prepare yourself for a salary tug-of-war, and of course, you psych yourself up to go at it, face to face, with your boss or supervisor.

In theory at least, the idea of a performance appraisal makes a lot of sense. It's an opportunity for you, the employee, and your boss to sit down and go over your performance on the job for the last twelve months or so. Conceptually, your immediate superior is supposed to give you lots of specific feedback on how you've done your work, what your strengths have been, where you've had some problems, how close you've come to meeting company goals or quotas, and what kinds of plans management has for you in the coming year.

And in most cases, there's usually some talk about a salary increment during this conversation (that is, of course, assuming you've merited a raise in pay).

So on paper at least, the idea of a periodic performance appraisal makes a lot of sense. Unfortunately, as with so many good ideas, the problems begin to crop up during the actual execution of the concept. And in recent years these employer-employee confrontations have resulted in lawsuits based upon faulty or flawed performance reviews. Ever so gradually, the sweaty palms, raised blood pressure, and nervous anxiety have begun to shift from the employee to—surprise!—the employer.

## The times are a-changin'

Consider, for example, the following performance appraisals that somehow went awry.

Remember the female marketing manager from chapter 6 who had earned glowing performance appraisals during the twelve years of her tenure with the firm? Each year, she had been rewarded with generous salary boosts and her superiors had consistently given her top ratings on her formal evaluation papers.

But then she started dating a salesman who used to work with her in the same computer company but who had since jumped to a competitor. Her boss requested that she be transferred out of her management job.

Angered by this development, the woman quit her job and then sued the computer company, claiming that she had been constructively fired. And in court, she brought along twelve years' worth of terrific performance appraisals to prove her point. Sure enough, the court agreed with the woman. She won her case and won big— $300,000 in damages. (*Rulon-Miller* v. *IBM*, 162 Cal. App. 3d, 208 Cal. Rptr. 524, Cal. App., 1984)

In a celebrated case, an airline fired one of its employees who had worked for the company for eighteen years. Angered by this sudden turn of affairs, he too fought back and took the airline to court, claiming wrongful discharge even though he had years of positive performance appraisals.

"I worked there for eighteen years," said the employee. "In all that time, they never gave me any reason to believe my performance was unsatisfactory. In fact, it was just the opposite. My ratings were always good."

And that's just what the California courts decided when they heard the case. Given the employee's record of solid years of service, and with the company's own reviews to back up that claim, the court decided in his favor. (*Cleary* v. *American Airlines,* 111 Cal. App. 3d 433, Cal. Rptr. 722, 1980)

Then there was the case of the employee who had worked for thirty-two years for a candy manufacturer. One day he walked in and was told his days were over in the candy operation. In court, he produced over thirty years of documents from the company that indicated that he had been a solid and dependable worker, with good evaluations and a history of promotions. In reviewing the papers, the court decided that the candy manufacturer acted capriciously in firing the thirty-two-year veteran, based upon his track record of service to the company. (*Pugh* v. *See's Candies,* 116 Cal. App. 3d 311, 1981).

---

## Hardly the exception to the rule

Don't for a minute think that these cases are exceptions to the rule. In the last decade since the employment-at-will doctrine has begun to erode in this country's legal system, more and more disgruntled employees are taking their bosses to court based on illegal or negligently handled performance appraisals.

Ironic, isn't it? Where in the past the employees have always had to worry about their periodic review sessions, now the tables are turning. The pressure is now on your supervisor to make certain that he or she handles your evaluation correctly—or else.

The courts are making it exceedingly clear that management is under a watchful eye when it comes to evaluating a worker's performance. No longer can a manager or supervisor just breeze through an evaluation session with a subordinate, make a few general comments, give a small raise, and then, a few months later, decide to stiff that same worker from the staff.

Increasingly, on a national basis, the courts are assuming that if an employee goes through a performance evaluation and receives generally good feedback along with any kind of raise, then there's a prima facie case that the company looks upon that worker as someone worth keeping on the payroll. And in exchange for that person's efforts on behalf of the company, the courts are now leaning toward the concept of an "implied contract" between the company and the employee.

Under the terms of this so-called implied contract, the courts are now pressing employers to present some sort of documented reasons to fire an employee. This means that whereas in the past a company could fire any employee for any reason (or no reason) whenever it wanted to, now the pendulum has swung to showing "just cause" for firing a worker.

## Implied contracts and performance appraisals

The implied contract stems directly from the performance appraisal itself. The courts look upon a performance evaluation as a quid pro quo between two parties—the employer and the employee. In essence, the company is saying to the worker, "If you do this, this, and this, we'll pay you so much, give you these benefits, and keep you on the payroll."

For his or her part, the employee has to meet the requirements of the job description as laid out by the company. But—and this is where the lawsuits begin—the courts are also saying that if an employer wants to break that contract, it had better have lots of documented records to prove that the employee didn't perform the job properly. Otherwise, the employer doesn't have just cause to fire that worker. That's when the employee can go to court and win.

In that classic case you first saw in chapter 2, where "just cause" was the issue, a marketing executive for a major publishing house was told one day that his services were no longer required. The old pink slip—despite the fact that the executive had plenty of good performance appraisals and salary boosts.

When he asked why he was being let go, the publisher simply said that it didn't need any specific reason. It just felt it could fire him at will. But upon taking the publisher to court, the marketing man pulled out the company handbook which stated that employees would only be fired for "just and sufficient cause." Since this was the case in this case, and no such cause was being provided, the Court of Appeals of New York State—the state's highest court—held in favor of the marketing executive. The publisher had indeed broken its implied contract with its employee, as stated in its very own company handbook. (*Weiner* v. *McGraw-Hill*, 57 N.Y. 2d 458, 443 N.E. 2d 441, 1982)

■ *Employee Rights Alert:* The company handbook, or employee handbook, is often the source of these implied contracts. Whenever the courts have to find some source of evidence in order to point to a company contract, the company handbook is often a handy and ready source, especially when it comes to performance appraisals.

# If you do them, do them right!

The oddity about performance appraisals is that although they are a well-established tradition in business management circles, such reviews are by no means required by state or federal law. That is, no company is under any obligation to conduct these reviews at all. And the courts recognize that there is no binding legal obligation on companies to do these evaluations.

However, the courts are just as quick to point out that if, in fact, a company does institute a policy of performance appraisals, then the company had better handle them right or else face the consequences.

A superintendent on a production line had been with the firm since 1948 and had held his current position since 1969. And like most employees across the country, he had undergone performance appraisals every year of his employment. Then in 1977, the employee was suspended and then placed on medical leave.

When he was finally reinstated, he found himself assigned to a different job and at a lower pay scale. He filed suit against his employer, saying he wanted his old job back along with the previous salary.

In his suit, the employee's attorney argued that the company had not only been malicious in taking away the superintendent's old position, but also that the company had carried out his last performance appraisal poorly and in bad faith, just so the company could justify his demotion and the lowering of his pay.

In its response, the company said in effect: So what? There's no law on the books that requires us or any company to carry out performance appraisals in a certain manner, so you can't hold us responsible for the way in which we conduct in-house performance appraisals.

But the court saw it differently. It ruled in favor of the employee, saying that true, there is no law requiring a company to do performance appraisals. But if a company does do them, then it's legally obligated to do them correctly. And in this case, the company did a slipshod job in reviewing the superintendent's performance and thus was held legally liable for back pay and damages. (*Schipani* v. *Ford Motor Co.*, 302 N.W. 2d 307, Mich. Ct. App., 1981)

The courts applied the same kind of rationale in a case in which a long-time employee was fired after many years on the job. When he took his former employer to court to show cause as to why he was dismissed, the employer could produce only one performance appraisal form from the employee's long tenure with the company. And on that particular evaluation sheet, the employee was listed as having been "above average" on ten of the eleven rated categories. As you might have suspected, the employee won his case hands down. (*Schulz* v. *Hickok Manufacturing Co.*, 358 F. Supp. 1028, 1973)

## State by state

There have been other decisions by state courts throughout the nation which have laid down the law for employers when it comes to handling employee performance appraisals. In Michigan in 1986, an employee actually sued his employer on the grounds of "negligent job evaluation."

In that case, the worker claimed that the company had been negligent in not conducting yearly performance appraisals as promised in the employee handbook, and further, that when the evaluations were conducted, they were done poorly. As it turned out, the Michigan Supreme Court decided in favor of the company in this case, but the justices made it very clear that the precedent of this case should not be counted on heavily in the future by management—meaning that in future similar cases the court might very well decide in favor of the employee. (*Carver* v. *Sheller-Globe Corp.*, 636 F. Supp. 368, 1986)

However, other courts are taking bolder action when it comes to loused-up performance appraisals. In one such case, an employee who had received positive comments in his most recent evaluation was stunned when he was let go just a few months later. When he sued on the grounds of a negligent performance appraisal, the court agreed with him—he won his case. (*Bonura* v. *Chase Manhattan Bank*, 795 F.2d 276, 1986)

And in another jurisdiction, a manager went too far in criticizing his subordinate in a performance appraisal. When the manager went overboard in his negative comments about the employee and then made them public, the employee sued for defamation of his reputation—and won. (*Hewitt* v. *Grabicki*, 794 F.2d 1373, 1986) So you can see that the pressure these days is really mounting on the supervisors and managers of the country—whether they like it or not.

## Thanks, have a nice life

In a performance appraisal-related case, a woman who had worked for a bank for twenty-eight years walked into her office one day and was told that she was being fired. No warnings, no reprimands, no counseling, no nothing.

The reason for the dismissal? The bank officer simply shrugged his shoulders and said, "Poor performance on the job, that's why!" The woman, angered by this shocking development, countered, "But I've been doing good work for this bank for years. . . ."

At this point, the bank officer took on an interesting strategy. "Well, that's the way you see it, but tell me—do you have any performance appraisals to support your claim?"

The officer knew quite well that the bank hadn't conducted any evaluations on the woman's work. But in her suit, she argued that it wasn't her fault that she hadn't undergone any appraisals during her employment—it was the bank's! In essence, she was claiming that the bank had been negligent in its failure to periodically review her work, and furthermore, dismissal without any prior notice was in violation of the bank's own written employment policies.

The bottom line in this case topped out in favor of the dismissed employee to the tune of $95,000 in economic damages, $100,000 for emotional distress, and $1.3 million in punitive damages. (*Flanigan* v. *Prudential Federal Savings*, 122 L.R.R.M. 2597, Mont., 1986)

## Evaluation systems must be fair

The same legal logic is applied to in-house performance evaluation systems that may not be intrinsically fair to certain employees. A utility firm in Massachusetts was taken to task because its appraisal system was based upon a "forced curve" strategy. Under this evaluation system, a certain percentage of all the rated employees had to fall into certain categories, including "poor."

That meant that no matter how good or bad each employee's performance had been, the system dictated that a certain portion of the employees had to be graded as "poor" performers in order to make the forced curve work. Even if all the employees had done terrific work, some would still have to be labeled as "poor" in order to justify the forced curve.

Even though the Massachusetts Supreme Court rejected the angry employees' claim on other grounds, the court did make it clear that such forced curve appraisal systems were inherently unfair. (*McCone* v. *New England Telephone*, 471 N.E. 2d 47, Mass., 1984)

The courts stress that performance appraisals must be handled fairly and objectively. And while judges realize that all evaluations involve some sense of subjectivity, they still are constantly on the lookout for unfair evaluation practices.

A company's motives were brought under suspicion when an employee who had been fired charged that his evaluations had always been delayed at his job, and even worse, his ratings always seemed to fall far below that of his peers—even though the employee knew he was doing good work.

The worker was sure that his supervisor had it in for him, but he could never prove it. However, when a new supervisor came in and took over, much to the employee's surprise, his ratings improved dramatically and suddenly. That, ruled the court, gave more fuel to the fire that the previous supervisor wasn't playing fair with the employee—and the court decided in favor of the worker. (*Hatton* v. *Ford Motor Co.*, 508 F. Supp. 620, 1981)

## The two-edged sword

"But the courts are asking the impossible," claim managers across the country. "They're insisting that during the course of a performance appraisal we must be brutally honest with an employee. That we say, 'Look, Joe, your work is slipshod, your on-time record is poor, and if you don't shape up within two weeks, we'll have to take drastic measures.' Now, honestly, how can you motivate any worker to do better if you tell him how lousy he is and that there's a good chance he'll be fired soon?"

■ *Employee Rights Alert:* True, motivation may be a problem, but that's why managers get paid the big bucks: Because they're supposed to be the experts on motivation. As far as the courts are concerned, if an employee goes through a performance appraisal and gets generally good reviews for his work, then the company had better have some awfully good reasons to want to dismiss that worker within the next six to twelve months based on a lack of satisfactory performance.

In one relevant case, a manager went only so far during an employee's performance appraisal. Here, the manager detailed all the employee's weak points in his work and explained how they had to be improved. But the manager made one fatal mistake: He didn't mention that unless the employee cleaned up his act in a hurry, that termination was imminent.

When the employee got his walking papers, he was stunned. "Hey, sure, I knew the boss had some problems with my work, but I never thought he was going to fire me." Upon taking his case to court, the dismissed employee won a judgment of thousands of dollars based upon this faulty performance appraisal. (*Chamberlain* v. *Bissell, Inc.*, 547 F. Supp. 1067, W.D. Mich., 1982)

## Performance appraisals and race

As is true on many occasions, performance appraisal records and documents are called upon by disgruntled employees who want to prove their case in court—either for an illegal evaluation, or in some situations, as evidence of racial, age, or sexual discrimination.

For example, one employee who happened to be black was hired by a major brewery and quickly started to earn favorable performance evaluations. But after about four years of doing excellent work on the job, it became increasingly clear to this employee that his name was constantly being bypassed for promotion and that even worse, the other employees who were being promoted were all white.

The black worker finally filed a complaint with his local chapter of the EEOC. In the lawsuit that followed, the brewery trotted out the exact performance reviews and, much to the surprise of the black employee, there were certain sections on the evaluations in which he was graded as having some deficiencies—mostly in the area of communicating with fellow workers.

But then the black's attorney pulled out the evaluations of the whites who had been promoted, and lo and behold, the whites had almost identical evaluation records to that of the nonpromoted employee: Mostly excellent reviews with a few minor criticisms. It didn't take the judge long to determine that the black employee was being discriminated against based upon the performance appraisal records. (*EEOC* v. *Miller Brewing Co.*, 250 F. Supp. 739, E.D. Wis., 1986)

In another case involving racial discrimination and performance appraisals, a Puerto Rican sales representative had been fired from his brand new position for two reasons: one, he had loused up his expense report, and two, his boss didn't think much of his sales habits when the salesman didn't sell harder while escorting a group of visitors.

In his lawsuit, the fired salesman claimed that he had been given a performance appraisal on the spot by his superiors, and that he had been given an overall score of 2.1 out of a possible 6. That was in direct contrast to his previous performance appraisal in which he had scored 3.7 out of 6—and that had been conducted only six months earlier. Because of this "drop" in productivity, the Puerto Rican was placed on immediate probation.

But to make matters worse, claimed the sales rep, he was told by his bosses that no matter what he did to improve, he was still going to be fired, case closed. And even though the salesman found another job within two weeks after this warning, he still sued his former employer on the grounds he was constructively dismissed.

Sure enough, although the trial judge dismissed the suit, on appeal a higher court ruled in favor of the fired sales rep, saying that he had indeed a case to be heard here on the grounds of discrimination and wrongful performance appraisal. The case was ordered back for a retrial. (*Lopez* v. *S. B. Thomas, Inc.*, 831 F.2d 1184, 1987)

## "Computerized" racial discrimination

In a case that involved performance appraisals, racial discrimination, and computers, a black computer operator became angry when she received her yearly performance appraisal. Oh, her marks were good, but they also happened to be just one level below the marks handed out to her five coworkers. She complained to the company, only to find herself placed on probation for her trouble.

From there she went to the EEOC charging that the company had discriminatory attitudes toward black employees. Sure enough, a local human relations agency reviewed the case and found that her claims had merit.

Then, about a half year after that ruling was handed down, the same woman discovered that her computer terminal was acting improperly. After some investigation into the computer's strange behavior, she found out that the company had placed an electronic security trace on her computer in order to scrutinize her work. This was too much for her to bear: She argued with her employers and was summarily dismissed.

She filed suit again, this time charging that the company was retaliating for her previous charges of discrimination. And sure enough, after several levels of appeals, the courts decided in favor of the black employee. (*Reeder-Baker* v. *Lincoln National Corp.*, No. 87-1287, 7th Cir., 1987)

## Just don't get old

In terms of age discrimination and performance appraisals, consider the case of an employee who was hired in 1972 at the age of thirty-eight to be a management training coordinator. He received terrific reviews for the next ten years until 1983 when he was suddenly let go. The reason? His performance ratings dropped precipitously and his boss claimed he had no choice but to fire him, based upon his lack of productivity.

The now forty-nine-year-old ex-employee filed suit under the ADEA, charging age discrimination and arguing that his firing was "set up" by management which had given him unreasonable work loads and unrealistic deadlines. That accounted for the drop-off in productivity. His claim: He was being made a victim of age discrimination.

To prove his point, the employee brought forth his long history of great performance reviews. The bottom line? The court awarded the employee over $67,000 in back pay, and for good measure, an extra $378,000 in damages. (*Domenic* v. *Consolidated Edison*, 652 F. Supp. 815, S.D.N.Y., 1986)

## No laughing matter

Anything that is heard in the office or plant or factory can, and will, be used in a court of law when it comes to these employee versus employer lawsuits—especially when it concerns age discrimination and performance appraisals.

A forty-nine-year-old foreman who oversaw a tree service crew was given his walking papers one day after eighteen years with the company. The company claimed it was firing the employee due to poor on-the-job performance. The employee countered that he had very good evaluations, and that furthermore, the company had replaced him with a guy who was in his early thirties—hence, a prima facie case of age discrimination.

The question then became whether or not the foreman did, or did not, have good evaluations. In court, the company attempted to build a case that the foreman had been guilty of some ongoing minor indiscretions, such as shopping for food during work hours and the like.

But the foreman brought forth numerous witnesses who testified that he was certainly a solid employee and that his work was in most cases better than average. Even more—and this went to support the age discrimination claim—several of the witnesses admitted that company officials used to say that the foreman was "just too old for the job" and that "guys over forty are too old to work here."

The company officials insisted that all these comments were in fact made, but that they were all made strictly in jest. Too bad, ruled the court. Those antiage comments combined with the foreman's solid track record give him the benefit of the doubt, and the foreman won. (*Cooper* v. *Asplundh*, Nos. 85-2316, 85-2369, 10th Cir., 1988)

In a similar case, a secretary who had been with the same firm for seventeen years was offered an early retirement package applicable to employees over the age of fifty-five. When she refused the deal, she found herself instead with a pink slip.

When the case got to court, the company defended its actions by claiming that the woman had not only been a poor performer on the job, but that she was in fact the weakest performer of any clerk in the entire company. It was for those reasons—a lack of performance—that she was being terminated.

But the secretary introduced her performance appraisals from her seventeen years with the firm, and in all that time, only two of the seventeen indicated any problem with performance. She'd even received merit increases in pay in recent years. The jury saw the case her way and she ended up winning $66,000 in back pay. (*Dreyer* v. *ARCO*, No. 85-3476, U.S. Ct. App. 3d Cir., 1986)

Then there was the case where an older employee was fired because, his boss claimed in court, the worker's performance had been "wholly inadequate." However, the boss had only conducted sporadic and superficial appraisal interviews with the employee over the course of his employment. In fact, the employee happened to be a sales clerk, but his boss couldn't even provide any sales records with which to compare the employee's efforts.

As a result, the employee won his case of age discrimination—with a good measure of poorly executed performance appraisals in the court's record. (*Schofield* v. *Bolts & Bolts Retail Stores*, 29 Empl. Prac. Dec. 12299, S.D. N.Y., 1979)

And as an employee, keep in mind that if your company should come up with documents and records of your performance after you file a lawsuit, well, it may be too little too late.

Along those lines, a sixty-two-year-old sales representative was eased out of his major accounts by his supervisor and eventually dismissed from his job. When the salesman filed a suit based upon age discrimination, his boss had no records or documents of the salesman's performance on the job. In other words, the company couldn't prove why they had decided to fire the sales rep.

Realizing this wouldn't look good to a judge or jury, the company then hastily put together a performance review of the salesman—after the lawsuit had been filed. Understandably, the court gave this poor evaluation sheet only "minimal consideration." And not surprisingly, the court found in favor of the sales representative. (*Bucholz* v. *Symons Manufacturing Co.*, 445 F. Supp. 706, 1978)

## By the numbers doesn't add up

Due to financial cutbacks, the manager of an engineering department was forced to lay off certain assistants. In order to be fair, he pulled out the company's performance appraisals on each of them.

In the ratings, which ranked workers from 1 (outstanding) to 5 (unsatisfactory), three of his five assistants had received ratings of 3. Of the remaining two assistants, both were ranked as 4. Obviously, one of the bottom two would have to be dismissed. Yet to make matters complicated, one was a white man and the other a black woman.

As it developed, the manager let the black female go. She fought back with a lawsuit based on racial and sexual discrimination.

In going over the performance appraisals in court, the judge examined carefully not only the records of the two employees who scored 4s, but also the other three workers as well. It turned out that the manager's method for rating the workers was entirely subjective and based upon personal emotions, rather than any sense of objective ratings system. In fact, the black woman's work was, in many cases, better than some of the assistants who had scored 3.

As a result, the judge ruled that "there is a strong inference that the low rating of the plaintiff was done to provide a stronger justification for the ultimate termination decision." In other words, the manager had consciously or unconsciously stacked the odds against the woman so that if he had to let someone go, she was going to be the one. (*Jackson* v. *Ebasco Services,* 634 F. Supp. 1565, S.D.N.Y., 1986)

■ *Employee Rights Alert:* This case points out the basic problem with conducting performance appraisals—no matter how objective a company may think its evaluations are, the bottom line is that they are still conducted by people. People with inbred outlooks, perspectives, and of course, prejudices.

## Sexual discrimination and performance appraisals

A forty-year-old female employee had been dismissed from a major automobile manufacturer. In its defense, the car company claimed that the woman had a long, documented history of poor performance evaluations and that the company even provided her with continuous employee counseling over several months to help her improve her on-the-job efforts.

But the woman charged that this was all a lot of baloney, that she had been fired simply because of her sex. Plus her so-called performance evaluations had all been fabricated by her supervisor who wanted her out, and the "continuous counseling" was in reality nothing more than a five minute conversation she once had with an in-house counselor.

The court decided in favor of the dismissed employee. The tab? The car manufacturer had to cough up $100,715 in back pay, was ordered to pay the woman's legal fees, and of course, reinstated her in her old job. (*Mills* v. *Ford Motor Co.,* 800 F.2d 635, 1986).

Then there was the case of a female employee who continuously complained to her company's bosses that she was being sexually harassed by her immediate supervisor. At first the company was very slow in responding to the woman's complaints, but eventually it got around to disciplining the sexist supervisor and then actually dismissing him.

In the meantime though, the female employee came up for a performance appraisal. As it turned out, she didn't score particularly well on her evaluation sheets and also ended up being summarily dismissed. But the woman felt she had not been able to perform her duties well because of the harassment she had suffered from her old supervisor.

Upon being let go, she sued the company on the grounds of sexual harassment and a negligent performance appraisal. The court found in favor of the dismissed woman worker and awarded her $36,000 in back pay. (*Lamb* v. *Smith International*, 32 E.P.D. 33772, S.D. Tex., 1983)

A similar case ended in the same fashion. Here, a woman who was an employee of the federal government claimed she had been a victim of sexual harassment by her supervisor and that the emotional trauma caused by this on-the-job friction made her work suffer. Regardless, the government had fired the woman based upon poor performance evaluations.

But in court, the woman pointed to the fact that she had worked hard and been promoted several times in her twenty-five years with the government. In its defense, the government's lawyers asserted that the woman had been given performance levels to reach and, quite simply, she had not reached them. Therefore, she was being dismissed. It had nothing to do with sexual harassment.

But the woman was able to bring forth lots of evidence that her supervisor "had intentionally discriminated against women, and that the discrimination resulted in a hostile working environment which prevented her from fully completing her assigned tasks." The court decided in favor of the dismissed female employee, ruling that the shoddy performance evaluations had been directly caused by the supervisor's harassment. (*Delgado* v. *Lehman*, 665 F. Supp. 460, 1987)

## Red flags to look for in your appraisals

Although it's clear that the laws concerning performance appraisals can change from state to state, it's also clear that within the last ten years, the courts have very much leaned in favor of the wronged employee.

The courts have made it clear that if your company does offer periodic performance appraisals, then your company's management assumes a legal liability to make certain these appraisals are carried out objectively, professionally, with no sign or indication of prejudice or discrimination, and within certain proscribed guidelines.

Here are some of the key indicators that the courts now consider very seriously.

## Before the appraisal

■ The presumption that if your boss or supervisor takes on the task of conducting a performance evaluation, that he or she handles it without bias. If you feel that your annual review was not handled in a professional, objective manner, you might want to discuss the matter with your attorney.

■ If, after several years of receiving good to excellent reviews, suddenly you receive a performance appraisal which drops precipitously. That kind of change in pattern can often spell trouble ahead—particularly if your work effort hasn't changed but your appraisal has.

■ If you feel that your company's appraisal system is inherently unfair in that no matter what kind of job you do, good or bad, the odds are always stacked against you. This kind of situation occasionally occurs when companies enforce a "forced curve" or "bell-shaped curve" on appraisals. This guarantees that a certain percentage of the working staff will always end up in the bottom half of the appraised pool. The problem with this kind of system is that because of the forced curve, good workers may end up being rated as poor, just to fulfill the company's curve.

■ Check out your company's employee handbook. Occasionally, there will be guidelines in that manual regarding the conduct and execution of employee appraisals, including the timing, content, rating systems, and so on.

For example, although there are no federal or state laws regarding the timing of a yearly performance appraisal, it's logical to assume that a court is not going to look favorably upon a company that attempts to stretch its evaluation period from, say, a twelve month period to an eighteen month or longer period. Particularly if you were promised when you were hired that evaluations would take place on a yearly basis, a company can't change its management tactics in midstream and now announce that they will take place at a later time.

## During the appraisal

■ Your supervisor has an obligation not only to go over what your strengths are on the job, but also (and perhaps more importantly) to detail specifically what areas you're lagging in. He or she has to explain how you are weak in these areas, and also provide you with an idea of what is expected of you and what the company considers to be satisfactory.

When you meet with your supervisor or boss, they should have in front of them a list of any incidents that were cause for reprimand or discipline since the last evaluation. These incidents, known as critical incidents, should consist of specific problems that cropped up during that time. For each incident the supervisor or manager should have the precise date of the incident, what the issue was, what you did, what the supervisor did in reaction to the incident, what the expected performance should have been, and any other pertinent comments.

In other words, if any legal action ever takes place, the burden is on the supervisor or manager to be able to provide careful, detailed records of any critical incidents. Just to say in court that "this subordinate was always a problem on the job" doesn't carry any weight with a judge or jury unless that manager can bring forth a list of critical incidents. Without that list, the complaints become a subjective matter, not objective.

Feel free to bring along a pad to take notes during your review, and if you want, when the appraisal comes to an end, take a few moments to review with your supervisor the precise areas in which you need to improve.

■ Don't be afraid to ask to see your employment file. Now, in some states, it's not legal to refuse employees access to their employment files. The trend in the majority of the states is to allow an employee to see his or her record, for better or for worse.

And your performance appraisal might be the perfect time to go over your personnel record. You might be surprised to find out what's in it.

Just to give you an idea, in Massachusetts, it's a state law that both private and public sector employers must allow their employees to review their personnel records at the employee's request. And if there is any disagreement or discrepancy in those records, the information in question must be corrected by mutual agreement of both employer and employee.

Massachusetts is just one example of this growing trend of allowing workers to see their employment records. Other states, like Arizona, Arkansas, Montana, North Dakota, and many others have already followed suit in protecting the rights of employees. Be sure to check with your company's and state's laws on your right to view your performance evaluation records.

## After the appraisal

If, for any number of reasons, you feel dissatisfied with your appraisal, don't run to your attorney first. Rather, give your employer the benefit of the doubt.

Schedule an appointment with your immediate supervisor to go over the appraisal again. If he or she refuses, or is not cooperative, then go to the company's director of personnel and file an official grievance there. Be specific as to your concern and why you think there was a problem with the appraisal.

If, after a reasonable period of time, you still haven't received a satisfactory reply, then and only then should you consider legal help. Remember, these employer/employee cases can become very long, very vitriolic affairs. So make certain that it's worth the battle before you start threatening a lawsuit.

## Personal performance appraisal audit

If you do find yourself with a pink slip in hand, be sure to ask your supervisor for the precise reason or reasons for your dismissal. If he or she mentions your poor performance records, then ask yourself the following questions:

- Does your company have a solid record of your so-called poor on-the-job performance? Have you ever seen these evaluations? Are they on record somewhere?
- Was your dismissal in direct keeping with the criteria as set

forth in your company's personnel handbook? Were the reasons for your firing based solely on objective criteria?

- Were you judged by any standards of performance that you were not familiar with? Were you the victim of a non-performance-related cutback or reduction in staff that was not fully explained to you?
- Do you feel that your poor performance reviews were due to a conflict in personality between you and your supervisor? Were you given a chance to prove that his or her appraisals were patently unfair or slanted against you?
- If your company used a combination of written and numerical evaluations, does the written part of the evaluation correlate with the numerical ratings?
- Did the company use a relatively current job description with which to judge your work? Or did they use a job description that hasn't been updated in years?

If there is any question in your mind that perhaps you've been treated unfairly, then there's no reason at all why you shouldn't pursue this issue. That might involve talking further with the personnel department, another manager or supervisor in the company, or even with your personal attorney.

# CHAPTER 9

# Discipline on the Job: Turning the Carrot-and-Stick Approach into Lawsuit Stew

"All right, we'll do it the hard way!" The manager of the chain restaurant was livid. Money had been stolen and he wanted to know which of the waitresses had been the culprit. But no one was spilling her guts. So, to get the tight-lipped employees to start talking, he had them all line up in a row in alphabetical order. And with each waitress, he asked if she had taken the money and if not, who had. And as each waitress said nothing or claimed innocence—just like that, she was fired on the spot.

The dismissed waitresses took the company to court for being treated so shabbily and rudely by their manager and guess what? The Massachusetts Supreme Court ruled that this kind of abusive discipline was intolerable and decided in favor of the fired waitresses. (*Agis* v. *Howard Johnson Co.*, 355 N.E. 2d 315, 1976)

## A right way—and a wrong way

A woman who had been hired as a clerical employee for an oil firm liked to dress stylishly in the office. The problem was, her bosses thought that she dressed up a bit too much—or too little.

It was true that the woman wore tight clothing, short skirts, and lots of makeup. Nobody denied that. But during the course of her three-month evaluation session, her supervisor commented about her dress style and also added that at a recent company party one of the company officials had complained that her behavior "was like that of a prostitute's." And that last comment really got the fireworks going. "You can't say things like that about me!" immediately protested the woman. "Why, that's so absurd I can't even believe it!"

"Yeah? Well, tell me this. How can you afford such snappy clothes on the salary you make here?" The woman was indignant. "How dare you! And I'm going straight to the EEOC to file a complaint." "You do that," threatened the supervisor, "and we'll make certain you never get another job in this city again!"

The woman did go to the authorities and filed a complaint of abusive discipline and discharge against the company and her former supervisor. In court, her attorney proved that the company had, in fact, no written or formal policy governing dress. That reality, coupled with the supervisor's comments about her behavior, her income, and her unfavorable impression with the other company officials paved the way for the court to decide in her favor in a suit based upon illegal personal appearance discrimination. She was awarded $72,000 in back pay and damages. (*Atlantic Richfield Co.* v. *District of Columbia Commission on Human Rights*, No. 1350, D.C. Ct. App., 1986)

A postal worker in Peoria, Illinois, was constantly being disciplined by his boss about spending too much time in the rest room. Not only was this criticism downright embarrassing to the worker, but he felt there was very little he could do about it. Except one day, he showed up at the post office wearing a cap on which he had pasted a picture of a toilet seat, evidently cut out from a store catalog.

Sure enough, the next day, other postal employees who felt that they, too, had been harassed about the time they spent in the bathroom joined in the pictorial protest. One female employee showed up to work wearing earrings with pictures of toilet seats pasted on them. "You jokers keep pulling this stunt and you'll lose your jobs," was the way in which the supervisor handled the situation. Sure enough, the workers kept on with their caps and earrings and they were summarily fired.

Upon the workers filing a complaint, the post office claimed that the toilet seat photos were indecent, hurt the post office's image, caused discipline and morale problems, and violated the dress code. But the administrative judge who heard the case disagreed, mainly because the dress code in the post office had always been lax and it had never caused a problem in the past in getting the work done. Furthermore, postal employees in this particular branch had been known in the past to have worn T-shirts to work with "unqualifiedly obscene and sexist" language printed on them and nobody in management had complained about those.

And so, the judge admitted that although the postal workers looked pretty silly with pictures of toilet seats hanging all over them, he had no choice but to rule in the workers' favor. After all, the court ruled, the employees have a right to protest the way in which they're treated on the job, so long as it doesn't interfere with productivity or image.

Then there was the case in which a federal judge ordered a motel to pay $7,200 in back pay to a former desk clerk who was fired because she refused to wear makeup on the job. A U.S. district judge ruled that the Montgomery, Alabama, clerk was a victim of overt sexual discrimination when she was first disciplined and then ultimately fired for being the only one of six female desk clerks who would not wear makeup.

"We fired her because of her lack of quality job performance," insisted the motel operator. "It had nothing to do with her lack of makeup." But the judge saw it differently, saying that the real "reasons for termination were a pretext for the woman's discharge, (that being) her refusal to wear makeup."

All these cases share one major theme—a boss wanted to discipline employees and did so. Unfortunately, it was done in a highly humiliating—and illegal—manner.

■ *Employee Rights Alert:* Being a manager or supervisor or boss means having to dispense discipline on the job from time to time. But as these cases illustrate, there's a legal as well as lots of illegal ways to handle employees. And if you as a company employee feel you've been treated unfairly, embarrassed, harassed, or disciplined wrongly, then you may have a legitimate legal beef.

Throughout this book you've seen the gradual erosion of the employment-at-will standard—that any worker can be fired at any time for any reason. More and more companies are becoming aware that discipline on the job is no longer just a passing fancy, but an integral part of every supervisor's charge. And disciplining a subordinate has to be handled in a fair, legally acceptable method that courts are going to uphold.

The days of seeing Dagwood Bumstead being kicked in the butt by his boss Mr. Dithers and thrown out the corporate door with the ringing words, "Bumstead! You're fired!" just shouldn't happen any more. And if it does happen—especially to you—then your former boss had better have some good reasons for his or her outrageous behavior.

## Way back in the good ol' days

Of course, these days employee rights are an accepted part of the give-and-take between employer and employee. But it wasn't that long ago that the employment-at-will doctrine was at full strength and an employer could discipline anyone on the job by simply carrying out that threat of immediate dismissal.

It took some very courageous employees who took it upon themselves to fight this centuries-old legal doctrine and pave the way for the expanding role of employee rights today. When it came to discipline before the 1970s, the bosses just said, "Either do it my way or else!" And the courts routinely backed them up.

But then a few chinks in the armor began to pop up. The courts were finding themselves presented with cases that involved the disciplining and ultimate firing of employees who were simply standing up for their legal rights. As mentioned in chapter 2 regarding public policy cases, that's when the courts started finding flaws with the employment-at-will doctrine.

One of the most celebrated cases, you might recall, involved an employee being called for jury duty. In this case, the woman's boss simply told her to get out of it, to think up some excuse for not reporting. But the woman wanted to serve, and besides, she felt it was her civic obligation. "Look," her boss finally said, "if you go to jury duty, then don't bother showing up here again for work." In essence, the boss got rid of this discipline problem by firing the woman.

The dismissed employee took the case to court and won, with the court saying, in essence, that it wasn't in the public's best interest to lose your job just because you got called for jury duty. (*Nees* v. *Hocks*, Ore. 210, 536 P.2d 512, 1975)

In another discipline-related case, a woman worker who had injured her thumb while at work was told by her boss not to file a worker's compensation claim. The boss evidently wanted to keep his department's safety record clean.

But the woman did file a claim, and because of her insubordination, this discipline problem was also handled with a quick dismissal. That's how discipline problems were handled ten years ago. But the fired employee sued and won her case. (*Kelsay* v. *Motorola, Inc.*, 384 N.E. 2d 353, 1978)

In another case you already read about, several farm workers decided to talk with an attorney about their employment contract with an agricultural employer. "You do that," they were warned by their employer, "and I'll fire you on the spot. I can't have any disciplinary problems on my farm."

But they did. And they were fired. In court, the judges ruled that being able to see one's personal attorney about an employment contract is hardly a matter of disciplinary upheaval, and as a result, found in favor of the farm workers. (*Montalvo* v. *Zamorra*, 7 Cal. App. 3d 69, 1970)

From fairly straightforward discipline-related cases like these, the rights of employees have mushroomed over the last few years. Of course, discipline is always a two-way street, but in many states today, that final threat of instant termination no longer carries as much weight with the courts. And quite frankly, most companies have tried to stay modern and keep up with the changes in disciplinary procedures.

## Discipline as an art form

Most companies these days understand that discipline is not only an essential part of management, but also that if handled poorly all sorts of problems (including legal) can develop. Motivation is always a delicate subject, and all managers know it's extremely difficult to criticize subordinates hoping that they will improve on the job.

That's precisely why some management teams have gone so far as to have included in their company policy handbook a definitive blueprint for discipline. In most situations (and you should definitely check your company's policy handbook to see if this is covered), a firm will outline that, in terms of discipline, an employee is given first an oral warning, then a written warning, and then, if there is a third infraction, a final warning which leads to termination.

This three-step "progressive discipline" policy, as it has come to be known, also works within the structure of yearly performance appraisals. During the course of a routine performance evaluation, as you saw in chapter 8, the supervisor must give specific and precise feedback, both positive and negative, on how the subordinate is doing on the job.

As you might imagine, the concept of progressive discipline varies from one company to the next. Some firms have a built-in grievance procedure to handle discipline complaints. Others keep track of on-the-job infractions by other means. But the basic concept of at least giving an employee warnings before termination tends to remain constant.

## Discipline in action

So far, progressive discipline sounds fairly straightforward, doesn't it? But you'd be surprised at how often this relatively straightforward disciplinary process goes awry. And that's when the lawsuits start to fly.

A case in point is that of the airline employee who had been on the job for eighteen years with a good track record which we mentioned in chapter 8. One day he was caught in a minor theft—taking some company property home with him. His punishment? He was fired on the spot by his supervisor. Feeling that his eighteen years of meritorious service shouldn't go up in a puff of smoke on one error, the veteran employee sued on the grounds that his discharge was improper and that the airline supervisor hadn't followed the company's long-standing policy of taking care of disciplinary measures through a "fair, impartial, and objective" procedure.

"Nonsense!" argued the airline's attorneys. "Not only is there no guarantee that, as an employer, we have to provide this kind of objective hearing. But furthermore, nowhere in the company policy handbook is that promise ever made. It's totally based upon oral history within this company—there's no legal requirement."

The court listened to the airline company's argument but disagreed and found in favor of the employee. In its ruling, the court decided that the employee's eighteen years of solid service should have counted for something when weighed against a minor theft, and more importantly, the company's own policy—although an oral policy and not written—guaranteed the employee a fair and objective hearing on the matter.

■ *Employee Rights Alert:* The decision here was significant on two counts. One, the court was saying that a company doesn't even need to have all of its personnel and disciplinary policies written in a handbook. A company is expected to follow its standard traditional procedures. And there's an "implied covenant of good faith and fair dealing" that exists between employer and employees. That implied covenant theoretically insures that an employer will not capriciously discipline—or fire—an employee.

Two, the court made it clear that if an employee has worked for a long time for a company and has done solid work, then the company is at least morally obliged to give that employee a fair shake. That pattern, although certainly not a law, does seem to hold up consistently from case to case. (*Cleary* v. *American Airlines,* 111 Cal. App. 3d 443, 168 Cal. Rptr. 722, 1980)

## And when it is in writing

Then there's the case where the company had its discipline procedures in writing and it still cost them big bucks.

In this instance, a loan officer at a bank in Minnesota had been hired at a time when the bank did not have a company policy handbook regarding disciplinary procedures. But six months later, the bank did institute a company handbook and among the topics covered in writing was employee discipline. The handbook required first an oral warning, then a written warning, and then finally termination.

A few months later, it was discovered that some bank funds were missing from the loan officer's account and the evidence seemed to point strongly toward the verdict that the employee had embezzled the dough. As a result, he was fired on the spot, although no proof of his being the actual thief was ever produced.

"You can't just fire me like that!" protested the loan officer, "Why, if nothing else, you didn't even follow the company handbook regarding discipline. You at least owe me that."

The bank argued that first of all, the loan officer had been hired before the company handbook had been adopted so that his employment wasn't covered by it. And second, a crime as terrible as embezzlement shouldn't have to go through the normal disciplinary procedures.

The Minnesota Supreme Court decided in favor of the loan officer. First, the fact that the loan officer had been hired prior to the company handbook being written made no difference. That's because the handbook itself made it clear that all employees of the bank were now covered regardless of when they were hired. So, under that ruling, the loan officer was covered.

Second, because of that handbook and its policy regarding discipline, the bank had indeed acted very hastily when it came to firing the loan officer. The bank had totally disregarded its own company policy, and as a result, had not given the benefit of the doubt to the employee. Furthermore, the bank had not followed its preprogrammed series of warnings to the employee. The court felt it had no choice but to decide in favor of the loan officer and awarded him $27,000 in back pay and damages. (*Pine River Bank* v. *Mettile*, 333 N.W. 2d 622, 1983)

A similar process was at work in a case in Michigan involving a hospital and a dismissed nurse. In that situation, the nurse had been disciplined because, in essence, she wasn't getting along well with her coworkers.

"We can't have those kinds of problems on our nursing staff in this hospital," the nurse's boss told her and promptly put her on suspension. And within a few weeks that suspension became permanent. She lost her job.

Understandably, the nurse then filed a grievance complaint, as outlined in the hospital's employee handbook. The rules were specific, and definite steps were laid out in the book regarding these grievance procedures.

But as the nurse made her case, it became evident that discipline steps were being forgotten and that she hadn't been advised of all her rights in the procedure. As a result, when she lost in the internal hearing, she decided to file a real lawsuit against the hospital, charging wrongful dismissal and a violation of the implied contract between her and the hospital based upon the employee handbook.

The appeals court in this case ruled in favor of the nurse, saying in its opinion that "it is reasonable for employees to expect that policies in force at any given time will be applied uniformly to all," and also that "while the hospital maintained the sole right to discharge employees, this right was expressly subject to the regulations and restrictions provided in the handbook." And the court made it clear that in this case, the handbook provided a detailed list of disciplinary standards and procedures, most of which had been ignored by the hospital's administrative staff. (*Renny* v. *Port Huron Hospital*, No. 74884, Mich. Sup. Ct., 1987)

## Personality conflicts and discipline

If there is one basic theme concerning discipline on the job, it's that the most common source of a lawsuit is a clash of personalities—usually between employee and supervisor. Case after case in this area of the law starts off with a difference of opinion between boss and subordinate, and then escalates into a series of disciplinary actions —actions, which the courts say, must be well documented and not petty.

Chances are you know someone (or perhaps even yourself) who has run into "personality problems" with their boss at the office or in the factory. The key to these cases is whether or not the actions for discipline (1) are substantial; (2) are well documented in the company files; (3) follow company guidelines; and (4) are fair and legitimate complaints by the supervisor.

To illustrate, here are a few typical cases involving a clash of personalities where the employee ends up being fired. Note in each case how the court decides and for what reasons.

An employee for a government agency was considered a hard and conscientious worker for her first two years on the job, but that was because she and her supervisor seemed to be such good friends. Those reviews, however, changed drastically when a new supervisor was appointed to the post and immediately dispatched new guidelines for productivity and standards of assignments.

The employee clearly resented these new directives, and before too long, she and her new boss were at loggerheads with each other. The reason? She didn't like the new orders or her new boss. Every time she balked, her new boss disciplined her, and duly noted it in a documented file. As time went on, the employee's attitude didn't change, her discipline file got larger, and she was ultimately dismissed.

In court, the fired employee claimed that she was let go simply because the new boss didn't like her. In the defense, the supervisor reported incident after incident of disciplinary problems in the office, all detailing work performance slip-ups. There was no mention at all of personality clashes or personal preferences. And that factor was important in the ultimate outcome of this case, because if there had been even the slightest hint that the new supervisor had been truly motivated by her personal dislike of the employee, then that prejudice would have strongly worked against her in court. Instead, she limited her disciplinary comments solely to on-the-job problems.

The court ruled in favor of the company and the new supervisor. Based upon careful inspection of the records, the court was convinced that the new supervisor had been fair in her evaluations, had not allowed personality conflicts to get in the way of discipline notices, and that the employee simply hadn't made enough of an effort to get her work done. In essence, the court ruled, there's no guarantee that employees have to be best friends with or even get along with their bosses. All that really counts is whether or not the employee does his or her work and does it well. (*Stanford* v. *Commission on Human Rights,* 37 Empl. Prac. Dec. No. 35, 261, N.Y., 1983)

An employee was caught drinking on the job by his boss and was duly dismissed from his job because of it. "That's not fair!" claimed the employee. "First of all, why isn't the company doing something for my alcohol problem, like offering me some alcohol-abuse program? I'm at least owed that. And second, with some other guys who had similar problems on the job, the company was a lot more lenient about letting them keep their jobs. I'm getting fired just because my boss doesn't like me and this gives him the perfect excuse to get rid of me."

The court didn't see it that way. In terms of discipline and alcohol or drug abuse while on the job, it was decided that this particular company had a very clear policy prohibiting drinking on the job. As a result, the company was under no legal obligation to put the employee in an alcohol-abuse program, nor was the company obliged to handle each drinking problem in the same manner. Furthermore, the charge that "the boss doesn't like me" didn't carry any weight with the court because the employee's supervisor had also kept solid records of the worker's past discipline problems on the job. The alcohol situation was merely the last straw. (*Reynolds* v. *Humko Products,* 36 Empl. Prac. Dec. No. 35, 050, 1985)

A black assembly-line worker was dismissed from his job in a food processing plant because, according to the detailed supervisory records, he was just plain incompetent. "That's crazy!" said the worker, "I lost my job because my boss is racist!"

But in court the boss produced carefully documented records that proved that the employee's dismissal had nothing at all to do with charges of racism but was a decision based squarely on poor performance. The issue here was not one of personality problems, but of lousy work effort. The case was decided in favor of the company. (*Gray* v. *Frito-Lay*, 30 Empl. Prac., 1982)

The three cases have two things in common: (1) they were all decided in favor of the employer, not the employee; and (2) the court made it clear that the only reason it decided in favor of the company was because the supervisor or manager in question had kept well-organized, detailed records of disciplinary actions and the only criticisms of the workers dealt with on-the-job performance—nothing more. There was never any mention that the supervisor "just didn't like the employee's attitude" or the way in which "the worker walked around the office" or the fact that the employee was of a different race, national origin, sexual preference, or religion.

■ *Employee Rights Alert:* If—and this is an important point—you feel you have been disciplined on the job and that the sole reason for the action is based on a difference in personalities and *not* because of a lack of performance, then you should consider complaining to the personnel office or, if discharged, to your attorney. Supervisors these days are expected to know the law regarding discipline on the job, and they know (or should know) that simple "personality problems" are rarely grounds for dismissal or censure.

## The seven basics of progressive discipline

While every management team has its own way or corporate method of handling discipline on the job, the concept of progressive discipline is the one style that seems to have caught on—both with top companies and with courts nationwide.

If you've been disciplined at work, take a look at the following seven-point checklist. Based on the principle of progressive discipline, check to see just how well (or not so well) your boss has handled your situation.

- Usually, with a serious disciplinary offense, you should receive a written notice of what you did wrong and why it was against corporate policy.
- The notice should describe the problem and why it is so serious.
- It should also set the standard for what is considered proper

corporate behavior, and if applicable, the notice should map out an expected deadline or progress schedule of when the problem should clear up.

- The notice should point out the future consequences (e.g., dismissal) if the problem isn't taken care of immediately.
- You should be notified that a copy of the notice will be placed in your permanent file.
- Accompanying that notice should be a written guarantee that if your behavior does improve, then the discipline notice will be expunged from your record.
- You should expect at least one more final notice before actions for dismissal are set in motion.

## A word about probation and procedures

If, due to the discipline problem at hand, you are officially placed on probation by your company, keep in mind that the purpose of probation is normally to give you a specific amount of time in which to correct a problem on the job or improve your behavior or attitude. Probation usually requires a special performance appraisal to be conducted at the end of the probationary period, which is commonly thirty to ninety days.

In terms of your rights, remember that you should be specifically notified why you are being placed on probation, what particular action or actions prompted the probation, how you are to correct the problem and in which way the resolution would be acceptable to the company, and for how long the probation period will last. Also remember that courts look suspiciously on probationary periods that last longer than three months (ninety days); there's an inbred feeling that individuals will either correct their problems on the job within that time frame or they won't at all.

Going by some of the above cases, can you assume that if your employer has a written internal grievance procedure you can expect it to be used? By most court decisions in this area, if you are being disciplined and your company does have a formal dispute resolution program, then yes—there is a reasonable expectation that you're entitled to be disciplined according to the company's standards.

In fact, because of this, some companies are hesitant to even adopt such a formal policy. After all, if discipline becomes a long drawn-out process, some bosses figure "Why bother with a formal system?" But the fact remains that most companies do have such policies, and as a full-time employee, you should read that company handbook to see exactly how the process works.

## Hey, does this mean I can never get fired on the spot?

Not quite. Most employees and employers alike would certainly agree that there's a wide range of disciplinary measures to be taken depending on the type of incident.

It's one thing if an employee has a chronic habit of being late to work or taking too much time at lunch or spending too much time on personal telephone calls. All those incidents are basic disciplinary problems, and certainly call for disciplinary steps.

But there are those incidents of serious magnitude which might include grounds for immediate dismissal, and in most cases a court of law would back up such a firing. In fact, many companies include a formal statement to that effect in their handbooks. A typical statement reads:

> IMMEDIATE DISMISSAL
> Flagrant disregard for policies and practices such as gross insubordination and physical violence warrant immediate discharge. Major offenses, such as dishonesty, breach of trust, unlawful distribution of drugs while conducting company business, and the possessing or transporting of firearms on company facilities, are so serious in nature that an employee can be discharged for the first violation.

Formal statements reserve the company's right to fire dangerous employees on the spot without any worry of legal retribution. While it is true that any employee can file a lawsuit for almost any reason, be forewarned that if you're caught selling drugs at work or showing off your .357 Magnum to your coworkers to impress them, then you'll have a tough time in court protesting your dismissal.

## Outrageous behavior in dismissal

While on the topic of angry dismissals, it's safe to say that firings rarely go down smoothly. Nobody wants to be fired, and booters (for the most part) don't enjoy the confrontations any more than the bootees.

And when things start getting hot, sometimes bosses can become enbroiled in what the courts refer to as "outrageous behavior."

What constitutes this kind of outlandish activity? Well, one judge has defined it as "whether the employer's conduct was sufficiently outrageous to offend the conscience of the community." That might be a bit too broad to be useful, but here are a couple of examples to clarify.

In one case, a laid-off employee returned for her final paycheck. But, upon returning, her former supervisor told her that some cash had been missing from her old cash register, and that to collect her pay, the former employee would have to pass a lie detector test. The employee did pass the test, but then her old boss decided not to pay her anyway. That, said the court, was definitely outrageous behavior, and ruled in favor of the fired employee. She got her money back and then some. (*M.B.M. Co.* v. *Counce*, 596 S.W. 2d 681, 1980)

Another example occurred in the course of a heated confrontation between a supervisor and employee where the supervisor made the outrageous mistake of hurling racial epithets at the dismissed employee. That, as you can imagine, was not received too well by the courts. (*Argawal* v. *Johnson*, 25 Cal. 3d 932, 160 Cal. Rptr. 141, 1979)

■ *Employee Rights Alert:* Again, the point is well taken. There's a right way and wrong way to discipline and dismiss a worker. Outrageous behavior just won't be tolerated by the courts.

## Discipline, rights, and the EEOC

If you hadn't guessed it by now, most supervisors are becomingly increasingly intimidated about how and when they can discipline a worker. Even if the supervisor is totally justified in confronting the worker and expressing displeasure with his or her performance, the execution of that disciplinary process has become the focus of corporate policymakers everywhere.

Indeed, whether you know it or not, corporate management teams are spending millions of dollars each year in the training of managers and supervisory personnel on how to discipline workers. Whether they send these supervisors to seminars or have them read books or newsletters on the subject, corporate management is convinced that discipline is not an easy subject to address. At best, discipline is necessary for productivity; at worst, it can be botched and end up costing the company thousands of dollars in court costs, legal fees, and lost man-hours.

That's why when your boss comes in to discipline you, he or she had better know the ropes. And these days, the courts are watching like hawks to make certain that a disciplinary move isn't just a thinly disguised maneuver to get around the EEOC laws.

As you know, the EEOC watchdogs are there to make certain your rights on the job aren't violated. How concerned are companies about the EEOC and discipline? Take a look at the following cautionary questions from a recent management seminar on the subject, prepared by a corporate attorney who is trying to prevent a company from being targeted for lawsuits.

*Race:* As a supervisor, do you have plans to replace a black employee with a white one? Has that black worker been a vocal advocate of minority rights? Does the discharge arise from a racial incident?

*Sex:* Will a male worker replace a woman who was fired? Was the woman a rights' activist? Did someone on the job make sexist remarks to her? Is sexual harassment part of the scenario?

*Marital status:* Have you, as a supervisor, made any presumptions about a married employee's willingness to travel or work unusual hours? Have you made any assumptions about an unmarried employee's lack of responsibility?

*Religion:* Have you tried to make reasonable accommodations, short of undue hardship, for the employee's religious beliefs? Has anyone on the job made any religious-oriented comments about the employee?

*Handicap:* Have you and the company made reasonable accommodations for any worker who is handicapped? Have any coworkers made any snide or derogatory comments?

*Age:* Do you plan to replace an over-forty worker with a younger employee? Has anyone made any comments about older workers on the job?

## Hard to believe, isn't it?

These questions may seem uncommonly blunt to you, but the attorneys who prepared them know exactly what the courts are looking for when it comes to discipline problems on the job. Particularly in this day and age where employee rights are growing in strength everyday, the Equal Employment Opportunity Commission is specifically there to investigate all violations.

What complicates matters even more is that supervisors and managers are beginning to be subtler in their disciplinary approaches. For example, in one gray-area case, a white supervisor told a black subordinate that "You're just not getting the job done. I'm giving you a very low rating on your evaluation sheet and also suggesting you get some counseling to improve your attitude and productivity."

Sure enough, the black employee went off for counseling and then returned to his job several weeks later. At that point, however, he was given the choice of either resigning or being fired on the spot.

"Let's face it," his boss told him, "neither your attitude nor your work has improved." So the worker resigned. But four days later, he found out that a fellow coworker, who had received just as lousy an evaluation as he, had not been terminated. Rather, that worker —who happened to be white—just received a minor demotion, nothing more.

Suspecting racial discrimination, the black employee filed suit. Sure enough, in court it turned out that the black employee had seven years of service to the company (compared to the white employee's three years) and both had similar performance records. It didn't take the judge long to see through the camouflage of race discrimination in this case, and promptly decide in favor of the black employee. (*Barnes* v. *Yellow Freight Systems*, 778 F.2d 1096, 1985)

## Sometimes, the company wins

When it comes to discipline and allegations of racial discrimination on the job, the courts always look to see if other workers of different races were treated differently. And unless there is solid prima facie evidence of that, the courts sometimes go along with the company. A case in point involved a Hispanic railroad worker who had injured his hand on the job.

He was told to file an accident report and to report back to work on a full-time basis within two days. He didn't report for another ten days, saying that he had stayed home on the advice of his own family physician.

His supervisor accused him of just taking a vacation, at the company's expense, and the supervisor suggested that the worker be fired. When the case got to court, the fired employee claimed that a fellow coworker—who happened to be white and had also suffered a similar injury—had taken off several days from work and nobody complained about him. Hence, this was a case of blatant racism.

"Not so fast," ruled the court. First of all, the white worker's injury and follow-up were not at all similar to this employee's case, and secondly, the Hispanic's dismissal was based upon "his dismal personnel record." The decision to dismiss, ruled the judge, was "clearly not based on race or national origin."

The key here, once again, was that the company had kept detailed records to back up its disciplinary action. Without those records, the court will usually work on a presumption of prima facie discrimination. (*Mata* v. *Southern Pacific Transportation Co.*, 36 Empl. Prac. Dec. 35, 199, No. 82-3088, Cal., 1984)

## Burnout? Or age discrimination?

As you can see, handling disciplinary situations can be extremely tricky. And in one instance, just because a manager forgot to add some key words, it ended up costing him and his company in court.

It was a situation in which an engineer had been with a firm for twenty-three years. Problem was, over the years, the engineer's productivity had declined by degrees—lots of degrees.

This was not lost on the company; in fact, in the course of its performance evaluations with the engineer, his supervisor had tried gently and politely to tell him about the work slippage.

But no one had ever directly said to the fifty-one-year-old engineer, "Look, you had better shape up or you're going to lose your job!" And when he got fired for lack of productivity, the engineer was stunned.

When the case got in front of a judge (you've seen the result already in chapter 8), he ruled in favor of the dismissed engineer. The court ruled that the company had done pretty much everything correctly and by the book. But when it came to disciplining the engineer, the company had fallen down on the job. No one had told the engineer that his job was on the line, or what the process was going to be that led to his dismissal. (*Chamberlain* v. *Bissell*, 547 F. Supp. 1067, W.D. Mich., 1982)

## Too much documentation?

Don't for a second think that management isn't taking all these legal strategies into consideration. The fact of the matter is that most supervisors and other bosses keep well-detailed files and documents on each and every disciplinary problem that erupts in the office or factory.

Of course, sometimes all this detailed record keeping can work against a firm's management. That almost happened in a curious case in which a black woman who had worked for eight years as a production line inspector was reprimanded repeatedly and finally dismissed.

She brought suit against her former employer, charging among other things that the company had built a trumped-up case against her and had recorded every petty detail of her tenure with the firm. "This isn't just a case of wrongful dismissal," argued her attorney. "It's really a case of racial discrimination in which management has used record keeping to prove its own self-fulfilling prophecy."

At first, the court looked at the records and had nothing to say. After all, the woman had run up a thick file of discipline infractions.

"But your honor, that's just my point," claimed the woman's attorney. "Take a look at some of the items included in that file and judge for yourself as to whether they are substantial charges or just frivolous." Sure enough, the file was filled with little items here and there—very few major incidents of discipline. And the court began to wonder, too, whether this was a situation in which management was, in fact, really trying to hide a latent case of race discrimination by building a file against the black employee.

The court realized it was in a pickle. After all, companies are always asked to document the reasons for dismissal, and this company had followed that policy—and then some. As it turned out, the court felt it could only agree with the facts as presented, and it found in favor of the company.

But significantly, the case was appealed and even though the lower court's decision stood, one of the appellate justices, in a strongly worded dissenting opinion, made it clear that such "overdocumentation" in order to get around the laws preventing racial discrimination will not be tolerated in the future. (*Weems* v. *Ball Metal & Chemical*, 753 F.2d 527, 1985)

## Union-busting tactics

Disciplinary firings can crop up for any number of reasons, and as an employee, you should be aware of all possibilities. Take, for example, the case of an employee who, the court admitted, had "an abysmal attendance and lateness record" and by all rights, deserved to be fired from his job.

But the court dug a little deeper into the case. It discovered another reason that the worker was fired. Turned out that nobody in management was in a great hurry to get rid of this particular employee, even though his work record was lousy. Until, that is, the word got around that he was involved in some union organizing talks. Suddenly he was given the bum's rush through the disciplinary process and was tossed out on his fanny.

The employee complained, claiming that not only had the company not followed its own handbook, but that the only reason he was being fired was because of his interest in a union being formed at work. "Not true at all," replied the company's attorneys. "We have a corporate policy regarding employee discipline and it's included in our handbook."

"Yes, you do," said the court, "but the problem here is that your company's supervisors didn't follow that policy when it came to disciplining this worker. Nobody bothered to formally acknowledge that the employee was officially late to work or missing too many days. And without that kind of official notification, you really can't come back and fire him after the fact. And besides, your company never bothered to discipline the employee at all until the union was being formed."

As you might imagine, the company lost the case—even though the court agreed that the employee most likely should have been fired in the first place. (*D. & D. Distributing Co.* v. *N.L.R.B.*, 801 F.2d 636, 1986)

## Discipline and you—unhappy together

The art of disciplining employees has always been challenging. And as this chapter points out, it's becoming more difficult with each passing day. But there are two basic themes that should run through your mind the next time your boss says that he "wants to see you in his office."

One, any disciplinary confrontation should be fully explained to you, as to why it is happening, what you can do to ameliorate the situation, and just how serious a discipline problem this is to you and the company. Further, all disciplinary conversations should relate strictly to on-the-job activities and not to either privacy matters or off-hours activities. The company generally has no right to pry into your off-hours or private life, as you saw in chapter 6.

Two, any and all disciplinary actions taken by the company against you should result in a report being written up and a copy enclosed in your permanent personnel file. If the particular problem is cleared up or if you are on probation, then you usually have the right to ask to have that disciplinary record removed from your file.

If, for any reason, you don't think you've been given a fair shake by your boss and company, or if you think you've been singled out for disciplining, or if you feel your personal privacy has become an issue, then you know where to go to find out your rights.

# CHAPTER 10

# Your Company's Employee Handbook: Reading Between the Lines

O f all the places where employee rights-based lawsuits have arisen, perhaps the most surprising place of all has been the employee handbook.

Certainly it's been surprising—and devastating—to corporate managers all around the country, because it was they who wrote these handbooks and distributed them to their workers in the first place. There's no law on the books that stipulates that a company must have a handbook for its employees. Yet traditionally, companies have put together these little handbooks and thought they were doing themselves and their workers a service.

Imagine the look on a boss's face when the fine print in his own company's handbook is thrown back at him in the form of a lawsuit. Believe us, it's not a pretty sight.

## The employee handbook?

Yep. That's right—the employee handbook. That little innocuous manual which is usually delivered to the new employee on his or her first day of work only to be tossed on a back shelf somewhere and seemingly forgotten. Forgotten, that is, until that fateful day arrives when the employee is summarily fired and he or she goes rummaging for that same handbook to see if any rights have been violated.

Now, up until about ten years ago, a dismissed worker could have read the employee handbook back and forth and upside down, but such efforts still wouldn't have done much good in a court of law. That old bugaboo of employment-at-will was still very much in effect, no matter what was written in that book.

However, the judicial system in our country has changed its views in the last decade. Judges and juries have started to read between the lines of those handbooks—handbooks, remember, that are written by management, not by employees.

Courts are beginning to look for "implied contracts" and other reasonable promises made by the company which are seemingly guaranteed in these handbooks. And, the courts are now saying, if a company or one of its managers doesn't follow its own handbook to the letter, then a worker who hasn't gotten a fair shake can win a cause of action against his former employer in a court of law.

Think we're kidding? Take a look at some of the following cases in which the employee handbook was the key element and you'll see who's laughing.

Here's a typical case: A company was experiencing some unexpected financial problems and the boss decided that in order to cut costs, he'd get rid of some of the higher-paid employees. In fact, he started his purge by giving one of his managers a pink slip.

When the boss called the manager in to give her the bad news, he simply said, "Look, if I don't let some of the top salaries go, the company will be looking at bankruptcy. Now, you don't want the entire operation to go under, do you?"

The manager didn't like this development, her being sacrificed just so the rest of the company could survive. And she pointed to the employee handbook to back up her argument, claiming an implied contract of employment.

"Forget the employee handbook," her boss shrugged. "None of that stuff in there applies to you because you were working here long before that book was ever written or distributed. So, there's no such implied contract between you and the company."

The manager went home, angry and confused—and out of a job. But a few days later, when she heard that her former boss had hired eleven new workers—all at lower wages—she took her case to a lawyer and ultimately to court.

The judge heard the evidence, read the employee handbook, and ruled in favor of the fired manager. As for the argument that the woman had worked for the firm long before an employee handbook was installed, the judge said, "As an employer, [the company] was freely able to enforce employee handbook rules of conduct. It likewise follows that [the manager], as an employee, could reasonably rely on the procedures outlined in the employee handbook during employment termination."

The fired manager was awarded $58,000 in lost wages and profit-sharing money. (*Kerr* v. *Gibson's Products Co. of Bozeman, Inc.*, 733 P.2d 1292, 1987)

Then there was the case of the airline executive from Colorado who walked into his office one day and was told by his boss, "I'm sorry, but we no longer need your services here. Please pack up your things."

"Hey, wait a minute," protested the executive, "you just can't fire me like that. According to the employee handbook, all airlines employees are entitled to a hearing before dismissal." "Oh, come on," replied the boss, "that kind of stuff is really designed only for lower-level workers—not executives like you or me. Forget it."

But the executive took his case to court, and used the company-written handbook as exhibit A. And sure enough, the language in the handbook specifically said that all employees of the airline were entitled to a hearing before being dismissed.

As it developed, the lower court held in favor of the airline. But on appeal, the higher court reversed that decision and held in favor of the dismissed executive. The court ruled that the handbook did constitute an enforceable contract between employer and employee and that there was an understood agreement that the contract would be in full force under the conditions spelled out in the handbook.

As a consequence, said the appeals court, the airline had breached its contract with the executive, and the executive was entitled to damages. (*Continental Airlines* v. *Keenan*, 731 P.2d 708, 1987)

The state's highest court in Illinois ruled that an employee handbook can be viewed as an implied contract. In that particular case, a nursing administrator found herself with a new title but basically the same job duties when a staff reorganization was announced. This bothered her, because she had been led to believe by her superiors that, with the new shake-up, she would be promoted to a new and more challenging position.

When she started to complain about this unfulfilled promise, her boss told her that not only was her complaint meaningless but that she wasn't doing a very good job in her new/old position to boot. Sure enough, the rapport between the nursing administrator and her superior began to sour, and within a few weeks, she was handed a formal report that severely criticized her work.

The report was called a probationary evaluation, but oddly, attached to that same report was another sheet of paper that listed the exact same complaints. Everything was the same—except that other sheet was labeled Final Notice. It, in essence, said the nursing administrator was fired and had to leave the hospital by the end of the day.

In court, the nursing administrator pointed to the employee handbook which contained a recently updated policy statement that established a probationary period of ninety days for any employee. Only during that probationary period, said the book, could an employee be dismissed without just cause.

But once that probationary period had passed, then an employee could be dismissed only "with proper notice and investigation." Furthermore, except for extremely serious offenses, the company policy required three formal warnings before a permanent employee could be fired.

In reviewing the case, the Illinois Supreme Court held in favor of the dismissed nursing administrator, saying that the hospital had indeed violated its own employee handbook when it fired her so quickly. (*Duldulao* v. *St. Mary of Nazareth Hospital Center,* 1 Indiv. Empl. Rts. Cases 1428, 1987)

The actual language of the Illinois Supreme Court's opinion in the nurse's case is worth reading, because the justices clearly spelled out how employee handbooks are now being viewed by a growing number of courts around the country.

> We hold that an employee handbook or other policy statement creates enforceable contractual rights if the traditional requirements for contract formation are present.
>
> First, the language of the policy statement must contain a promise clear enough that an employee would reasonably believe that an offer has been made.
>
> Second, the statement must be disseminated to the employee in such a manner that the employee is aware of its contents and reasonably believes it to be an offer.

Third, the employee must accept the offer by commencing or continuing to work after learning of the policy statement.

When these events are present, then the employee's continued work constitutes consideration for the promises contained in the statement, and under traditional principles a valid contract is formed.

■ *Employee Rights Alert:* The court's opinion is fairly clear cut. And with each day, more and more cases based on this "implied contract" concept are being filed.

From Alabama, where adherence to the doctrine of employment-at-will has been rock solid for over two hundred years, came this earth-shattering decision in 1987: An employee handbook can be construed as an implied contract between employer and employee.

In that landmark case, a sales representative for a pharmaceutical firm had been in poor health because of an injured leg. As his leg got worse, surgery was needed. Unfortunately, his employers weren't too sympathetic to his medical problems, and while he was recuperating from the surgery, they started disciplinary action against the sales rep for poor performance leading to dismissal.

That's just what happened. The sales rep was ultimately fired. But he sued, waving the employee handbook as solid evidence that he had an implied contract with the firm that he could only be fired for poor performance when he was physically able to conduct business.

But the pharmaceutical company wasn't too concerned with the lawsuit; after all, Alabama had decided case after case like this one in favor of employers throughout the state. But lo and behold, the Alabama Supreme Court changed direction better than an open-field breakaway halfback and decided in favor of the sales rep. It said that an implied contract did exist (thanks to the handbook) and that it was most unreasonable to expect that the salesman "could be discharged for unsatisfactory performance when he was not physically capable of satisfactorily performing." (*Hoffman-La Roche, Inc.* v. *Campbell,* 512 S.2d 725, 1987)

## How the companies are reacting

As you might imagine, corporate management around the country isn't taking all these proemployee decisions lightly. In addition to constantly warning their managers and supervisory personnel to follow the disciplinary procedures of employee handbooks correctly, some corporate bosses are calling upon their legal beagles to nip this so-called implied contract problem in the bud.

A recent case highlights what some companies have done. One corporation had its counsel add a disclaimer to its employee handbook that read, in part, "that nothing in this policy manual should be construed as an employment contract or guarantee of employment."

Sure enough, a case came up that tested that exact statement. Two employees of the firm were terminated because a company official had discovered that they (a married male and an unmarried female) had gone on an out-of-town trip together. The official, who had strong religious beliefs about such things, fired the two employees for carrying on in this manner.

The two employees sued the company on the grounds of breach of an implied contract of employment based on the company's employee handbook. They referred to a section which said the company promised to provide "fair and uniform treatment to all employees" and to that end, it was written that the company could fire employees only for good cause. The manual also said that an employee's off-duty conduct was not grounds for termination except under specified circumstances.

The lower court ruled in favor of the company, agreeing that the statement in the handbook said that nothing should be construed as an implied contract. But the Kansas Supreme Court reversed that decision, saying that the company had written this disclaimer into its employee handbook to create an unqualified employment-at-will situation, and that ran totally counter to the rest of the handbook's provisions.

In other words, the effectiveness and usefulness of such a disclaimer to discount the employee handbook was really short-circuited. (*Morriss* v. *Coleman Co.*, 738 P.2d 841, 1987)

## When employee handbooks get in the way

What's really scary about employee handbooks and their impact is that sometimes they can cause tremendous harm—legal and otherwise.

Take the case of the junior manager who was working the front desk one wintry night in rural Virginia. A man came through the front door into the lobby and inquired about getting two rooms and paying for them with a personal check.

Uncertain about what to say, the fledgling manager checked out the company policy manual. "I'll need some personal identification in order to accept a check," he told the visitor. But when the man said he didn't have any, the junior manager, although sympathetic to the man's plight on a cold night, refused him: "I'm sorry, but company policy is very strict about accepting checks without identification."

The junior manager then made some calls around to other neighboring motels but with no luck. Disgusted, the man finally walked out.

About a week later, the chairman of the board of the motel chain received a hostile letter from the man who was turned away. Turns out that the man ran a local shelter for kids. Apparently, on that winter evening, the shelter had experienced a power failure, and the man was attempting to find shelter for his kids for the night.

The chairman, of course, was outraged by the junior manager's behavior. First he issued an immediate apology to the man, then he issued direct orders to fire the manager on the spot.

When the firing order came down, the junior manager protested that he was being fired for merely following the company handbook. Furthermore, he said, according to that same handbook, he was entitled to three formal warnings before dismissal. And here, of course, he had received none at all.

When the case went to court, the judge ruled in favor of the junior manager, pointing to the fact that the company had made certain promises in its handbook regarding termination procedures and had simply ignored them. In sum, the court said: "Employees were essentially instructed that as long as they abided by company policy, their continued employment was guaranteed." (*Thompson* v. *American Motor Inns*, 623 F. Supp. 409, 1985)

## What about "protective language"?

As mentioned earlier, some companies attempt to get around the legal dilemma of implied contracts in employee handbooks by inserting specific language in the handbook that flatly refutes the contract. Sometimes the wording will say "nothing in this handbook is to be construed as a binding contract between employer and employee" or that the employee acknowledges that he or she is "being employed as an at-will employee only." That means, of course, that the employee theoretically acknowledges that he or she can be fired at any time, no matter what it says in the handbook.

And on occasion, the courts will enforce these disclaimers. For example, in one such case a company had placed a clause in its manual that said, "this handbook does not form an employment contract between employer and employee." And even though the employee in this instance was fired on the spot after twelve years on the job, the court accepted the company's defense that it could dismiss any of its workers at will.

However, it should be pointed out that the circumstances of this case were a bit peculiar. Specifically, the employee in question had been fired because he had deliberately covered up the underhanded conduct of a fellow worker. And the court certainly didn't want to be placed in the situation of condoning some potentially criminal behavior by an employee who was now suing based upon a wrongful termination. (*Dell* v. *Montgomery Ward & Co.*, 811 F.2d 970, 1987)

The legal changes regarding employee handbooks have been coming fast and furiously. Keep these thoughts in mind the next time you leaf through your company's employee handbook.

- There is definitely an increasing movement among state courts to regard an employee handbook as a binding contractual agreement, or at least as a promise from your employer to abide by the stated policies. In exchange, the boss expects you to follow the rules as well. This quid pro quo serves as the basis of the implied employment contract.
- If, in the course of the employee handbook, there is listed a series of progressive disciplinary procedures, then the courts usually expect management to follow these procedures, step by step. After all, as the courts point out all the time, it was the company which wrote these disciplinary procedures in the first place.
- As far as employment contract disclaimers are concerned, don't be misled. Not very many states recognize disclaimers, such as that employment is at-will or that no contract exists between employer and employee. If you think you've been wronged and that your boss hasn't followed written procedure, then check with the personnel department.
- And there's a very strong movement over the last decade from courts nationwide to curtail capricious firings—especially when

such dismissals conflict directly with the best interests of public policy, good faith employment, and proper on-the-job conduct.

## A word about New York State

Curiously, the Empire State has been a maverick when it comes to this growing national trend. Ever since the landmark *Weiner* v. *McGraw-Hill* case, the Court of Appeals in New York State (the state's highest court) has sharply curtailed the scope of that decision which found an implied contract between the book publisher and its employee. That contract, said the court, simply said that the company couldn't fire any employee except for just cause and only after several measures had been pursued to ameliorate the problem or problems.

In that case, the employee had been summarily fired one day without any warning or just cause being given. Because of that scenario, the court ruled in his favor and he was awarded a substantial amount in damages.

However, that decision has been very much the exception to the rule. Since then, several decisions have been handed down in favor of the employer, not the employee, when it comes to wrongful discharge.

### *What you need in the Big Apple's orchard*

Currently in New York State, an employee has to find a precise clause in the handbook that openly says that the employer expressly agrees to limit its right to fire employees. Then, after that stipulation, the New York–based employee also has to find the exact elements of a legally enforceable contract in the employee handbook. That includes a communication of an offer through distribution of the employee handbook, a reliance by the employee on that handbook, and evidence that the employer intended to be bound by that handbook.

To illustrate just how New York State is proemployer in these employee handbook cases, consider a case from 1987 in which an employee filed suit against his firm after his division had been shut down and he was ultimately let go.

He claimed he was fired because he wouldn't participate in some sleazy dealings in which his bosses were involved, including various slush funds and a tax avoidance scam. Naturally, the company denied all these allegations.

The fired employee relied upon the argument that the company handbook provisions regarding dismissals had been overlooked, that his dismissal was not in the public's best interest, and so on.

However, the Court of Appeals wouldn't buy any of this. The justices distinguished the decision in the *Weiner* case from this one by saying in that case, the employee handbook had expressly guaranteed that dismissals would be based solely on just cause, and only after extensive efforts had been pursued by the company to correct the employee's situation. Other decisions have also confirmed and strongly defined the court's very narrow scope of employee handbooks as implied, binding contracts.

As a result, the Court of Appeals turned down this employee's claim of wrongful dismissal, and with it, New York State has remained steadfastly in the boss' corner. (*Sabetay* v. *Sterling Drug, Inc.*, 121 L.R.R.M. 2716, N.Y. Sup. Ct., 1987)

## New Jersey and you . . . perfect together

But don't let the stuffed shirts in New York State get you down. Just across the Hudson River in New Jersey, one of the classic cases regarding employee handbooks was decided just a few years ago—in favor of the employee.

A major chemical company had written and distributed its employee handbook to all its workers. The language was very clear. It was the company's policy to retain employees. The handbook even listed the only seven reasons an employee would be terminated, including: layoff, discharge due to poor performance, disciplinary discharge, retirement, resignation, resignation requested, and mutual agreement. In addition, company policy made it clear that the chemical firm would do everything it could to help an employee stay on in cases of disciplinary action.

Sure enough, this employee handbook got a real good workout when a worker was asked for his resignation by his boss one day. There was no reason given, just that the boss had lost confidence in the employee. When the worker refused to resign, he was fired.

The worker sued on the grounds of wrongful dismissal and relied on the "handbook-as-contract" principle in court. Unfortunately, he lost both in the trial court and then at the appellate level. But when his attorneys pleaded his case in front of the New Jersey Supreme Court, the court reversed the lower courts and found in favor of the worker.

In essence, the New Jersey Supreme Court ruled that the employee handbook did constitute a valid contract between the employer and employee. Furthermore, even if there had been good reason to fire the worker, the company was still bound to abide by its procedures of discipline as spelled out in its own book.

The case was sent back to a lower court to be retried, but in the interim, it was settled out of court with a large cash settlement. (*Woolley* v. *Hoffman-La Roche, Inc.*, 491 A.2d 1257, 1985)

## Company policy and record keeping

At this juncture, let's take a brief stroll down a side avenue that runs through company policy, though not specifically handbooks. We'll call this street, Reject Road.

Ever apply for a job only to be rejected with a form letter saying something like, "Your application will be kept on file in the event future openings should occur for which you are qualified"?

Ever think someone took that last line seriously? As if someone in the company actually maintained a real file for your application —a file that wasn't circular!

Well, in a case in Tennessee, somebody did take that rejection letter seriously and wanted to hold that company to its word about having his application kept on file.

Basically, a job candidate was turned down for a position with a company form letter which added that his application "will be kept on file in the event future openings should occur for which you are qualified." Sure enough, the applicant—who happened to be black—found out that a year and a half later, another opening occurred for which he was qualified but for which he wasn't considered. The company had apparently reneged on its own word—ignored a policy promise made to an individual who wasn't even an employee.

The angry job candidate filed suit, claiming that the company had indeed not followed its own stated policy. And the court agreed with him. It had no problem with the company's policy-making; but it did have a problem with the fact that the company didn't follow its own policy.

What did this nonemployee end up costing the firm? Some $13,000 in back wages plus attorney's fees. (*Williams* v. *Hevi-Duty Elec. Co.*, 688 F. Supp. 1062, 1987)

## Modifying the handbook

Don't think for a moment that these legal precedents are not being carefully scrutinized by corporate attorneys everywhere. But despite some clever legal maneuvering, employees are still winning their share of days in court.

Case in point. In Virginia, an amusement park owner decided to sell his operation. In 1980, the original owner of the park had published and distributed an employee handbook that covered the standard fare, including a section on employee dismissal. The handbook stated that "dismissal" was to be defined as "separation initiated by [the amusement park] for cause only."

However, in 1985, when the new owner took control, he put out his own employee handbook which said that either the employer or employee "may terminate employment at any time with or without cause and with or without notice." Whereas the old handbook had said dismissal could be triggered only by cause, the new boss wanted to reclaim the doctrine of employment-at-will.

Sure enough, a dispute developed. An employee, a sign painter, got fired on the spot, and protested that the old handbook still ruled. "Nonsense," said the new owner, "the rules changed when I came in."

In court, the judge rejected the new owner's argument and held in favor of the sign painter. The court ruled that the new handbook might indeed amend the old handbook. But trying to pawn off a new handbook as gospel just wouldn't fly.

To come to this conclusion, the court referred to the old handbook as—guess what—an implied contract between employer and employee. Just because a new owner came into the picture doesn't allow him or her to automatically and totally change the working agreement with the preexisting employees. If the new boss wanted to fire the sign painter, he would first have to show just cause—as stated in the old employee handbook. (*Thompson* v. *King Entertainment Co.*, 653 F. Supp. 871, 1987)

## Read the fine print

The fact that employee handbooks are being read literally is having serious impact everywhere. Imagine, for example, the embarrassment of corporate management in an East Coast firm when a recently hired (and then seven months later fired) employee brought suit against his former employer based upon the handbook.

The employee took the company to task over a simple provision in the handbook which read that an employee could be fired during the company's 180-day probationary period, but that once the employee had passed the 180-day mark, he could only be fired for just cause.

When he got sacked seven months later, the employee pointed to that 180-day probation period and how it had elapsed after six months had passed. He was now, he claimed, past the probationary period.

"No, no, no," exclaimed the company's attorneys, "you've got that all wrong. You've counted 180 days in a row; our policy meant 180 working days only. Therefore, you were still on probation when you were dismissed."

So, it was up to the court to decide, and the court simply said to the company, "Look, if you had meant 180 working days in your employee handbook, you should have added that extra word—working." Case decided in favor of the dismissed employee. And the price tag for that one missing word? About $70,000.

■ *Employee Rights Alert:* This case, and others like it, are significant in the sense that when it comes to making a determination about misleading or ambiguous language in a written statement, the courts usually rule against the party responsible for writing the ambivalent language in the first place. And in the case of employee handbooks, that usually means the court decides against the company; after all, the companies wrote them—not the employees.

For example, certain words—unless specifically defined in the handbook—can be downright misleading in termination cases. Sometimes, for example, a handbook might refer to a job as being "permanent," as in full-time. However, some employees have interpreted "permanent" to mean that they have the job until retirement age.

In an extension of that ambiguity, in the classic *Toussaint* v. *Blue Cross* case, the employee was told by his boss in effect, "Don't worry about your job. As long as you do good work, you'll always have a job here."

When there was a cutback in jobs years later, Toussaint was sure he wouldn't be affected. After all, he had been assured by his boss. So when he got his pink slip, he sued—and won his case. He had, ruled the Michigan Supreme Court, been verbally guaranteed a life-time job with the company (and you thought verbal contracts weren't enforceable). (*Toussaint* v. *Blue Cross/Blue Shield of Michigan*, 292 N.W. 2d 408 Mich. 579, 1980)

## Hoist with its own petard

There are countless examples of management's best intentions going astray via its own written word. In one curious case, a major airline had the following statement inserted prominently into its own em-ployee handbook.

> If legislation of a state, territory, or country served by [this airline] is more favorable to the employee than policies in this booklet, or if any policies in this booklet are in violation of the legislation of any state, territory, or country, that legislation will be applied to noncontract employees stationed in the state, territory, or country.

Gee, wasn't that nice of the airline? This provision was added, no doubt, to resolve any potential conflicts that might pop up among the laws of the various jurisdictions the airline flew into and operated out of.

But a couple of customer service agents who happened to be sta-tioned in San Juan were told that their jobs were "surplus" and they were being let go. The airline, however, made it clear that while the positions in Puerto Rico were excess baggage, the two employees could keep their jobs if they transferred to New York City.

Not particularly happy with this development or with the prospect of moving to New York, the customer service agents took the airline to task on its provision regarding prevailing state law. Sure enough, in federal court, the judge looked at the above statement and applied Puerto Rico's Wrongful Discharge Statute which said, in essence, that the airline couldn't wipe out the San Juan jobs and transfer these two employees to New York.

The upshot? A federal judge ruled in favor of the two airline employees. After all, it was the airline's policy to begin with.

## Both in writing and verbally

A company can run into problems with its employees simply by condoning a worker's on-the-job behavior—even when the employee handbook disapproves of such activity.

That was the issue being litigated in a case in Michigan in which a long-term employee was fired because her on-the-job behavior was forbidden by the handbook. However, in this case, the woman, whose job centered primarily on customer service and billing problems, had been following a relatively unorthodox but widely accepted means of correcting bills for customers. Indeed, some of her activities were not only accepted by her immediate supervisor, but downright encouraged in order to get the job done.

Then, one day, the office manager inquired into these unusual activities and when she found out that the employee handbook was not being followed totally correctly, the woman was fired.

When the case got to court, a jury decided that, fundamentally, the woman had been dismissed due to company policy "violations" that had taken place for years and were overlooked as just part of doing business. Due to this inconsistency between the strict written word of the handbook and the actual day-to-day business practices, the jury ruled in favor of the dismissed employee. In essence, a case in which the language of the employee handbook was disregarded. (*Ritchie* v. *Michigan Consolidated Gas Co.*, 413 N.W. 2d 796, 1987)

■ *Employee Rights Alert:* The significance of this decision shouldn't be treated lightly, because here was an example where the company had a handbook which specifically forbade certain kinds of behavior. And yet, when this particular employee violated a specific policy, because her bosses overlooked that violation time and time again, when it came time to finally enforce the rule, it was too late. Actual daily practice had overruled the written handbook.

## But don't get too itchy

A word to the wise. While these numerous cases are based on the "implied contract" theory of the employee handbook and more and more are being decided in favor of wronged employees, there are still many court decisions which go against the employee. Keep in mind that most companies don't like to give in to employees who file lawsuits, and the fact of the matter is that sometimes, employees file suits that seem to smack of a bit too much brass.

In one such situation, a marketing executive of a company in Ohio saw the handwriting on the wall. The firm was being bandied back and forth as a takeover target, and so the employee figured he'd be smart and jump on the bandwagon of the outside group which seemed to have the best shot at being victorious in the takeover.

However, at the last second, a surge from within the company's own employees saved the day, and the employees put together enough cash to purchase the operation and fight off the outside group. Of course, the marketing executive knew he was now a dead duck, and figured he'd soon be in the unemployment soup.

And he was. He also thought he should get some severance pay. Which he did. But then he wanted more. He took the severance, and then filed a wrongful dismissal suit based upon the company's employee handbook, saying in essence that he had been wrongfully asked to leave.

That was too much, said the court, and threw the case out. The marketing executive had left on his own, he had received a generous severance to which he really wasn't entitled, and the company handbook was not to be perceived in this case as an implied contract of employment. In other words, the marketing executive had bitten off more than he could chew, and the court wouldn't swallow it. (*Harknett* v. *The Smithers Co.*, No. CA-12974, Ohio Ct. App., 1987)

---

## What if my company doesn't have a handbook?

Good question. Some companies don't provide these written rules of behavior. But relax. Unless you're in a state which strictly and staunchly believes that an employee can still be fired at any time (and those states have become a shrinking minority), then most courts will apply prevailing state law to such employee rights cases. That means, for example, that if the judicial system in the state in which you work has decided in the past that an employee cannot be fired except for just cause, then the chances are good that the court will apply that same measure of implied contract for your situation—even if your company doesn't have an employee handbook. Look over figure 10 to find out how your state lines up in the handbook-as-contract controversy.

## Figure 10. State Handbooks and Manuals Trends

Status: Y = This state often recognizes a contract obligation in a policy manual.

U = This state does not have a clear or established policy. In many cases, the state observes traditional employment-at-will in the absence of any definitive decision to the contrary.

N = Manuals are not recognized as contracts, or are recognized only under unusual circumstances.

| State | Status |
| --- | --- |
| Alabama | U |
| Alaska | Y |
| Arizona | Y |
| Arkansas | Y |
| California | Y |
| Colorado | U |
| Connecticut | Y |
| Delaware | U |
| District of Columbia | U |
| Florida | U |
| Georgia | Y |
| Hawaii | U |
| Idaho | U |
| Illinois | Y |
| Indiana | U |
| Iowa | U |
| Kansas | U |
| Kentucky | Y |
| Louisiana | U |
| Maine | Y |
| Maryland | Y |
| Massachusetts | U |
| Michigan | Y |
| Minnesota | Y |
| Mississippi | U |
| Missouri | Y |
| Montana | Y |
| Nebraska | Y |
| Nevada | U |
| New Hampshire | U |
| New Jersey | Y |
| New Mexico | Y |

| | |
|---|---|
| New York | U |
| North Carolina | U |
| North Dakota | U |
| Ohio | Y |
| Oklahoma | U |
| Oregon | U |
| Pennsylvania | Y |
| Rhode Island | U |
| South Carolina | U |
| South Dakota | U |
| Tennessee | U |
| Texas | U |
| Utah | U |
| Vermont | U |
| Virginia | Y |
| Washington | U |
| West Virginia | U |
| Wisconsin | Y |
| Wyoming | Y |

## To sum up

Take a few moments to dig out your company's employee handbook. It's certainly more than worth your while to read through it. See if there are any so-called disclaimer statements saying, in essence, that nothing in that handbook should be construed as a binding contract between employer and employee. Or if there is any language which says that you, as employee, work strictly on an employment-at-will basis.

Check through the entire book for any other language that seems strange or suspicious. If you have any questions, be certain to have all the details explained slowly and carefully by someone in the personnel office.

And if you still have questions, then by all means check with your attorney. You may have more rights on the job than you ever thought possible. Employee handbooks have become increasingly important documents in recent years and neither the courts nor the country's corporations are treating them casually any longer. You shouldn't either.

# CHAPTER 11

# Name-calling, Mind Games, and Unemployment Lines

D efamation. Unemployment benefits. Stress. You've got certain rights in each area that can't be stomped on by your employer. It's the law. Here's the scoop.

"Sticks and stones can break my bones, but names will never hurt me." That childhood expression has a new tag line used by employees referring to their employers. "But I can sure make sure they hurt you."

An insurance broker for a major firm in Houston was fired. And to his continued consternation and puzzlement, his ensuing job hunt was shot down again and again. Determined to unearth the reason, he hired a private investigator. That enterprising gumshoe called the former employer, under the guise of being a future employer, and asked the ex-employee's supervisor about that worthy's employability. What he got was a diatribe.

The former insurance broker was described as ruthless, disliked by his coworkers, and a failure as a businessman. The coup de grace: He "was a classical [sic] sociopath, a zero, a Jekyll and Hyde personality who was lacking in scruples."

When those taped comments were played to a mesmerized jury, it agreed that libel and slander had indeed occurred and its $1.9

million judgment against the company began to wind its way through higher courts. (*Frank B. Hall* v. *Buck*, 678 S.W. 2d 612, 618, Tex. Ct. App. 1984; cert. denied 472 U.S. 1009, 1985)

A technical writer and his supervisor argued long and loud. Said the top gun: "You're extremely difficult to work with, can't take criticism, have tied this department in knots, and haven't shown any signs of improvement."

No beating around the bush here. Both individuals agreed to a termination. But there their agreement ended. The reason on the employment record for the separation was lack of cooperation. The writer saw that, rebelled, and sued for defamation. The company moved to have the case dismissed on grounds that the statement wasn't defamatory and hadn't been published.

Here's how I see it, said the judge. The use of the phrase "lack of cooperation" standing alone could lead members of the community and other persons to believe the employee was unremediably insubordinate, obnoxious, and antagonistic. Plus it had been communicated to the supervisor, managers, and members of personnel. Grounds exist for a jury to hear case. (*Elbeshbeshy* v. *Franklin Institute*, 618 F. Supp. 170, 1985)

## Defamation by the numbers

Early in 1987 *Newsweek* magazine ran a scoreboard headlined THE HIGH COST OF CRITICIZING AN EX-EMPLOYEE. Some of the results:

- Four employees fired for gross insubordination over expense accounts—$515,000
- Worker accused of falsifying invoices—$278,000
- Employee accused of forging checks—$185,000

Some other numbers for thought:

- Estimate: Libel suits filed by discharged workers account for one-third of all defamation suits, a category called the "work-horse of termination litigation."
- Estimate: Employee victory percentage in California libel and other job termination trials is a whopping 72 percent, with jury awards averaging over half a million dollars.
- Estimate: The average award in eight thousand defamation cases

over five years rose from a little over $100,000 to half a million dollars

Don't let those dollar signs lighting up your eyes blind you to the facts. Defamation cases are hard to win. Employers have lots of defenses. Before we get to the defenses, let's go through the ammunition you'll need for your offense.

## Defamation by definition

The majority of defamation cases pop up in the reference area, but they can also be generated by internal meetings, open arguments, and exit interviews. Usually the suit stems from language that implies the employee committed a crime or is an incompetent bumbler.

Strictly speaking, libel is the written end of defamation and slander the spoken aspect. They are torts of negligent or intentional harm to another's reputation which involve the unprivileged publication of a false communication about an individual to a third party. Sounds confusing.

To have a defamation case, you need to prove that:

- Your employer made a defamatory statement
- It is about you, or concerns you, or is understood to be either
- It is published to a third party
- The result damaged your reputation
- There is a degree of fault on their part

At first blush, those five elements of a defamation case may seem pretty obvious. But as in all things of a legal nature, nothing is simple. Take the case of degree of fault.

Some courts are much tougher than others in demanding a significant measure of fault. One standard: One who publishes false and defamatory communications about a private person is liable only if he knows the statement is false and is defamatory to that person, or if he acts in reckless disregard of those matters, or if he acts negligently in failing to ascertain them.

There is no uniform federal law laying out such elements of defamation. Mostly it's a matter of common law actions governed by the states, which means the usual diversity of activity. For example, some states (like Indiana) hold that intracorporate communications are not publications for the purpose of defamation. Others (like Illinois) hold that communications even to fellow employees can satisfy the defamation case for cause. Pennsylvania lists four elements required for a cause of action in defamation. Kansas has three.

In general, to be actionable (that means to have a case), a statement must be both false and defamatory. It's defamatory if it tends to harm your reputation so as to lower you in the estimation of the community or to deter third persons from associating or dealing with you. Simple so far.

Also, in general, defamatory statements contain language that adversely affects an individual's reputation. In employment, it may imply commission of a crime or cast doubt on your ability to perform certain tasks successfully or conduct yourself according to the requirements of your trade or profession.

## Defamation complications

Statements which question or impeach your trustworthiness may be defamatory, even when they are not direct accusations. So may statements which adversely affect your ability to perform your duties. And a statement which on its own may not be defamatory can be converted into an actionable case if you can demonstrate it was defamatory based on extrinsic facts or that others understood it to be defamatory. Not so simple.

■ *Employee Rights Alert:* In most jurisdictions, if language is susceptible to more than one interpretation, a cause of action exists if one interpretation is defamatory.

Many defamation cases are linked to the privacy rights you saw in chapter 6, like unreasonable intrusion into seclusion and public disclosure of embarrassing facts. One big difference: You usually need to prove that a bigger audience received the "bad" word for a privacy suit than for a defamation case.

And in workplace defamation, the situation itself can now be a contributing factor; for example, when an employer has someone removed from the premises by security personnel so it looks like the employee committed a criminal act. One firer circulated a firee's picture to all the company guards and told them to apprehend and remove the subject of the picture if they saw him on company property. That strategy certainly supported defamation charges.

## Defamation for the defense

As we promised, here are the defenses an employer can use against defamation charges, along with some cases that flesh them out and give you an idea how to proceed if you're in the same boat.

## Defense #1: Truth

The traditional defense against defamation. Not only is truth sometimes in the mind's eye, it's also in the ear of the listener. One court ruled it must be truth in its broadest sense, not just in a technical way. While speaking with a reporter, a media executive used the word *terminated* in describing an employee's departure. In defending the truth of the statement, the executive pointed out that the word termination referred to any separation of employment, voluntary or involuntary. Maybe, said the court, but the word termination does leave the impression that the employee was fired. And that's the truth. (*Denny* v. *Mertz*, 318 N.W. 2d 141, Wisc., 1982)

■ *Employee Rights Alert:* Even if a statement of fact is literally true, if you can prove a reasonably foreseeable inference drawn by the receiver of the statement was false, you may have a case.

## Defense #2: Privilege

Absolute privilege is usually reserved for big cheeses like members of Congress, public officials acting in a government capacity, and the like. Some courts have expanded that concept to include employers' responses in "official" situations, such as EEOC inquiries, unemployment insurance commission questioning, and labor arbitration proceedings.

But the most common—and strongest—defense for employers, managers, and supervisors is *qualified privilege*. That means they are granted a qualified privilege to speak candidly, even derogatorily, about employees as long as they:

■ Exhibit good faith in doing so
■ Have an interest or duty to be upheld
■ Limit the scope of their statements to the purpose of the inquiry

- Make the information available on a proper occasion
- "Publish" the information in a proper manner only to an appropriate audience with a common interest

Thus a Kansas employer was protected by qualified privilege when it acted in good faith, on the basis of interest and duty, with a communication to a party with a legitimate interest. (*Polson* v. *Davis*, 635 F. Supp. 1130, D. Kan., 1986)

But a Pennsylvania employer lost its defense when it acted out of malice and communicated information to persons without a need to know. (*Jackson* v. *J. C. Penney Co.*, 616 F. Supp. 233, E.D. Pa., 1985)

## Privilege won and lost

Privilege is available in most normal business conditions, especially dissemination of in-house material necessary for personnel administration. It can even extend to nonsupervisory employees whose duties create an interest in the subject, and to reports to unions on actions of its members in, say, the disciplinary area.

Privilege is most easily lost when information is broadcast to individuals without a need to know. It doesn't usually matter how, or even sometimes how many. In one case, an employee won a defamation suit even though the offending memo never left one building and only eight executives saw it. That constituted circulation. (*Pirre* v. *Printing Developments, Inc.*, 468 F. Supp. 1028, S.D.N.Y.; aff'd 614 F.2d 1290, 2d Cir., 1979)

Most of the time, publication is a lot more widespread and thus decidedly tilts the defamation scales in the employee's favor.

A chain store official sent a letter to every store manager reporting a woman had been fired for theft. She found out that even nonmanagement personnel had seen the missive and that helped her get a jury trial. One company reported the reasons for an employee's suspension to three hundred coworkers. Another reported in a reference request that an employee had been discharged for stealing company property, when in fact he had never been convicted.

A pharmacist was convinced an employee was responsible for the disappearance of drugs. And he said so in front of the entire staff when he fired the suspect. That gave the employee grounds for a suit. (*Sokolay* v. *Edlin*, 65 N.J. Sup. Ct. 112, 167 A.2d 211, 1961)

Sometimes it's the words rather than the publication, when accusations get heated. The quote that inspired one lawsuit was: "He was a thief and a crook who stole us blind." (*Bobenhauser* v. *Cassat Avenue Mobile Homes, Inc.*, 344 S.2d 279, Fla. App., 1979)

Usually the name-calling won't be quite that obvious. But liability may be generated even by implication. That happened when a compensation board was told an ex-employee had to be continually watched when handling money. That implied the employee was not trustworthy.

■ *Employee Rights Alert:* Before you depend on derogatory names for your case, better make sure you have one. Name-calling in and of itself is not always defamatory. A few that have been judged inflammatory but not defamatory are *regular nut, screwball,* and *meshugganah.* To qualify to defame, in such cases, the "name" must relate directly to the employee's ability to do the job.

## Different strokes for different defamatory statements

Here are some examples of cases when statements were—and were not—defamatory.

Yes:

- A business administrator of a school district was labeled *dishonest.*
- An employment agency was told an individual was discharged for being a *poor salesman and bad worker.*
- An unemployment commissioner heard that store sales fell drastically after the employee took command, indicating she was *unable to perform the job.*
- A farm labor organization organizer *didn't know anything about farming.*
- A union organizer was accused of *untoward sexual advances* with females, when the union had a heavy female membership.
- A teacher was accused of *introducing Communist literature* into schools.
- Language that implied that a person was *not reliable,* and by innuendo was *guilty of unpardonable public or private misconduct.*

No:

- The statement that *your lawyer is an asshole* is not actionable.

- A defamatory letter sent between offices of a corporate employer is not published.
- Checking a box in an internal memo indicating an employee's loss is minor was judged not published, just a routine memo.
- Dictation of a defamatory letter to a secretary is not published.

## Problem of publication—self

Another twist to the publication problem in defamation was reflected in a landmark case in Minnesota. Common sense would tell you that if you publicize your own defamatory information, you wouldn't have grounds to sue anyone but yourself. But as in most employment law areas, exceptions pop up. In fact, at least three other states besides the Gopher State (Georgia, Michigan, and California) at some point recognized the theory of self-publication in defamation.

This well-known case involved four insurance employees who returned from a business trip and filled out their expense vouchers in the normal manner. Their supervisor told them to refile for lower expenses. But they considered the initial forms honest, and so refused. The supervisor fired them for "gross insubordination." Then he informed them that they were to use that very phrase when prospective new employers asked why they had left their last jobs.

The quartet filed suit, claiming they were maneuvered into a position to defame themselves. Lo and behold, the court ruled the company responsible for libel. Even acknowledging it was contrary to traditional legal principles, the court held that exceptions were justified in certain cases—and this was one. Why? The individual is compelled to repeat a defamatory statement, and the defendant who originated the statement could reasonably foresee that situation occurring. The judgment: Half a million split four ways. (*Lewis* v. *Equitable Life Assurance Society of America*, 361 N.W. 2d 875, Minn. App. No. C8-84-1065, 1985)

"Foreseeability" doesn't always carry the day however. A woman was discharged for dishonesty involving medical records and work days. A company review board upheld the dismissal. Her contention in court: When she came to the line on new employment application blanks with the query "reason for leaving last job," she was forced to defame herself by writing "dishonesty."

The company shrugged its corporate shoulders and pleaded not guilty by way of not publishing the information to any outside party.

The ex-employee's lawyer argued that it could easily be anticipated that the woman would have to do that publishing herself in her job quest. And there are states that hold employers liable for the natural and probable consequences of their actions, even when they keep information in confidence.

The trial judge ruled foreseeability could be applied, but it hadn't been proven in this case. An appeals court said there was no foreseeability exception and the company was right in claiming a "no publication" defense. (*Churchey* v. *Adolph Coors Co.*, 725 P.2d 38, Col. App., 1986)

## When privilege punches out defamation

Among the instances when qualified privilege has won the day for employers:

■ The description of a manager for a reference inquiry labeled him intelligent and hard-working. That was the positive. On the downside, he was called dictatorial, quite devious, and often demoralizing. And, it was said, he could only be effective under close supervision. The court: No ill-will or malice, just a good-faith response to a legitimate inquiry. (*Zuschek* v. *Whitmoyer Laboratories, Inc.*, 430 F. Supp. 1163, E.D. Pa. 1977; aff'd 571 F.2d 573, 3rd Cir., 1978)

■ Some courts take qualified privilege to the limits. A South Carolina manufacturing plant laid off eleven workers and nine immediately trundled off to another area plant and applied for work. The second plant's personnel manager called his counterpart at the first plant to inquire about recall rights. He was taken aback when the old employer's manager launched into a dissertation on the drawbacks of the laid-off workers. Larded in with the comments were descriptions like "militant," "NOW organizer," and "emotional problems."

Those allegations made their way into a memo at the second plant which made its way into the hands of the former employees from the first plant. They charged defamation and blacklisting, and the initial jury awarded substantial damages. But an appeals court reversed that decision.

For one thing, it was an exchange of reference information of common interest that only reached publication because a security guard friend of one of the applicants glommed it out of company files.

For another, the information was not slanderous. On top of that, the failure to recommend was not proof of malice. And to add insult to injury, there is no South Carolina law against *preparing* a blacklist per se, just against making deliberate malicious use of such a list to injure a former employee. (*Austin* v. *Torrington Co.*, No. 85-1740, 4th Cir., 1987)

■ *Employee Rights Alert:* No matter how strong a case you think you have, the first step in any employment litigation journey must be at the doorstep of a competent local attorney specializing in your type of case.

## Defense #3: Opinion

Also merits some umbrella "truth as I see it" protection in defamation cases. But few employers want to risk having a jury decide what is true and whether the opinion falls under the protected aegis of free speech or management privilege. They know most juries are made up of your peers, not theirs.

The pure opinion defense is based on the theory that there is no such thing as a false idea. But you may be able to kick in liability if the opinion reasonably implies the existence of underlying facts that can be proven false or defamatory. That usually occurs when speakers combine facts with opinions and state or imply that there are other facts that they are not disclosing which make their opinions true. Also, if the opinion is based on undisclosed facts, and those facts are proven false, then the opinion isn't protected. (*Raffensberger* v. *Moran*, 485 A.2d 447, 450, Pa. Sup. Ct., 1984)

Even the rich and famous are not immune to the slings and arrows of defamation charges. Diana Ross hit a few sour notes when she wrote a letter about seven former employees. She crooned: If I let an employee go, it's because their work or personal habits are not acceptable to me. I do not recommend these people.

The letter was widely circulated in the entertainment industry, and one former employee sang the blues in court after she saw it. The letter made it sound like she had failed at her job and been dismissed, she said, when in reality she was a good worker who quit voluntarily.

Rebuffed in her retraction efforts, the former employee sued for a million in compensation and a million in damages. Diana's defense: Not defamatory because it expressed a subjective opinion and never made an outright statement that the ex-employee herself was professionally unfit.

A Manhattan federal judge agreed, but a court of appeals demurred. Let a jury decide. Thanks, said Ross, but we'll settle out of court.

*Voluntary opinions* can get an employer in trouble. An executive answered some telephone questions in reference to an ex-employee. Then without being asked, he offered his opinion that the worker in question might not be all that trustworthy handling money. The mantle of qualified privilege fell from this manager's shoulders because he had gone beyond the bounds of the inquiry with his opinions, and in fact had not even bothered to determine that the caller had a valid interest in the information being gleaned. (*Costas* v. *Olson*, N.J.L.J. 2d 552, aff'd 52 A.D. 1975; 382 N.Y.S. 2d 287, 1976)

■ *Employee Rights Alert:* Another defense employers will try to build is consent. Agreeing to the content of, say, a letter of reference makes a defamation claim a hollow one. Chapter 13 covers your rights in signing releases and such. One quick word on the subject: Don't. At least until you've seen a lawyer.

## Defamation audit

Think you've got a defamation suit on your hands? Ask yourself:

- Does the company keep its reference system reined in, with one person or department designated to handle all requests?
- Are there any state laws that restrict the type or amount of information your employer can disseminate about you? Are they being followed? What about company policies about information distribution? Are they adhered to?
- Do you have any evidence of obvious malice or ill will or bad faith on your employer's part?
- Were you forced into a position of having to defame yourself because of something the company did or said?
- Were you told the truth about the reasons you were fired, and are those statements being relayed appropriately to potential employers?

- Does your employer have documented proof to back up the facts it is spreading?
- Did you sign any forms that authorized your employer to release information about you?

## Disemployment dilemmas

Your rights don't end once all the loose ends of your dismissal are tied up. In many cases, unemployment benefits and worker's compensation claims turn into a loose cannon that turns a done deal into a courtroom battle.

Unemployment benefits are the less deadly of the two, because situations are more clear-cut. The law is fairly clear about who gets what, when. You just read your booklet from the local unemployment office.

Sometimes you do get a fly in the ointment in the form of the company contesting your claim. If it's doing that just to get back at you, you may have a retaliation case like you'll read about in chapter 12. In many states, as well as the District of Columbia, the employer must prove the employee was fired for wanton and willful misconduct to contest a claim. And as always, each of those states has a mind of its own.

Speaking of wanton and willful. A jury in Illinois broke the bank when it awarded a manager $3.5 million. Seems he had been ordered by the high command at his firm to fire his own father. When he gave his padre six months severance, the company invited him to join his dearest daddy on the unemployment lines. Then it made the whole thing a family affair by axing the manager's mother, a part-time bookkeeper. Jury found the employer guilty of willful, wanton, and reckless misconduct.

Back to unemployment. On the East Coast, a Virginia employer received an anonymous tip that a worker was using drugs. Urinalysis confirmed marijuana in his system. A search of the employee and his car came up empty. His claim: He didn't use it himself, but was with others who did. He didn't challenge his discharge, but did challenge his ex-employer's challenge to his unemployment claim.

The Virginia statute in question denied unemployment compensation benefits to an employee discharged for "misconduct committed with work." After much legal Ping-Pong before an agency, a hearing examiner, and two courts, an appeals court ruled that discharge for cause and discharge for misconduct are not the same. There was no evidence of a problem "with work." (*Blake* v. *Hercules, Inc.*, No. 0818-86-3, Va. Ct. App., 1987)

On the West Coast, it was an appeals panel of the California state unemployment insurance agency that voted in favor of a company which had discharged an employee who refused to take a substance abuse test. Written company policy called for such a test when on-the-job suspicion of use existed. Refusal could detonate termination.

The worker in question self-destructed one morning when he couldn't get his locker open. Instead of asking for help from security, he beat the locker to a pulp. Witnesses agreed he displayed all the signs of being intoxicated. Plus his job required observance of safety procedures which if not followed could endanger his life and those of other employees. After refusing to take the mandatory substance abuse test, he was sent home. Twice he showed up for work, but both times refused testing. The third time he was discharged. The judgment in this case: Individual privacy rights yield to legitimate job concerns. He was fired for work-related misconduct and not eligible under state law for unemployment benefits. (In re: Vernon Ables, Schultz Steel Co., No. 86-05446, California Unemployment Insurance Appeals Board, 1987)

The moral of the stories: Be very careful to check your post-employment rights with appropriate agencies.

## Stress and compensation: A marriage made on the job

Psychological disorders are becoming the fastest-growing segment of occupational ills. The National Council on Compensation Insurance offered this statistic: Stress accounts for about 14 percent of all occupational disease claims. Burnout heads the list of more and more workplace crises. Technostress is the latest buzzword describing the mental plight of white collar, service industry, and computer workers. In California, a Work Trauma Hotline informs callers about compensation laws and puts them in touch with legal and medical counselors.

Worker's compensation judgments are following trends in liability and negligence, basing awards on damages for pain and suffering and even loss of life enjoyment. Or in some cases, loss of life.

A newspaper sports editor said he felt funny while attending a ball game. But it wasn't a laughing matter five days later when he suffered a massive stroke. And it wasn't the losing ways of his favorite team that caused his death, said his widow. It was that infernal deadline stress and those long working hours. The state ruled she was entitled to worker's comp ($55,000 and $200 a week for life). The job stress aggravated the editor's high blood pressure and diabetes. (*Mulcahey* v. *New England Newspapers, Inc.*, 488 A.2d 681, 1984)

There are basically three types of mind claims in this rights mine field.

- When a physical injury causes a mental neurosis or disability. Fairly easy if you have the physical part of the evidence.
- When a nonphysical stimulus, such as stress, causes physical injury with clear symptoms. A heart attack caused by job stress is the classic here.
- When a purely mental stimulus causes a disabling mental illness. Example: A negative performance evaluation pushes an employee over the edge to a mental breakdown.

Those last so-called mental-mental claims, in which both the cause of the condition and the condition itself are mental or emotional, are the trickiest and the closest to the stress areas we're stressing. About half the states recognize some form of mental-mental claims, under a dozen require a physical element to a mental claim, and about a third have no standard for mental disability claims.

Even fear has teamed up with stress to bolster employee compensation claims. A report out of Washington told how an asbestos worker feared he would contract an asbestos-related disease. He filed under the Federal Employees' Liability Act. A jury offered him over $330,000 for the anxiety and stress associated with his fear of getting cancer. In another West Coast case, a San Francisco nurse was awarded five grand in a settlement of a worker's comp claim linking her fear of AIDS infection to a stress-related ulcer.

## Skipping through the states of stress

State legislatures and courts often put out the welcome mat for stress-related disability claims. By one count, only three states balk at compensating employees disabled by stress. Standards, though, differ. Some states require a sudden shocking occurrence, such as seeing a coworker die, before they'll offer stress-related compensation. Most states merely demand that the source of the stress-related injury be unusual and not a normal workplace happening.

Pennsylvania, for example, revised its worker's comp statute in the 1970s. It deleted the word *accident*, which usually connotes some type of physical violence, and replaced it with *injury*, a much wider-ranging word.

Since states have jurisdiction over most worker's comp claims, you need to know just where your state stands in order to assess your stress case strength. Here are just a few examples.

*Pennsylvania.* Going back to the Quaker state, here are some cases when job-related stress has popped up in court and generated successful claims for compensable mental "injuries."

- A sheet-metal worker in a family business ascended from the ranks to the throne when his father retired. The new responsibilities—supervising, estimating, paperwork—just weren't his cup of tea. He suffered a mental breakdown. (*Bevilacqua* v. *W.C.A.B. [J. Bevilacqua & Sons]*, 475 A.2d 959, Pa. Commonwealth, 1984)
- A supervisor was all over an employee's case with constant public criticism. The worker developed an aversion to work, showed up late, took vacation days to avoid confrontations. The supervisor left, but the memories remained. Eight years later, the worker snapped: breakdown. His psychologist testified the employee's work experience was a substantial cause of his mental disorder.
- An employee went on vacation. Work piled up on his desk. After his return, even more paperwork was added to his daily regimen. Then he lost an assistant's assistance. Those job pressures caused a severe depression resulting in suicide. So said his widow. So affirmed a worker's comp referee. (*Allegheny Ludlum Steel Corp.* v. *W.C.A.B. [Fisher]*, 498 A.2d 3, 1985)

*Minnesota.* Workers may sue employers for intentional infliction of emotional distress. Such suits are not banned just because there are other remedies for workplace maltreatment. Standard of proof is higher than for traditional discrimination cases. Physical injury is not necessary, but you must provide evidence that a continued pattern of harassment persisted in the workplace and caused psychiatric disturbance.

Case: Female employee alleged that she was forced to have sex with her supervisor, called names, and physically assaulted, and forced to watch as her coworkers tortured and killed rats and birds. Company turned a deaf ear to her complaints. After she finished project, she sought psychiatric counseling. Claimed this left her with serious and permanent emotional damage. (*Pikop* v. *Burlington Northern Co.*, Nos. C7-84-1333, C4-85-1431, Minn. Sup. Ct., 1986)

*Oregon*. Has a measure that, among other things, disallows claims for stress due to reasonable employer actions like firing, discipline, and appraising performance. However, when the president of a company in Oregon managed his company into bankruptcy, he got depressed. The whole situation drove him to drink. He filed a worker's compensation claim and got it.

*Massachusetts*. Has a series of measures that ban stress claims based on transfers and layoffs.

## Stress audit

If you're stressed out and thinking of putting more stress on your employer in terms of your rights to worker's comp, keep these things in mind.

- You must have a strong and verifiable link between stress and the job, and the stress must be real, not imaginary.
- Your case is weakened if you haven't been in a position for long or you have a history of psychological problems.
- Your case is strengthened if you can dig up evidence that will instill a sense of outrage or elicit a sense of sympathy from a judge, jury, or examiner.
- Your case is further strengthened if you can present objective evidence about stressful conditions of the workplace, including previous cases, witnesses, etc.
- You're also dealing from a position of strength if you can obtain medical evidence that it was a work-related illness that disabled you, and that the results and cause are related to stress.

Finally, depending on your state and particular situation, it's helpful to the cause if you can tie the cause of the stress condition to abnormal or greater-than-regular day-to-day tensions. Among the "abnormal conditions" that have precipitated stress claims in various jurisdictions are:

- Inconsistent job performance evaluations
- Inconsistent supervision
- Unwarranted criticism of job performance by supervisors
- Disciplinary actions not in line with standard practices
- Layoff notices and plant closings
- Internal investigations
- Lack of adequate communications
- Lack of clearly defined job responsibilities
- Rejection of employee proposals
- Transfers or reductions in salary

## Fear of not flying

Here's a capper for our psychological disorder section. A national news magazine came up with this one. Seems a Philadelphia real estate manager spent eleven years as a student and teacher in a transcendental meditation group. He claimed he suffered psychological disorders when he wasn't able to attain that perfect state of life the group had promised.

One alleged promise that never got off the ground: He was told he would be able to fly through self-levitation. Turned out, he only got to the stage where he could hop with his legs folded in a lotus position. Not satisfied with such maneuvers, he bopped into a U.S. District Court in Washington, D.C., where a jury dropped nearly $138,000 in damages in his lap. And so it comes.

# CHAPTER 12

# Everything You Always Wanted to Know About the EEOC but Were Afraid to Ask

D iscrimination charges and the Equal Employment Opportunity Commission (EEOC) go together like a horse and carriage. It's the primary agency for enforcing this country's equal employment opportunity laws. Different laws apply to different situations, but most which affect employment fall under the aegis of the EEOC.

We could go on forever about the EEOC. But we won't. At least not here. You'll find a more extensive explanation in the Appendix. It will outline time constraints, intake interviews, fact-finding conferences, cause determinators, how each type of suit is handled. You'll find there a more formal explanation of the EEOC, its structure, mission, and policies. And if you want to know what guidelines are given the individuals who come before it to register a complaint, look over the information sheet the Agency gives all aggrieved parties to get the ball rolling in an employee discrimination suit.

But as long as we're running on about the EEOC, let's forge ahead in this vein for a couple of pages. The better you know your EEO "stuff," the better your chances of filing a winnable lawsuit, or forcing your employer to settle with you on your terms.

We'll be brief. The EEOC considers five basic theories of discrimination in analyzing cases.

*One: Disparate treatment.* When similarly situated individuals of a different race, sex, color, national origin, or religion are accorded different treatment in the context of a similar employment situation. Famous case: *International Brotherhood of Teamsters* v. *U.S.*, 431 U.S. 324, 14 E.P.D. para. 7579, 1977. (Note: For each of these theories, we'll give you a case the EEOC feels is very important. It's just another entry in your knowledge bank that will give you an edge if you find yourself in a similar situation.)

In less formal terms, disparate treatment occurs when you are treated less favorably than others because of your age, sex, etc. This "theory" has been translated into practical application in a variety of instances. It's been used to claim discrimination not only in discharge, but in discipline and promotions as well. In fact, any employment decision favoring one person over another may hold the seeds for a disparate treatment claim.

In a well-known case in Michigan, (*EEOC* v. *J. C. Penney Co.*, 632 F. Supp. 871, 873, E.D. Mich., 1985) a court listed six factors to consider in analyzing such a situation. You be the judge about your own case:

- Does the employment decision have a disparate impact?
- What is the historical background?
- What were the specific events leading up to the decision?
- Was the decision a departure from normal procedures?
- Was the decision a "substantial" departure from normal practices?
- Were contemporaneous statements made?

Even more recently, the Supreme Court ruled that a disparate impact analysis in which statistics are used to show a policy or practice has a discriminatory effect (even unintended) can be used to challenge *subjective* promotion decisions. That puts managerial judgment or discretion right in the sights of this theory. (*Watson* v. *Ft. Worth Bank & Trust*, No. 86-6139, Sup. Ct., 1988)

*Two: Adverse impact.* When seemingly neutral employment policies and practices have a disproportionately negative effect, not justified by business necessity, to the effect of excluding women or minorities. Famous case: *Griggs* v. *Duke Power Co.*, 401 U.S. 424, 3 E.P.D. para. 8137, 1971.

A number of prime suspects have emerged over the years in the adverse impact arena, among them height and weight requirements, grooming standards, arrest and conviction records, physical strength and capability, customer preference, subjective evaluation procedures, unwed parenthood, military service records, and credit records.

*Three: Perpetuation of past discrimination.* When a neutral policy reinforces past discrimination. For example, when jobs are usually filled by internal word of mouth, and the work force is all white. Famous case: Commission Decision No. 75-281.

*Four: Failure to accommodate.* Usually in a religious or handicap situation. Based on section 701 (j) of Title VII. Famous case: *TWA* v. *Hardison*, 432 U.S. 63, 14 E.P.D. para. 7620, 1977.

*Five: Retaliation.* When an individual suffers discriminatory or adverse actions for being involved in a Title VII claim or in another legal right or privilege, such as filing for worker's compensation. Famous case: Commission Decision No. 72-1883.

That last is one of the most practical of all the theories. It includes the growing concept of *constructive discharge*, another employer thorn in the employee rights side. You'll see more on both retaliation and constructive discharge later in this chapter.

Let's get back to the EEOC. The Appendix spells out the charge filing process. But in a nutshell, the overall process works like a Ping-Pong game. You serve. Allege race or sex or whatever discrimination. It has to be a good serve. You have to establish a prima facie case, that is, on the face of it (and you thought Latin would never come in handy), you have a valid case.

The employer returns your first serve. The company articulates a legitimate, nondiscriminatory reason for its actions. At least, it claims it does.

Now you move in for the put-away. The stated reason is a pretext. You offer statements, documents, witnesses to show discriminatory motives, or evidence that undercuts the employer's proffered reasons. That's a winning return.

## Putting yourself in the EEOC's wingtips

What does the EEOC itself look for in terms of cases and investigations? Here are some tips to keep in mind that will make your efforts stronger.

*Job interviews*. The EEOC looks for hints of discriminatory attitudes here when:

- The employer pushes minority or female candidates toward jobs held by those groups
- Questions are asked of females but not of males, especially on pregnancy and family planning
- Remarks are passed about appearance or dress
- Comments are made about age, sex, color, etc.
- Personal prejudices surface
- Condescending or familiar terms are used, like honey, dear, boy, girl
- Assumptions are made, like women won't accept jobs with relocation probabilities

*Priority issues list*. The EEOC regularly issues this menu of transgressions for which it would like to eat an employer's lunch. Some types of cases make this list regularly; others are added at intervals. Figure 11 gives you a taste of what you'd find on this list.

There are also five general case categories which fall under the EEOC's National Litigation Plan. These also get the EEOC spotlight.

- Cases having the potential for promoting the development of law favorable to the antidiscrimination purposes of statutes enforced by the commission.
- Cases seeking to protect the integrity of the commission's charge investigation and conciliation process, which would include, for example, cases involving retaliation.
- Cases involving violations of established antidiscrimination principles, whether on an individual, class, or systemic basis.
- Cases designed to provide services to localities, protected groups, and individuals in need of enhanced commission services.
- Cases involving issues of special concern to the particular geographic region served by each of the commission's district offices.

## Figure 11. EEOC Compliance Manual Priority Issues List

### *Title VII of the Civil Rights Act*

■ Charges raising the issue of hazardous substances or conditions which may affect the *fetus or the reproductive health* of males or females in the work force.

■ Charges raising the issue of religious accommodation where the respondent claims that accommodation would require more than a *de minimus* cost.

■ Charges where the employer raises a business necessity defense for its use of a blanket *convictions policy*.

■ Charges raising issues regarding abortions.

### *Current Title VII Pending Issues List*

Items on this list are relatively current and so are published as a separate category.

■ Charges involving an affirmative action issue(s) regarding plans developed in reliance on state or local government agencies other than a state or local 706 agency, under a law other than a state or local fair employment practices statute or ordinance.

■ Charges alleging adverse impact from the denial or limitation of *child care leave*.

■ Charges involving discrimination on the basis or manner of *speaking or accent*.

*Stereotyped views.* To bolster any discrimination case, you should try to prove a mind-set, as well as to establish facts. Courts are human, too, you know. So are EEOC investigators. You'll strengthen any case you have if you can produce quotes like the following (taken from actual EEOC files, by the way) that reflect stereotyped attitudes.

■ "The blacks are always assigned outside. The heat doesn't bother them like it does the white workers."
■ "We look for young, aggressive, go-getter types."
■ "Women have a natural aptitude for typing."
■ "Women aren't aggressive enough for our marketing jobs."
■ "Older workers are too set in their ways. You can't teach them anything."
■ "We put all women in this department because they're good at routine work. They don't get bored like the men do."
■ "We couldn't promote her. She's too aggressive."

- "Women have child-care problems. We need people in this department who are reliable."
- "Women won't work for a woman supervisor."

*Attention to detail.* You can see in the Appendix explaining the EEOC structure and procedures that the Agency places great emphasis on rules. The EEOC, of course, is there to help you if your employee rights have been violated. But its help will be more helpful if you play by the rules of the game. Before you raise any hackles or waste anyone's time, make sure:

- You've filed within time limits, usually 180 days for the EEOC under Title VII
- Your employer falls under EEOC jurisdiction, fitting the fifteen-employee category and other requirements (Note: it's twenty for ADEA claims)
- You have what is called a standing to file, that is, an employee/employer or applicant/employer relationship
- Your discrimination claim falls under a law administered by the EEOC
- You've picked the correct grievance route; besides the EEOC, you can go to your state fair employment agency for discrimination claims of race, sex, age, etc. In your area it may be called a human rights commission or civil rights unit or whatever

There are other avenues for employee complaints too. You've got state or federal labor departments to handle minimum wage or overtime questions; the Office of Federal Contract Compliance Programs for charges of discrimination involving federal contracts; and the Veteran's Employment Service of the U.S. Labor Department to handle job complaints from veterans.

Enough on the EEOC background, already. Bring on the cases.

## Getting down to cases with the EEOC

It may be the opposite of Diogenes traveling the highways and by-ways with his lantern trying to turn up an honest man. Discrimination. You don't have to look far to find it. It's everywhere. Seems you can't get away from it—or with it. Even in the dimly lit recesses of that age-old mecca of equality, the drinking establishment.

Out in the formerly wild West, a "cowboys" bar displayed a few idiosyncrasies it thought would boost business. For one, it refused to hire males as bartenders, or females as managers. For another, it placed only blond employees in one bar, redheads in another, and brunettes in a third.

Whoa there, hold your horses, said the EEOC as it filed for injunctive relief and back pay for all applicants who had been refused work based on those discriminatory standards. (*EEOC* v. *Robert Johnson & Assoc., a.k.a. "Cowboys,"* D. Ariz.)

Then there's the Anchorage bar that reportedly boasts a sign denying entrance to "pimps, prostitutes, and pushers." Happens to say nothing about Hells Angels in full battle regalia. Seems one of the Angels was kicked out for refusing to doff his jacket. Result: A courtroom rumble.

The offended plaintiff pleaded a case based on freedom of speech and equal protection provisions of the U.S. Constitution. The defendant defended with contention that such apparel was known to spark fights, which in turn gave the bar a black eye before the state's liquor license powers-that-be.

Open the doors and leave on the jackets, ruled a judge, to the chagrin of bar management and the delight of Hells Angels everywhere.

---

## The real thing

Okay, so most EEOC discrimination cases don't have nearly as much color in them. As you saw in other chapters, such cases do include some sex, and a little age, and maybe even drugs. But the main discrimination law which the EEOC enforces is Title VII, explained in figure 12. And four of the main no-no's in that law—national origin, race, and religion plus retaliation—are covered here.

### National origin

Take a couple of cases:

- A Hispanic with a noticeable accent was applying for a managerial position. He never even got through the interview. Other Hispanics, without accents, were hired. The EEOC found unlawful national origin discrimination. (Case No. A1-68-1-155-E, 1 F.E.P. 92, 1969)
- A Filipino was demoted. Reason: His accent. Retort: It didn't

## Figure 12. Title VII Prohibits Employment Discrimination

Title VII of the Civil Rights Act of 1964, as amended, is the federal law that prohibits employment discrimination based on race, color, sex, religion, or national origin. Title VII was extended to cover federal, state, and local public employers and educational institutions by the Equal Employment Opportunity Act of 1972. This amendment to Title VII also gave the Equal Employment Opportunity Commission the authority to file suit in federal district court against employers in the private sector on behalf of individuals whose charges were not successfully conciliated.

In 1978, Title VII was amended to include the Pregnancy Discrimination Act, which requires employers to treat pregnancy and pregnancy-related medical conditions the same as any other medical disability with respect to all terms and conditions of employment, including employee health benefits.

### Under Title VII

Employment discrimination by any of these groups having fifteen or more employees is prohibited:

- Private employers
- State and local governments
- Educational institutions
- Labor organizations

Employment discrimination by any of these groups also is prohibited:

- The federal government
- Private and public employment agencies
- Joint labor-management committees for apprenticeship and training

It is unlawful for an employer to discriminate with regard to:

- Job advertisements
- Recruitment
- Testing
- Hiring and firing
- Compensation, assignment, or classification of employees
- Transfer, promotion, layoff, or recall
- Use of company facilities
- Training and apprenticeship programs
- Fringe benefits such as life and health insurance

- Pay, retirement plans, and disability leave
- Causing or attempting to cause a union to discriminate
- Other terms and conditions of employment

It is unlawful for employment agencies to discriminate with regard to:

- Its own employees on the basis of race, color, religion, sex, or national origin
- Receiving, classifying, or referring applications for employment
- Job advertisements

It is unlawful for labor unions to discriminate with regard to:

- Applications for membership
- Segregation or classification of members
- Referrals for employment
- Training and apprenticeship programs
- Other discriminatory conduct, including causing or attempting to cause an employer to discriminate
- Job advertisements

It is unlawful for employers, employment agencies, and labor unions to retaliate against individuals who oppose unlawful employment practices or attempt to exercise their rights under the statute.

### Remedies Available under Title VII

Remedies under Title VII are tailored to specific findings of discrimination by the EEOC or by the federal district courts. These remedies may include requiring an employer to end discriminatory practices and systems, institute equal employment practices and systems, and in some cases, provide specific make-whole compensation for victims of discrimination.

Remedies may involve reinstatement, hiring, reassignment, promotion, training, seniority rights, back pay, and other compensation and benefits. (Back pay awards under Title VII cannot accrue from a date more than two years prior to a filing charge.)

interfere with performance of the duties of his job. Result: EEOC found it was not a legitimate reason for the employer's adverse action. (*Carino* v. *University of Oklahoma*, 36 F.E.P. 826, 1984)

- A Polish-born employee was the butt of a constant stream of "Polack" jokes and derogatory comments from fellow employees. EEOC: Management should be held accountable as it knew of the discriminatory activity, but took no steps to put a lid on it. (EEOC Dec. No. CL-68-12-431-EU, 2 F.E.P. 295)

- *Employee Rights Alert:* Don't get in a legal huff every time someone denigrates your ancestry. In analyzing this type of case, the EEOC examines the nature of the derogatory remarks, their frequency, and the effect on the individual. In that vein, a football coach was exonerated for his anti-Italian remarks. The use of those ethnic slurs were part of a casual conversation that "did not rise to the level necessary to contribute to a violation of the law."

In a nutshell, Title VII bars employment practices which subject individuals to different or unequal treatment on account of their national origin. The squirrely part comes when the Immigration Reform and Control Act (IRCA) of 1986 gets tossed into the potion. It requires verification of all individuals to see that they are legally authorized for employment in the United States.

If you want to see the exact language that the EEOC uses in its fact sheet on national origin, read through figure 13. If you'd accept less exact, but more understandable language, take a look at these rights and wrongs:

- Employers can't seek IRCA documentation from you only because you're "foreign looking." They have to ask everyone. And they can't avoid IRCA simply by refusing to hire all individuals of a certain national origin.

- Employers can't refuse to hire you because you display physical, cultural, or linguistic characteristics peculiar to one national group. And they can't refuse to give you a job because you're married to or associate with members of a particular national group.

- It's unlawful to discriminate because of your accent or manner of speaking, unless the employer can show a legitimate, non-discriminatory, business reason for the action.

- The law is also flouted when English fluency rules are adopted for discriminatory reasons, or are not applied equally to all, or

## Figure 13. Fact Sheet: Discrimination Because of National Origin

Title VII of the Civil Rights Act of 1964, as amended, protects individuals against employment discrimination on the basis of race, color, religion, sex, or national origin.

### Definition of National Origin Discrimination

The commission broadly defines national origin discrimination as including, but not limited to, the denial of equal employment opportunity because of an individual's, or his or her ancestor's, place of origin; or because an individual has the physical, cultural, or linguistic characteristics of a national origin group. The commission will examine with particular concern charges alleging that individuals within its jurisdiction have been denied equal employment opportunity for reasons which are grounded in national origin considerations such as (a) marriage to or association with persons of a national origin group; (b) membership in or association with an organization identified with or seeking to promote the interests of national origin groups; (c) attendance or participation in schools, churches, temples, or mosques generally used by persons of a national origin group; and (d) because an individual's name or spouse's name is associated with a national origin group. In examining these charges for unlawful national origin discrimination, the commission will apply general Title VII principles.

### Speak-English-Only Rule

The commission will presume that a rule requiring employees to speak only English at all times in the workplace violates Title VII as a burdensome term and condition of employment. Requiring employees to speak only English at certain times would not be discriminatory if the employer shows that the rule is justified by business necessity. When the employer believes that the rule is justified by business necessity, the Guidelines on Discrimination Because of National Origin, 29 C.F.R. 1606.7 (1983), would require the employer to clearly inform employees of the circumstance in which they are required to speak in English and the consequences of violating the rule.

Notice of such a rule is necessary because it is common for individuals whose primary language is not English to inadvertently slip from speaking English to speaking their native language. Any adverse employment decision against an individual based on a violation of the rule will be considered as evidence of discrimination when an employer has not given effective notice of the rule.

### Accent

In a unanimous decision on August 4, 1986, the five-member commission determined an employer must show a legimate non-discriminatory reason for the denial of employment opportunity because of an individual's accent or manner of speaking.

Investigations will focus on a claimant's qualifications to do the job and whether the claimant's accent or manner of speaking had a detrimental effect on job performance.

Requirements that employees or applicants be fluent in English may also violate Title VII if they are adopted for discriminatory reasons, applied in a discriminatory manner, or if they have the effect of excluding individuals of a particular national origin and are not related to successful job performance.

### Harassment

The commission has consistently held that harassment on the basis of national origin is a violation of Title VII. It holds that an employer has an affirmative duty to maintain a working environment free of harassment on the basis of national origin. This rule which has been adopted by the courts in race and sex cases clearly applies equally to national origin.

Ethnic slurs and other verbal or physical conduct relating to an individual's national origin constitutes harassment when this conduct (1) has the purpose or effect of creating an intimidating, hostile, or offensive work environment, (2) has the purpose or effect of unreasonably interfering with an individual's work performance, or (3) otherwise adversely affects an individual's employment opportunities.

An employer is responsible for its acts and those of its agents and supervisory employees under Title VII, regardless of whether the employer knew or should have known of the acts under the commission's Guidelines on Discrimination Because of National Origin (Title 29 of the Code of Federal Regulations, Section 1606).

The guidelines distinguish the employer's responsibility for the acts of its agents or supervisors from the responsibility it has for conduct among fellow employees. Liability for acts of national origin harassment between fellow employees in the workplace exists only when the employer, or its agents or supervisory employees, knows or should have known of the conduct, and the employer cannot demonstrate that it took immediate and appropriate corrective action. In certain circumstances, where an employer may be shown to have the necessary control, it may also be responsible for the acts of nonemployees with respect to harassment of employees in the workplace on the basis of national origin.

### Immigration-related Practices Which May Violate Title VII

In complying with the Immigration Reform and Control Act of 1986, an employer should remember that it is unlawful to discriminate against any employee or applicant due to that individual's national origin. The Immigration Act requires employers to verify that all employees are legally authorized for employment in the United States. An employer who requests verification of employment status only from individuals of a particular national origin or only from individuals who "appear to be foreign" or "sound foreign" may have violated both the Immigration Act and Title VII. Moreover, employers who impose citizenship requirements or who grant a preference to citizens of the United States in hiring or other employment opportunities may violate Title VII if such a requirement or preference has the purpose or effect of discriminating against individuals of a particular national origin.

disproportionately disqualify certain groups and are not job-related.

- Speak-English-only rules also bump the boundaries of legality, especially when they unduly place a burden on employees whose primary language is not English, when they are not job-necessary, or when they create a hostile environment.
- That hostile environment characteristic also pushes ethnic slurs and other verbal or physical conduct based on national origin into the realm of the EEOC. When such conduct creates an intimidating, hostile, or offensive working environment, unreasonably interferes with employees' ability to do their jobs, or adversely affects employment opportunities, you're talking the EEOC language.

■ *Employee Rights Alert:* An employer in some cases will be held responsible for its managers' and supervisors' actions, even if it did not know about the discriminatory behavior. Some courts will even expand that responsibility to include coworkers' actions if the employer is proven to have known about the discriminatory behavior and not to have acted to stop it.

## Racial discrimination

Many will claim that this is where it all began in terms of discrimination. And it is true that many original EEOC staffers cut their eyeteeth on the civil rights activities of the 1950s and 1960s. But with so much emphasis on the black movement that resulted and carries over today, racial discrimination is rarely as high profile as in the past. Today it usually serves as a supplement to a case rather than the crux of a claim.

The nature of today's complaints are different too. It's more a case today of individual rather than institutional racism. It's no longer formal policies and practices, like segregated washrooms or blacks in the fields and whites in the offices. The bias leans more toward personally vindictive supervisors, unrealistic job expectations, faulty employment testing, and interview areas that reinforce discrimination or disproportionately segregate.

■ *Employee Rights Alert:* Many employers are learning to their chagrin that even without conscious intent, liability still exists. If policies and practices are not truly job-related, and they limit the opportunities of minorities, the inference is discrimination. Actual intent is not the overriding factor.

Despite all the publicity and all the attitude alterations and all the changing social mores, you still get:

A black employee was sacked. Reason: White coworkers wouldn't sack out with him in motels when they all had to hit the road on company business. Forget the company objection that it couldn't afford the business cost of providing separate accommodations or of replacing the intolerant white workers, said the court. The bottom line was the guy was fired for being black. That's illegal race discrimination and he's entitled to damages. (*Sylvester* v. *Callon Energy Services, Inc.*, No. 85-4127, 5th Cir., 1986)

One of the very few blacks employed as an engine tester for a manufacturing firm consistently outperformed his peers. That didn't win him any popularity contests. It did win him a tool box shut tight by glue, a number of his tools hidden around the premises, and some sabotaged engines he was supposed to test. To add insult to injury, there were racial epithets ("The KKK is not dead, nigger") that appeared on bulletin boards and restroom walls. He complained repeatedly to company management, and then took his claims to the state Fair Employment Practices Commission. Soon after he got management's attention—but not in the way he wanted. He began receiving disciplinary sanctions, culminating in his discharge for falsifying test records.

In court the engine tester revved up his case with the claim that there were discrepancies in the company's claims of records falsification. And anyway he had evidence that mistakes in the test records were common, and no testers before had ever been disciplined for them.

The court concurred that he was hitting on all cylinders. The supposed falsification was a pretext for the firing. The company was negligent in not dealing with a vicious campaign of racial harassment. It was liable for the barrage of racist acts, epithets, and threats directed at the employee by fellow workers. And it would suffer: $25,000 in punitive damages, $25,000 for emotional distress, and three years back pay. (*Hunter* v. *Allis-Chalmers Corp.*, No. 85-2401, 7th Cir., 1986)

You already read the one about the black female computer operator in Indiana who complained her white coworkers received better performance marks strictly because of their pigmentation. She was put on probation, denied an opportunity to apply for a management position, and eventually had her computer bugged with a tracing device.

Her day in court took into account race, retaliation, and some testimony from company managers that the court labeled "unworthy of credence." The damage award: $88,000. (*Reeder-Baker* v. *Lincoln National Corp.*, No. 87-1287, 7th Cir., 1987)

Sometimes employment practices are placed under racial scrutiny even when they seem to have a basis in business. Hitting close to home at work was the case of the black female who applied for a position in a bindery department. A glance at her resume stopped the interviewer. She had moved four times in four years. Reason for rejection: A history of geographic instability is incompatible with employer's goal to hire long-term employees.

The unhappy applicant had a prima facie case. She was black; had applied for the job and was qualified; was rejected and the employer continued to seek applicants. Now, the legal Ping-Pong game went into high gear.

The employer had to prove it had a legitimate, nondiscriminatory business reason for the rejection. It thought it had with its geographic stability defense. Not so, said court. The company never asked her about her background or reasons for moving. In fact, it hired non-minorities whose work histories demonstrated instability at least as pronounced as the black applicant's. Judgment: pretext for racial discrimination. (*State* v. *Scientific Computers, Inc.*, 44 F.E.P. Cases 539, Minn. Ct. App., 1986)


## *Religious discrimination*

This type of discrimination may be even older than racial, but new twists are being added to it almost every day. *Accommodation* may be the most important. You can see how the EEOC explains its guidelines for this tricky issue in its religious fact sheet in figure 14. In general, accommodation obligations take into account an employer's size, composition, and structure of the work force, and the nature and cost of the needed accommodation.

You can see in figure 14 how specific the EEOC can get in this area. This is especially true when it comes to determining "undue hardship." The case in figure 14 is a precedent setter that indicates that anything more than a *de minimis* cost to a corporation may constitute that undue hardship. (*Hardison* v. *TWA, Inc.*, 432 U.S. 63, 1977)

The EEOC allows broad definitions of what constitutes religion. It's not confined to theistic concepts or traditional religions only. It includes moral and ethical beliefs as well. Under EEOC conventions, a belief is religious not because a certain group professes it, but because an individual sincerely holds that belief with the strength of traditional religious views. So something like atheism is protected, but beliefs that derive solely from political or social associations are not.

Basically, an employer has to be flexible when it comes to the religious practices or beliefs of its employees or applicants. As an employee, you can't be discriminated against because of a religious

## Figure 14. Fact Sheet: Discrimination Because of Religion

Denying or limiting equal opportunities to individuals without reasonable effort to accommodate their religious beliefs or practices is a violation of Title VII of the Civil Rights Act of 1964, as amended, which prohibits discrimination in employment based on race, color, religion, sex, or national origin.

### Background on the Revised Guidelines

Section 701(j) of Title VII established an obligation by employers to reasonably accommodate the religious practices of an employee or prospective employee unless to do so would create an undue hardship upon the employer. The need for a revision of EEOC's Guidelines on Religious Discrimination arose from the confusion following the Supreme Court's decision in *Trans World Airlines, Inc.* v. *Hardison* in 1977. In that case, the Court ruled against a religious observer because the accommodations would have involved the seniority rights of other workers and regular payment of premium wages to the employee who would have had to replace him. Although the *Hardison* decision left intact the responsibility of business to accommodate, many employers and unions were unclear as to the extent of their duty to provide reasonable accommodation for religious practices under Title VII.

The revised guidelines were developed following a year-long examination of public testimony and commentaries submitted by business, labor organizations, religious groups, employees, and the general public. Hearings held in 1978 in New York City, Los Angeles, and Milwaukee had demonstrated a need to clarify the duty to accommodate various religious practices, such as observance of religious holidays, prayer breaks during working hours, observance of dietary requirements, religious prohibitions against medical examinations, and membership in labor unions.

The revised guidelines cite examples of available alternatives which would accommodate religious practices without significantly increasing cost. These include securing voluntary substitutes, permitting lateral transfers, and creating flexible work schedules. The guidelines state that preselection inquiries which determine an applicant's availability to work during scheduled working hours will be considered to violate Title VII unless the employer can show that the inquiries did not have an exclusionary effect on its employees or prospective employees needing an accommodation for the same religious practices, or the inquiries were otherwise justified by business necessity. After selection, an employer must attempt to accommodate the employee if feasible.

EEOC first published Guidelines on Discrimination Because of Religion (31 F.R. 8370) on June 15, 1966, less than a year after the commission became operational. Those guidelines were superseded by revised guidelines (32 F.R. 10298) on July 13, 1967.

The commission approved the revised final guidelines for publication on October 28, 1980 (Title 29 of the Code, Federal Regulations, Section 16050).

### Revised Guidelines

The revised guidelines provide clarity in the following areas:

*Accommodations.* The employer is obligated to accommodate an employee's or prospective employee's religious practices once the employer has been notified of the need. The employer must offer the alternative which would least disadvantage the employment opportunities of the requester and not cause undue hardship to the employer.

*Alternatives.* Examples of alternatives specified by the guidelines include the use of voluntary substitutes and swaps, flexible scheduling, lateral transfer, and change of job assignments.

*Union Dues.* When an employee's religious practices prohibit payment of union dues to a labor organization, the employee must not be made to pay union dues but may be permitted to pay a sum equivalent to the dues to a charitable organization.

*Undue Hardship.* Under the guidelines, an employer may assert undue hardship to justify a refusal to accommodate an employee's need to be absent from his or her scheduled duty hours if the employer can demonstrate that the accommodation would require more than a *de minimis* cost, which would be determined within a factual context but in accordance with the *Hardison* decision. Also, undue hardship may be shown where a variance from a bona fide seniority system is necessary in order to accommodate an employee's religious practices when it would deny another employee his or her job or shift preference guaranteed by that system.

*Selection Practices.* Under the guidelines, if an employee or prospective employee cannot be present at the scheduled time for a test or other selection procedure because of his or her religious practices, the employer has an obligation to accommodate that individual unless undue hardship would result. Additionally, preselection inquiries addressing an applicant's availability to work during certain time periods will be considered to violate Title VII unless the employer can show that the inquiries do not have an exclusionary effect or are otherwise justified by business necessity.

belief, and you can't be forced to choose between employment opportunities and the fundamental precepts of your religion.

*Religious claims and cases.* To get from the definition to setting up your religious discrimination claim, you need to:

- Show that your religious practice conflicts with a requirement of employment
- Inform your employer of the religious nature of your activities and the nature of the conflict
- Show that any detrimental job action taken against you resulted from your failure, because of religious beliefs, to comply with the company's requests

In line with the landmark case involving accommodation discussed in figure 14 came another case a decade later. It involved the usual religious problem of time off for faith required observances. And it also involved the time-honored question: Whose suggestion for accommodation is better than whose?

A Connecticut public school teacher was a member of the Worldwide Church of God. The three days off allowed for religious observance in his collectively bargained contract weren't enough, so he wanted to use his paid personal days to cover the remainder. School hierarchy deplored that ploy.

Okay, said the teacher, you hire a sub and I'll pay for him or her. Nope, no good, said the school, you'll have to take unpaid leave like everyone else.

The ultimate court decision was full of dissension, but a few noteworthy items emerged:

- The policy underlying Title VII's reasonable accommodation theory calls for flexibility and bilateral cooperation.
- But it doesn't demand that the employer automatically accept the employee's alternative for accommodation. If the employer offers a reasonable alternative, that's usually all she wrote. Case closed. No need to look into degrees of hardship on employer —or employee.
- About the only across-the-board agreement came on the matter of when a religious policy was actually discriminatory. It's not when an employer offers *no* paid leave for any religious purposes, or offers a *precise* leave for every proven religious belief. It's when *different offers are made for different beliefs.* (*Ansonia Board of Education* v. *Philbrook*, No. 85-495 U.S. Sup. Ct., 55 U.S.L.W. 4019, 1986)

*Accommodation in the act.* Weekend work is also a common spark for religious troubles. Another member of the Worldwide Church of God was comfortable working the usual Monday to Friday routine, but informed her boss she couldn't handle Saturday overtime because her beliefs didn't abide it.

As luck would have it, mandatory overtime was instituted. When the assembly line worker failed to report that first Saturday, she was duly disciplined. Both she and the company looked for a way out. A job transfer seemed the ticket to accommodation, but that strategy got canceled quickly when the waiting list for that particular job was found to be two hundred strong.

More absences provoked more discipline, and finally a discharge. The trial court sided with the employee and proffered $73,000 in lost pay and benefits, plus reinstatement.

At the appeals stage, the court laid out the case in two stages. First a prima facie case of religious discrimination was there: sincere religious beliefs, church-forbidden Saturday work under threat of excommunication, conflict conveyed to employer, discipline of employee on basis of religious beliefs.

Then came the question of reasonable accommodation and undue hardship. We tried, said the company, pointing to the transfer attempt. Then we went strictly by the book in discipline.

Didn't try hard enough, contended the worker. For one thing, she proved her job was easily learned and could be handled by a substitute. Also, subs didn't adversely affect the assembly line operations. And in the coup de grace, she pointed out that the company itself employed a roving band of relief operators whose services could have been used to ease her circumstances.

You should have tried harder, said the court. You failed to make reasonable accommodation. (*Protos* v. *Volkswagen of America*, F.2d, 41 F.E.P. Cases 598, 3d Cir., 1986)

Another facet of accommodation reared up when a worker refused to work Sundays and was fired. The company, said the court, did its level best. It had to employ a reserve work force on that day, and it tried to fill it with a skeleton crew of volunteers. When it had to dip into the nonvolunteer sector, it did so on an equitable rotating basis. Everyone received the same consideration. That was reasonable. It would seem unreasonable to allow a worker to demand that other workers be discriminated against. (*EEOC* v. *Ithaca Industries*, No. 87-2526, 4th Cir., 1987)

*Religious discrimination: From gay to funny.* Religious discrimination has even involved the gay movement. A nineteen-year bank employee, a branch manager in fact, was elected president of a local gay Christian group. He informed his superiors that in such a position, he would have to speak out on the issues.

Bank management was in a quandary. One of the bank's iron-clad policies was to forbid outside activities that might undermine public confidence in the bank. Management's decision: Drop the presidency, keep your membership quiet, and keep your job.

The bank manager resigned and filed a religious discrimination suit. The bank claimed the religious nature of the manager's involvement in the gay group was never established, and that it had not been notified of the religious bent of that particular organization.

An appeals court shook a skeptical head and ordered a trial court to decide (*a*) would a reasonable employer under these circumstances know that an accommodation for religious beliefs was being sought and (*b*) had the employee made the religious aspects of this case crystal clear to upper management. (*Dorr* v. *First Kentucky National*, 796 F.2d 179, 1986)

Religious discrimination is a serious business, but it has its stranger side as well.

A report out of Florida told of a worker for a temp agency who toted around a lunch sack wherever he went. His edible of choice: cat food. Every time he cracked open a can, coworkers began holding their nose and opening their mouths to complain. Part of my religion, claimed the man when fired, so you can't discriminate against me because of it. An EEOC district director indicated his paws were tied: Anyone can file a case with us and we are required to investigate it.

From North of the border comes word of a religious discrimination case involving—a male witch. Employed at a Canadian college, this high priest of the temple of Elder Faiths in Toronto followed a religion called WICCA which calls for belief in reincarnation, the practice of magic, and rejection of the inferiority of women. An independent arbitrator ruled he was entitled to a paid religious holiday to celebrate his pagan religion, since his employment contract said such leave shall not be unreasonably denied.

And speaking of North, as in Pole, even Christmas has come into the firing sights of religious discrimination. A Kentucky company ordered its employees to answer the phone during the season with a cheery "Merry Christmas." A Jehovah's witness refused. Compromised her beliefs. Fired, she cried religious discrimination. An appellate court agreed: She could have been accommodated without undue hardship to the company. (*Kentucky Commission on Human Rights* v. *Lesco Manufacturing & Design Co., Inc.*, 86-CI-143, Ky. Ct. App., 1987)

## Retaliation

Two employee actions involving retaliation are protected under Title VII and these come under EEOC jurisdiction. One is when you oppose a discriminatory practice. So if you file an EEOC claim, and suffer because of it, you're in the retaliation realm. Also, if you participate in a state or federal proceeding you're protected against retaliation.

Those are the easy black-and-white cases. In reality, retaliation is infused with shades of gray. And lots of big-name cases contain some hue of retaliation in them.

Case in point: A Northeastern fast-food chain manager was forced to take a lie detector test to investigate drug use. He failed and was fired. A court decided that wasn't the whole story. The polygraph failure may have been the obvious straw. But the one that broke the camel's back was the manager's refusal to promote the president's godson. The fact that the company omitted any reference to retaliatory motives in the discharge was proof of misrepresentation of facts, said the court. That contributed to an almost half million dollar award. (*O'Brien* v. *Papa Gino's of America*, 780 F.2d 1067, 1986)

*Concepts to embrace.* If you do have a black-and-white situation that falls under the spectrum of EEOC retaliation charges, you must prove the circle *concept of participation.* That means:

- You participated in a Title VII proceeding
- You suffered an adverse action by your employer
- The adverse action was generated by your participation
- The employer would not have taken the adverse action but for your participation in the EEOC proceeding

There is also the *concept of opposition* which covers a broad range of activities outside the direct participation realm. Before you can claim protection under this concept you must prove:

- Your conduct was not unlawful in itself or excessively disloyal, hostile, disruptive, or damaging to your employer's business (like the whistle-blowing you saw in chapter 2).
- You must reasonably believe that the practice or policy you are opposing violates Title VII. You may be proved ultimately mistaken, but if you erred in good faith, you are usually forgiven —judicially, that is. Your employer may be less sanguine (sounds like the makings of a retaliation cycle).

The opposition concept also pulls in the requirements of the participation one. You've got to oppose a policy or practice you in good faith believe unlawful under Title VII, suffer an adverse action based on that opposition, and have only been the subject of the action *because of* your opposition.

*The states in the retaliation fracas.* Even the states are getting in on the retaliation act. A worker took his young son to visit his supervisor's home. While there, a neighbor's dog attacked the lad and puncture wounds in his leg had to be treated at the local hospital. Several months of stewing provoked the worker into having his lawyer write both his supervisor and the neighbor, informing them that he held them responsible for the injuries.

Two days later, it hit the fan at work. The supervisor waved the letter in the worker's face and then waved good-bye. Security personnel dogged the worker's heels as he cleaned out his desk and hit the road. A court conversation ensued, as in:

WORKER: You can't do that. No cause.

EMPLOYER: Can so. Employment-at-will.

STATE COURT: Cannot. Employment laws have changed over the years, reflecting legal, social, and economic conditions. Courts cannot ignore the prevailing climate. The worker was penalized because he took steps to ensure a right granted by the *state constitution*. We hold that a termination by an employer of a contract of employment-at-will that is motivated by bad faith or malice based on retaliation is not in the best interests of the economic system or the public good and constitutes a breach of employment contract. So there. (*Fulford* v. *Burndy Corp.*, 623 F. Supp. 78, 1965)

*Rising emotions in distress.* Three other related elements make retaliation a fertile ground for employment snafus. They are individual liability, emotional distress (related to chapter 11 stress), and the exploding area of constructive discharge.

Normally you wouldn't sue an individual. Managers are usually protected by the broad umbrella of acting within the scope of employment. As you saw in the defamation section in chapter 11, they also get qualified privileges for their communications.

But some courts have expanded recognition of individual liability in tort cases when a corporate officer is liable even when the corporation isn't. Usually those tort claims are based on interference with contract, infliction of emotional distress, and defamation.

To get to individual liability, you may have to prove a corporate officer was acting for individual advantage and not the company's interest, out of personal animosity, in bad faith, or without business justification.

One company not only terminated an employee but contacted his new employer and through veiled yet intimidating threats got him fired. He received $150,000 in compensatory damages and half a million in punitive for tortious interference of contract. (*Bagley* v. *Iowa Beef Processors*, 797 F.2d 632, 8th Cir., 1986)

A motel owner short-sheeted a new manager less than two months after the latter started his assignment. Two days later, the owner had the manager's car towed and placed him under citizen's arrest for trespassing. A jury gave the ex-employee the keys to the kingdom, $111,000, less on the termination than the overall handling of the situation. (*Breedlove* v. *Plantation Inn*, San. Fran. Sup. Ct. No. 789829, 1987)

Individual liability is even creeping into nontermination actions, like a retaliation-generated six-month disciplinary suspension without pay. It would seem liability is created by conduct that is spiteful and harassing and goes beyond the bounds of business and decency. (*Garcia* v. *Rockwell International Corp.*, 187 Cal. App. 3d 1556, 232 Cal. Rptr. 490, 1986)

*Motions based on emotions.* Woven into the fabric of individual liability is the recurring thread of emotional distress. This is also a fairly tight tort claim to tackle. Again, it depends on conduct, not merely termination. You'd want to be able to depict the conduct surrounding the discharge as extreme, outrageous, beyond the bounds of public decency, intolerable to a civilized community. You get the picture.

Most termination situations are not so cut-and-dried. In fact, in many cases they involve an individual manager who retaliates against a worker creating emotional distress for the express purpose of sparking a "quit," rather than undergoing a messy termination. The result: *constructive discharge,* a claim that can be even messier.

Basically, constructive discharge occurs when an employer knowingly permits conditions of discrimination so intolerable that a *reasonable person subjected to such conditions would resign.* Both Title VII and other aspects of the Civil Rights Act may come into play on this one, and you can recover back pay, future lost earnings, pension and other benefits, and reinstatement.

Cases in point.

A female sales manager had family plans. But her supervisor expressed doubts that she could handle both motherhood and a career. After suffering a miscarriage, she took two weeks sick leave. On returning, she found her old position occupied by a new sales rep. She had two options: transfer to a less lucrative sales territory or resign. She opted for a third, lawsuit.

A court awarded her about a hundred grand in damages and front pay (future lost pay, benefits, pension). The reasoning: It's not necessary to prove specific intent on the part of an employer, just a reflection of the reasonable person theory. (*Goss* v. *Exxon Office Systems Co.*, Nos. 83-1557 and 83-1598, 3d Cir., 1984)

A black man hired as a "casual sweeper" was promised a permanent position based on seniority when an opening occurred. It never happened. Not only were whites interviewed for those permanent positions on a regular basis, but the black was occasionally asked to train those new employees.

Convinced he could never expect the promised promotion, he resigned and sued, hauling the Civil Rights Acts of 1966 and 1971 into the fray. The court: The purported reason for denying promotion—lack of experience—was a pretext. This is constructive discharge because a reasonable person would have found such working conditions intolerable. Back pay award: A little over $99,000. (*Satterwhite* v. *Smith*, 36 F.E.P. Cases 148, 9th Cir., 1984)

A female bartender in a Nebraska restaurant was elated. She gave thanks at Thanksgiving because she was pregnant. But when she gave that message to her employers, they stuffed her happiness. Because your job entails heavy lifting and working on slippery floors, they intoned, you won't be able to work behind the bar after the first of the year.

She weighed the option offered: part-time cocktail waitress with irregular hours. She needed full-time work, so she resigned, looked for another job, then sued. A district court ruled she failed to show constructive discharge because the employer had not taken a discriminatory job action with intent to cause her to resign.

Wake up and smell the coffee, an appeals court responded. The reality of the situation is this: The ex-bartender reasonably believed her employment would end in January, or become sporadic at best. Plus it was the employer's outdated perceptions of the limitations of pregnant women that led to the reassignment of duties, the reduced work, and irregular work schedules. (*Schneider* v. *Jax Shack, Inc.*, F.2d No. 85-1653, 1986)

In another pregnancy-related constructive discharge case, a manager scolded a subordinate for pursuing a career while having two small children at home. He also made some derogatory comments about the problems that arose when women got too much education. Then he demoted her from an associate's position to a clerical one. The courts bandied this one about, but on appeal it was held that there was evidence the demotion stemmed from the supervisor's bias against women. (*Derr* v. *Gulf Oil Corp.*, F.2d Nos. 85-1056 and 85-2341, 10th Cir., 1986)

*Retaliation audit.* To retaliate against retaliation, ask yourself this series of questions:

- Were any threats of adverse action made against you if you didn't stop opposition to what you considered unlawful or discriminatory practices?

- Did your employer refuse to allow you to join or represent other employees in protesting practices?
- Did you suffer what you believe was a forced resignation?
- Were any of the following harassment or intimidation tactics used on you?
  Transfer to a lower paying job, less lucrative territory, more menial position
  Denial of overtime, bonuses, perks
  Undeserved reprimands
  Surveillance
  Coercive questioning
- Were there any postemployment tactics?
  Unfavorable references
  Denial of benefits usually granted a departing employee
  Opposition to legitimate unemployment compensation claims
  Refusal to allow you to be eligible for rehire
- Is the timing of events such that it reflects you being caught in a retaliatory spiral?
- Can you produce evidence that evidence against you in a discipline or discharge situation was manufactured?
- Did your employer accelerate a discipline process to get rid of you, or ignore standard procedures other individuals have enjoyed?
- Were you subject to disproportionately harsh treatment not in line with previous similar situations?

# CHAPTER 13

# After They Sharpen the Axe, How Can You Dull the Pain?

Your *rights as an employee* have been hacked and slashed. You're bloody but unbowed, determined to exact a measure of revenge against the unfeeling corporate monolith that has caused you this pain. A few words of advice: Don't do anything rash lest you reopen those wounds.

If you've been reading along carefully, you should have a good feel for whether or not you really do have an employee rights case. Before you take the *final* plunge, give a quick look-see at these *last* three considerations:

- Releases after you've been terminated (they may be just what the doctor ordered, much less messy than a lawsuit)
- The pros and cons of the lawsuit route (they may give you second thoughts about traveling it)
- Suggestions for dealing with lawyers (they'll put you on the right track if you do decide to forge ahead with a suit)

## Getting relief in releases

That's what *employers* are looking for. They're not having much luck. Negotiating waivers of lawsuits, especially in federal age discrimination claims, is a tricky business, particularly without EEOC approval. Employers must take extraordinary strides to cross the release finish line as a defense to subsequent age litigation.

Case in point: One company learned the hard way that a general release of claims doesn't always cut the mustard. The employee had signed an official termination letter which outlined the terms of his departure in exchange for specific enumerated benefits.

Not so fast, ruled two courts. The release was not valid because:

- It did not expressly refer to a waiver of a federal right, in this case ADEA protection
- The employee didn't sign the letter as a settlement of a claim dispute
- He wasn't represented by his own attorney
- He didn't sign the release knowingly and voluntarily

The rule of thumb handed out on this case: A release must be the result of a bargaining process in which the terms and consequences of the agreement are made clear, and there is a genuine intent to release claims without threat, duress, or coercion.

Judgment: $360,000 plus reinstatement. Why? No bargaining process, no clarification of terms, no realistic explanation of consequences, no negotiation of terms or conditions. Sound familiar? (*Valenti* v. *International Mill Services, Inc.*, 45 F.E.P. Cases 1054, 3d Cir., 1987)

## On the "rights" side of releases

Even the EEOC is struggling with this controversy. And Congress has poked its finger in the pie, demanding a review of a regulation that would allow unsupervised (by the EEOC) waivers of age discrimination claims if:

- The agreement is set "write" down there in black and white for all to see
- It's written so it doesn't take a rocket scientist to figure it out
- Adequate time is given to review all the ifs, ands, or buts
- Appropriate counsel in terms of the employee's legal gunslinger is available to review
- The added compensation bargained for goes beyond standard entitlements

That last one is important. You're being asked to give up a great deal. Your job for one. And the right to legal redress for another. Look for at least a financial bonus above severance, maybe a deferred payment schedule. How about some nonmonetary concessions, like a good price (or no price) on the company auto or computer you've been using? You might want a promise not to give out unfavorable references.

You can also negotiate for the timing of your termination benefits, making them more valuable for you (and sometimes the employer too) by spreading them out. What about seeking remuneration that offers the most favorable tax treatment? Check vesting dates on your pension and insurance coverage. Maybe your old employer will recall happier days with you and move up those dates even if you're not technically eligible.

This is basically a contract situation. It can't be one-sided, and it must include an exchange of benefits for both parties. A judge will look at all the circumstances of each case, including:

- The relationship between you and your employer
- The types of rights you are being asked to give up
- The situation that surrounded your signing of the release
- Whether the release request suggests an employer may have violated a law
- How the employer handled similar previous cases

## Courts agree to disagree

As usual, courts are in disagreement on certain aspects of releases as contracts. A California court ruled that an employer's existing severance pay policy was itself a contractual obligation. Merely paying the standard amount was not enough to enforce a separation agreement. But a federal judge in New York ruled that severance pay policies don't create binding contracts.

■ *Employee Rights Alert:* Whatever they say, they all agree that you can't have anything that may be construed as wages held back as an inducement to sign a release. New York State labor laws include severance and termination allowances among the wages a departing employee gets. And in California, a statute says that if the employer holds up pay pending the signing of a release, not only can the release be wiped off the books, but he could have the book thrown at him in criminal court.

Before you conduct a little release audit on yourself, here's a brief audit of what a standard release contains, so you'll know how to spot the species. If anything else is included, check it out with your attorney.

- An acknowledgment that the termination is voluntary.
- A list of the pay and benefits offered in return for the release. This should include the amounts of salary and severance pay and the payment period.
- An agreement by the employee not to sue or start any administrative proceedings.
- A statement that the employee has a right to review the release and to consult an attorney before signing it.
- An agreement that the terms of the release will be kept confidential.
- Provisions for the return of company property and confidential documents.
- A statement that the employee is due no other pay or benefits.
- A clause that cancels any existing employment contracts.

## Release audit

Think about your own release situation.

- Is there a chance arbitration could settle any differences you have?
- Did you ever receive any pressure from anyone in authority to sign the release? Did they say "sign this release or else?"
- Did they offer you sweeteners over and above what you had coming?
- Did they give you the time and opportunity to consult an attorney?
- Were there any witnesses to your "voluntary" signature?
- Were there any verbal agreements or promises that got lost in the written shuffle? Can you prove that they were made?
- Did they make a single nonnegotiable offer (no bargaining makes

them look bad)? Did they make different offers to others in similar circumstances than they did to you?

## Being resigned to resigning

Resignations, like releases, are legally sensitive. You get the same kinds of circumstances, involuntary actions, contract breaking, bad faith. Here's a classic.

Without warning, an employee was placed between a rock and a hard place. Have a heart, she pleaded. Cut it out, company responded. Either resign or be discharged. Okay, she sighed, how about a positive letter of recommendation to help me find another job? I guess I can do that, grumped her supervisor.

So she handed in her letter of resignation, and asked for her letter of recommendation. I promised only a letter saying you had been employed, smirked the boss. Then give me back my resignation letter, demanded the ex-employee.

Well, she never got her letter, either one. But she did get $50,000 from a sympathetic jury hearing her claims of breach of implied contract of good faith and fair dealing. Here's what the state supreme court said in sustaining the award:

> The respondent is not being assessed punitive damages for failing to provide a warning prior to the firing. Rather respondent's conduct in obtaining a letter of resignation and refusing appellant's demand for return forms the basis for a jury finding of fraud, oppression or malice . . . resignation, rather than discharge, may protect an employer from immediately becoming liable for unemployment compensation benefits . . . the employer may, by obtaining that letter of resignation, be insulating itself from a claim of wrongful discharge. (*Gates* v. *Life of Montana Insurance Co.*, 668 P.2d 213, 216, No. 82-468, 1983)

■ *Employee Rights Alert:* References often go hand in hand with resignations, as in this case. Keep your options open when they are related. Negotiate for the language in the reference. Watch for company practices. If it gives good references to employees it likes and no references to employees it doesn't, chalk it up in your proof of malice column.

## Pros and cons in actually suing

By this time you may be champing at the bit to ride off to battle. But take a good hard look at the big picture. Balance these pros with the cons which follow.

### *Positives*

- Most juries tend to side with the employee, if a suit gets that far. After all, they're more your peers than those of big bosses. The trend: When in doubt, the benefit of the doubt goes to the employee.
- Juries also are human. They side with the underdog and may in fact ignore judicial instructions and let their feelings dictate their decisions.
- Despite the legal concept that the burden of proof usually rests with the plaintiff (that's you, the employee), it often gets shifted to corporate shoulders.
- Courts are placing great weight on companies toeing the line, adhering not only to legislative strictures but to their own policies as well.
- Courts are reading between the lines of company actions, turning thumbs down on sudden decisions, looking askance at unreasonable tactics, imposing their own views of fair play on the corporate playground.
- Personalities sway decisions, especially when it's a three-piece suit versus a shirt-sleeve worker.
- Managers who hack and slash, instead of encourage and teach, receive negative jury reviews.
- Some juries decide to teach the corporate community as a whole a lesson by imposing huge awards against one of its members.
- Finally, a sympathetic jury can really open the coffer doors. You can win back pay, including overtime, vacation, shift differentials, pension, retirement, and severance. You can be awarded front pay—money from future loss of earnings. You can get attorney's fees, compensatory damages for pain and suffering, for emotional and psychological distress, for loss. Then again, you can also end up with egg on your face from a courtroom loss. But that's not the worst of it.

## *Negatives*

- You're going to lose lots of time, which could be used more constructively, like in finding a job. You'll spend hours investigating, compiling evidence, being interviewed.
- Then there's the lawyer's time, which of course you pay for. You'll be getting up close and personal with him or her if you want to develop the best case. Consider a cot.
- What about court time? Can you afford to turtle your way through an endless series of delays, discoveries, challenges, changes, and court calendar fill-ups?
- Then there are the costs. Financial is apparent. Even if you get a lawyer on a contingency basis, you'll bleed from the pocketbook: copying material, travel, out-of-pocket expenses. You're probably up against deeper pockets than your own. Or maybe those pockets aren't so deep, and you may be wasting your time trying to turn them inside out.
- And suppose those pockets are in big corporate breeches. Inhabited by fat legal departments. With a bevy of heavy hitters. Pugnacious combatants who have been through the employee-rights wars—and returned.
- There are other costs beside financial. Try psychological. One discharged employee called his lawsuit "emotionally draining . . . like suing your father." You can easily make enemies of former colleagues and associates. And if it's tough on you, what about your family?
- No matter how strong your case, you're rolling the dice. Courts are unpredictable. From state to state and jurisdiction to jurisdiction. What are your chances of winning? And if you do, remember the law is there to give you *appropriate relief*, not to make you a sultan or queen.
- Finally, you're opening up a can of worms. Make sure you're not going to be the one on the hook. Your workplace activities, and even some extracurriculars, will be placed in the spotlight. Any business skeletons you might have in the closet won't stand a ghost of a chance of staying hidden. Ready to stand naked in court?

## Preparing the evidence for your case

If you're not daunted by that preview of the pitfalls that could befall you in pursuing an employee lawsuit, here are a few words to the wise in compiling the evidence for your case. You've already seen a slew of specific questions to ask and short audits to conduct that will strengthen your hand in preparing to go to war in court. Add the following to your preparation stage.

Even the EEOC admits that the number one problem in most employee rights cases is lack of evidence. To bolster your case, consider:

- Dragging out the personnel files, yours and anyone else's with a related situation.
- Grab any other documents you can. Memos, performance appraisals, supervisors' notebooks, recorded interviews, logs.
- Conduct some interviews yourself. Your immediate supervisor, the person who fired you, anyone involved in the decision up the corporate ladder, witnesses to the "execution," other employees who may have suffered similar fates.
- Check history. Does the company have a "record?" Are there others who might have been soured by the same pickle you're in?
- Check policy. Did the company violate its own? Was there inconsistent application? Are infractions common but unreported? Was progressive discipline adhered to? Should you have been given the opportunity to improve? Did you violate a policy that wasn't common knowledge?

In collecting your evidence, you needn't go quite as far as one woman reportedly did in upstate New York. Seems she had found her pet Maltese (that's a dog, not a falcon) bitten to death on a neighbor's property. She suspected her neighbor's collie or hound was responsible. But her day in court was scheduled six months after the tragedy. So in order to preserve the evidence for as strong a case as possible, she—yep—put the puppy in her freezer and popped him out a half year later in front of a startled judge.

# Looking for a lawyer

Okay, you're not daunted by the drawbacks of suing and you think you can come up with the evidence. It may very well be time to take the plunge and hire yourself a legal beagle to set on your lawsuit trail.

There are a number of places to look. You could:

- Hit up friends and associates for referrals. Beware of relatives, tennis partners, and nephews of long-lost friends. You need a specialist, not a comrade.
- Check with other "suers." If someone has gone through the experience, ask for a reference. Also pick their brains about that experience. It may give you second or third thoughts about charging into battle.
- Ask state or local fair employment practices commissions and agencies for suggestions. Maybe a firm they know of specializes in employee rights cases. Other organizations go under such monikers as Neighborhood Legal Services or Legal Aid Society (check the Yellow Pages, too). There's also the National Resource Center for Consumers of Legal Services in Washington, D.C.
- Go the professional route. Ask local judges or practicing lawyers or court personnel you may know. Check with the local bar association or the national American Bar Association for other avenues to pursue. Even publishers of legal information may be able to guide you in the right direction. Then again you could dial a toll-free number and ring up LawPlan, a prepaid legal advice and counsel program from Hyatt Legal Services advertised on cable TV. Just have your credit card handy.

Even after you've tentatively decided on your legal hero, you may want to go back to some of these sources, especially the "industry" ones. Ask about your choice's reputation in the field. Whether the firm has direct or indirect contacts that are going to help your case along.

No matter which menu you choose to choose from, take it with a grain of salt. Whether you uncover a name from wee-hours-of-the-morning advertising for free consultation or look up the richest lawyer in your town, enter the situation with your eyes wide open. That way, there'll be no surprises for either side.

## Grilling your barrister

While you're involved in this case, you and your lawyer(s) are going to get close. Very close. Like in a marriage. So before you fall head over heels in love with an esquire, cover some "pre-judicial" areas:

- Discuss strengths and weaknesses of the case. Ask for a list of scenarios and likely outcomes, with estimates of time and work-load for each type of settlement.
- Check billing rates. Are they negotiable? Does a flat fee option exist? What about billing procedures? How much do you have to pay and when? You may want to ask for a letter of engagement laying out the details.
- Ask about monetary differentials among senior and junior part-ners, associates, and paralegals. If you're paying by the hour, you don't want to be charged full-time lawyer rates when work (research, interviews) is being done by a paralegal or clerk.
- Probe for hidden costs. Document copying or mailing and mes-senger costs? Do rates include overhead and incidentals? What about the cost of expert witnesses or transcripts?
- Keep a wary eye on procedures. Are there any limits on "ex-pense" items, such as traveling first class, computerized re-search, or overtime? Do they assign two lawyers to take depositions and interview when you only need one? Do they itemize all their bills so you know exactly what you're paying for, so there's no duplication?
- Look into personalities. Who will be handling your case in court and in out-of-court negotiations? A high-ranking partner? The associate you're used to dealing with? Who prepares the doc-uments and attends the meetings? Is the individual you've be-come comfortable with in initial meetings merely the pitchperson, who hands off your case to the "grunts" in the inner sanctum?
- Check out communications. How are they handled? How often do you hear from your lawyers and in what forms? Do you get calls, copies of documents? Will they discuss every point of strategy before embarking on it, or just major decision points?
- Get a little background. How's their track record in the em-

ployee rights area? Not just wins and losses, but settlements and satisfied customers. Does the firm sometimes spread its resources too thin? Does it have an adequate backup? Just how important will your case be in the overall scheme of things?

After you walk out of any lawyer interview, look inside for your gut feelings on such questions as:

- Am I comfortable with this firm's lawyers—do I feel I can trust my legal life to them?
- Does he or she exude competence, look organized (including the office itself), act professional?
- Are they experienced in this type of employee rights case; and did they appear interested in my particular situation?
- Can I afford—literally—to pursue this case with this firm?
- Did the lawyers make my case, and my alternatives, perfectly clear to me?
- Did they inspire confidence in me? Communicate well?
- Were they completely honest, with a minimum of double-talk and legalese?

# Appendixes

## APPENDIX I. THE EQUAL EMPLOYMENT OPPORTUNITY COMMISSION

The U.S. Equal Employment Opportunity Commission (EEOC) was created by Title VII of the Civil Rights Act of 1964, which prohibits employment discrimination on the basis of race, color, sex, religion, or national origin. The EEOC has enforced Title VII since July 2, 1965.

Since 1979, the EEOC has also been responsible for enforcing the Age Discrimination in Employment Act (ADEA) as amended, which protects workers forty years of age or older; the Equal Pay Act (EPA) of 1963, which protects women and men performing substantially equal work against pay discrimination based on sex; and, in the federal sector, Section 501 of the Rehabilitation Act of 1973, as amended, which prohibits handicap discrimination.

Executive Order 12067 of 1978 directs the EEOC to provide oversight and coordination of all federal equal employment opportunity regulations, practices, and policies.

### The Commission

The EEOC has five commissioners and a general counsel appointed by the president and confirmed by the Senate. Commissioners are appointed for five-year staggered terms. The term of the general counsel is four years. The president designates a chairperson and a vice-chair. The EEOC's chairperson is responsible for the administration of the commission. The five-member commission is responsible for making equal employment opportunity policy and approving all litigations undertaken by the commission. The general counsel is responsible for conducting commission enforcement litigation.

*The work of the commission* EEOC staff receive and investigate employment discrimination charges or complaints. If the commission finds reasonable cause to believe that unlawful discrimination occurred, the staff attempts to conciliate the charges or complaints. The EEOC staff also conducts commission-initiated investigations under Title VII, ADEA, and EPA. When conciliation is not achieved, the commission may file lawsuits in federal district court against employers (private employers only under Title VII; only the Department of Justice may sue a state or local government for a violation of Title VII), labor organizations, and employment agencies.

*EEOC's mission* To ensure equality of opportunity by vigorously applying federal legislation prohibiting discrimination in employment through investigation, conciliation, litigation, coordination, regulation in the federal sector, and through education, policy research, and provision of technical assistance.

*The commission's policy* In pursuing its mission of eradicating discrimination in the workplace, the commission intends that its enforcement be predictable, provide effective relief for those affected by discrimination, allow remedies designed to correct the sources of discrimination, and prevent their recurrence.

## Headquarters Offices and Their Functions

*General counsel* Recommends and conducts all EEOC litigation in class, systemic, and individual cases of discrimination by means of direct suit, intervention, and *amicus curiae* (friend of the court) participation in litigation brought by private parties. The general counsel also enforces commission subpoenas.

*Legal counsel* Serves as principal advisor to the commission on nonenforcement litigation matters, represents the commission and staff in defensive litigation and administrative hearings, and carries out the commission's leadership and coordination role for the federal government's EEOC enforcement program.

## Field Operations

In 1984, the commission reorganized its field structure to make it a more effective and professional force in the civil rights arena. Under the new structure, fewer charges have to be transferred from one office to another in order to complete administrative processing.

The EEOC has a three-tier field structure consisting of twenty-three district, sixteen area, and nine local offices.

District offices are full service units handling charge processing and have units which can do extended investigations necessary for potential litigation vehicles. Local offices process charges but forward cases for litigation to district offices for litigation development.

### Filing Your Employment Discrimination Charge Under Title VII *(Race, Color, Sex, Religion, or National Origin)*

In many places, you must file an employment discrimination charge within 180 days of the alleged discriminatory act. Where there is a state or local fair employment practices agency in your area, you generally have up to 240 days, and in some cases up to 300 days, to file your charge with EEOC, but you should check with the commission. If your charge is not filed on time, EEOC may not be able to investigate it, and you may not be able to secure any relief.

You may file your charge in person, by mail, or by telephone. However, most people prefer to come into an EEOC office.

If you believe that you have been discriminated against by an employer, a labor union, or an unemployment agency when applying for a job or on your job in the terms or conditions of your employment because of race, color, sex, religion, national origin, or age, you may file a charge of discrimination against the employer, labor union, or employment agency.

Charges or complaints of employment discrimination may be filed at any field office of the U.S. Equal Employment Opportunity Commission (EEOC). Field offices are located in forty-eight cities throughout the United States and are listed later in this appendix and in most local phone directories under U.S. Government.

*The intake interview* You will be interviewed by an Equal Opportunity Specialist (EOS). During your initial contact with EEOC, you will be:

■ Asked to complete a questionnaire for information such as name, address, and telephone number of your employer, or the place you applied for a job, the name of your supervisor, the date the alleged discrimination occurred, and the nature of the discrimination.

- Interviewed about your allegations so that the charge may be properly written.
- Asked to provide information about other potentially aggrieved persons (this "class" information will be included on the face of your charge).
- Counseled so that you will understand what to expect while your charge is being investigated.
- Counseled as to your rights, if any, under ADEA and EPA.
- Referred to the proper agency if your complaint cannot be handled by EEOC.

*Review of your charge* After you have filed your charge, it will be reviewed by a senior manager to determine whether it should be assigned to a rapid charge unit or an extended unit, which conducts full-scale investigations, including on-site visits. An individual determination will be made on how your charge should be processed (even charges assigned to rapid charge processing units may be considered for more extensive investigations).

*The fact-finding conference* After your charge has been filed, your employer will be notified that you have filed a charge of discrimination. Under Title VII EEOC must notify your employer after receiving your charge. When the employer receives notification of the charge, the employer will normally be asked to come to EEOC for a fact-finding conference to discuss the allegations in your charge. You will also receive a copy of that notification.

The fact-finding conference is conducted by an equal opportunity specialist who is trained to conduct these conferences and to investigate employment discrimination charges. At the fact-finding conference, evidence will be presented by both you and your employer. Your employer will be asked to bring only those witnesses who have actual knowledge of the incident. Your witnesses will be interviewed prior to the conference. Only those people who have knowledge of the incident are permitted to speak at the conference.

Information obtained at the fact-finding conference will be used to help resolve your charge with a settlement satisfactory to both you and your employer. If settlement is impossible or inappropriate, your charge will be investigated further.

*After the conference* While most charges filed with the EEOC are resolved without lengthy investigation, some charges require investigation beyond the fact-finding conference. If your charge is one of these, or if it is a charge which is not appropriate for a fact-finding conference, it will be investigated by either a rapid charge unit or an extended investigation unit.

*Extended investigation* If your charge is assigned for extended investigation at any stage following its receipt and is identified for possible litigation, it will be processed by a team that includes an attorney. The attorney will be involved in all critical decision points as the investigation proceeds and will work on the case from beginning to end. To the extent possible, extended investigations will include a visit to the facility in question.

*Cause determination* If the investigation shows that there is reasonable cause to believe that discrimination has occurred, the commission will notify you and your employer of this decision. At this point, EEOC will begin the conciliation efforts required under the statute.

*No cause findings* If the commission concludes that there is no reasonable cause to believe that discrimination has occurred, you and your employer will be notified of the findings. You have a right to request a review of the findings with EEOC in Washington, D.C. All appeal rights and instructions for filing a request will be sent to you along with the notification of findings. You will also be informed of your right to take your case to court if you choose.

*Litigation* Most charges filed with EEOC, even those where the commission decides to sue, are conciliated or settled before the case actually goes to trial. At all stages of the investigation, the commission, as required by statute, will attempt to bring the matter to a resolution agreeable to all parties without costly litigation.

If, however, EEOC finds that there is reasonable cause to believe that discrimination has occurred and is unable to conciliate your charge, it will be considered by the commission for possible litigation. If the commission decides to litigate your case, a lawsuit will be filed in federal district court.

If the commission decides not to litigate your case, a "right-to-sue" letter will be issued, which permits you to take your case to court, if you choose.

*The state or federal fair employment practices agency* Title VII requires that the federal government defer charges of discrimination to a state or local agency if that agency meets certain criteria. EEOC has work-sharing agreements with many state or local agencies. Depending upon the agreement, your charge may be processed either by EEOC or the state agency. In any event, your employment discrimination charge will be handled under tight management and quality controls.

## Under the Age Discrimination in Employment Act (*Protects Workers Forty Years of Age or Older*)

During your initial contact with EEOC, you will be:

- Interviewed by an EOS who has been trained to handle age discrimination charges.
- Counseled as to your right to file either a charge or complaint (see Confidentiality).
- Interviewed about your allegations so that your charge may be properly written.
- Counseled as to your rights, if any, under Title VII.

If you decide to file a charge or complaint under ADEA:

- EEOC will investigate your charge or complaint.
- In the case of a charge, you and your employer may be asked to attend a fact-finding conference to discuss your charge.
- EEOC may initiate court action if a violation of the law is found and conciliation fails.

*Private suits* Individuals may file suits on their own behalf but not until sixty days after filing their charge of unlawful discrimination with EEOC and, where there is a state age discrimination law, with the state agency. Should EEOC take legal action, however, the individual may not file a private suit.

## Under the Equal Pay Act (*Pay Difference Because of Sex*)

During your initial contact with EEOC, you will be:

- Interviewed by an equal opportunity specialist trained to handle equal pay discrimination complaints.
- Interviewed to determine if there is reason to believe that you have an equal pay discrimination complaint and to determine whether other individuals may also be affected.
- Counseled as to your rights, if any, under Title VII and EPA.

Your complaint will be investigated on a sufficiently broad basis so that your identity (see Confidentiality) will not be disclosed to your employer. If a violation of the law is found, EEOC will attempt to obtain appropriate prospective wage increases and back wages for all aggrieved individuals.

If the attempt to settle is not successful, the commission may file suit to enforce the Act.

*Private suits* Under the Equal Pay Act, you have the right to file suit for back pay, liquidated damages, attorney's fees, and court costs. However, you may not bring suit if you have been paid full back wages under supervision of the commission or if the commission has filed suit to collect the wages. A two-year statute of limitations applies to the recovery of unpaid wages, except in the case of willful violations, for which there is a three-year statute of limitations.

## Confidentiality

Under Title VII, except in unusual circumstances which will be discussed with you, your identity must be revealed.

Under ADEA, if you wish confidentiality, you may file a complaint or have a charge filed on your behalf. The filing of a charge protects your right to file a private suit. If you file a charge, your name will be given to your employer.

Under EPA, EEOC will not disclose your identity without your written consent. However, if you elect to file a charge under both Title VII and EPA, your identity will be revealed.

## Retaliation

Under Title VII, ADEA, and EPA, employers are prohibited from retaliating against any employee who files a charge or complaint or participates in an EEOC investigation.

If an employer retaliates against you for filing a charge or complaint or for participating in an investigation, the commission can ask for a temporary restraining order which, if granted by the court, would prevent the employer from retaliating further.

## Additional Information

If you need further information, you may call EEOC toll free on (800) USA-EEOC. EEOC's TDD number (for the hearing impaired) is (202) 634-7057.

### U.S. Equal Employment Opportunity Commission
### Information Sheet for Charging Parties and Complainants

*EEOC procedures* The Equal Employment Opportunity Commission (EEOC) will investigate the allegations you have made. The EEOC investigator will ask you questions, will ask the respondent questions, may ask witnesses questions, and may review records. Based on the evidence gathered, the investigator will prepare a recommended determination for the office director on whether discrimination has occurred. You will be given a Letter of Determination which will state whether there is reason or not to believe that discrimination has occurred. If you have filed a complaint, rather than a charge, or if you have had a charge filed on your behalf, your identity as a complainant will be kept in confidence throughout EEOC's handling of your case.

- If the director believes that the allegations you have made are supported by the evidence, the Letter of Determination will say this and will ask the respondent to meet with EEOC and work out an agreement which will provide relief for the harm caused by the discrimination. If an agreement cannot be worked out, the investigation file will be reviewed in EEOC headquarters and EEOC (or the Department of Justice in some cases) will either sue on your behalf or notify you of your right to sue (see information below about your private suit rights).

- If the director believes that some or all of the allegations in your charge are not supported by the evidence, the Letter of Determination will say this and will notify you of your right to request EEOC headquarters review of the determination and of the date that the determination will become final if you do not request review. A Request for Review form will be sent to you with the Letter of Determination.

If you do not request review within fourteen days of the determination, it will become EEOC's final determination on the fifteenth day and the investigation will be ended. You can then decide if you want to file a private lawsuit to enforce your rights in court (see the information below about your private suit rights).

If you request EEOC headquarters review of the determination within fourteen days, and your request is accepted, a final EEOC determination will be sent to you after the review is complete. This determination will notify you if EEOC will take any further action and the effect on your private suit rights.

*Your responsibilities* Please inform EEOC of any prolonged absence from home or change of your address. Please claim any certified mail which EEOC may send you. If EEOC cannot locate you or if EEOC asks you to do something necessary to its investigation, and you decline to do so, EEOC may notify you that the investigation will be discontinued and notify you of your right to sue (see the information below about your private suit rights). You may retain a lawyer while your case is investigated, but you are not required to do so.

*Your private suit rights under Title VII* If you filed a charge with EEOC under Title VII of the Civil Rights Act, you have preserved your right to sue the respondent named in your charge. If we cannot resolve your charge, we will notify you of your right to sue. You may then file a lawsuit in U.S. District Court within ninety days from receipt of our notice in order to enforce your rights in court. Once this ninety day period is over, your right to sue is lost. EEOC may give you notice of your right to sue in the following circumstances:

- *If you ask for a notice of right to sue.* You may not wish to wait for EEOC to complete its investigation or your attorney may recommend that you file your own lawsuit. You can obtain a

Notice of Right to Sue in such cases by asking the office where you filed your charge to issue a notice to you, even though our investigation is not finished. If you ask, EEOC will issue a notice to you after 180 days have passed from the date you filed your charge. In some cases, if you ask, we will issue the notice to you at an earlier time, if it is known that the investigation will take a long time to complete. You will have 90 days to file suit from the day you receive the Notice of Right to Sue.

- *If EEOC finds no violation with respect to all the allegations in your charge.* Before this happens, you will be interviewed by EEOC and given an opportunity to provide additional evidence. If, at the end of investigation, you are given a Letter of Determination stating that there are no violations, you will be told that you may, within fourteen days, ask EEOC headquarters to review the determination. You will have ninety days to file suit from the day a determination in your case becomes final—either after the fourteen day period is over if you do not ask for a review or after final EEOC action at a later date if you do ask for a review.
- *If EEOC finds a violation, fails to obtain relief, and decides not to sue on your behalf.* If EEOC finds a violation but does not succeed in obtaining relief under the law, the investigation is reviewed by EEOC's commissioners to decide if a lawsuit will be filed. Sometimes the commissioners decide that a lawsuit will not be filed. If this happens, you will be notified and receive a Notice of Right to Sue. You will have ninety days to file suit from the day you receive the notice.
- *If your charge is dismissed.* EEOC regulations require a charge to be dismissed when (1) an investigation shows that the law does not apply to your case, (2) it is not possible to continue the investigation due to an inability to locate you, (3) you did not cooperate in some way necessary to the investigation, or (4) you did not accept a settlement offer which afforded you full relief for the harm which you alleged. EEOC may discontinue its investigation by notifying you that it has dismissed your charge. You will have ninety days to file suit from the day you receive the Notice of Right to Sue.

**Your private suit rights under the Age Discrimination in Employment Act (ADEA) or Equal Pay Act (EPA)** If you filed a charge or complaint under the ADEA or EPA, the above rules on your private suit rights do not apply. However, as stated under EEOC Procedures, you may request an EEOC headquarters review of a no violation finding under these laws. Please note that such a request for review will not extend the time you have for filing a lawsuit. You must file suit within two years of the alleged discrimination (three years in cases of willful violations). You must wait sixty days from the day you filed an ADEA charge before you can sue under that law.

If you have any questions, please call the EEOC office which last handled your case.

## Offices of the U.S. Equal Employment Opportunity Commission

*Nationwide toll-free number*     1-800-USA-EEOC
              (1-800-872-3362)

*Headquarters*

Columbia Plaza Office Building, 2401 E Street, NW, Washington, DC 20006           (202) 634-6922

*District, area, and local offices*

Albuquerque Area Office, Western Bank Building, Suite 1105, 505 Marquette, NW, Albuquerque, NM 87102    (505) 766-2061

Atlanta District Office, Citizens Trust Bank Building, 75 Piedmont Avenue, NE, Suite 1100, Atlanta, GA 30335    (404) 331-6091

Baltimore District Office, 109 Market Place, Suite 4000, Baltimore, MD 21202           (301) 962-3932

Birmingham District Office, 2121 Eighth Avenue, North, Suite 824, Birmingham, AL 35203       (205) 731-0082

Boston Area Office, JFK Federal Building, Room 409-B, Boston, MA 02203           (617) 565-3200

Buffalo Local Office, Guaranty Building, 28 Church Street, Room 301, Buffalo, NY 14202       (716) 846-4441

Charlotte District Office, 5500 Central Avenue, Charlotte, NC 28212           (704) 567-7100

Chicago District Office, Federal Building, Room 930A, 536 South Clark Street, Chicago, IL 60605     (312) 353-2713

Cincinnati Area Office, Federal Building, Room 7015, 550 Main Street, Cincinnati, OH 45202      (513) 684-2851

Cleveland District Office, 1375 Euclid Avenue, Room 600, Cleveland, OH 44115 (216) 522-2001

Dallas District Office, 8303 Elmbrook Drive, 2nd Floor, Dallas, TX 75247 (214) 767-7015

Denver District Office, 1845 Sherman Street, 2nd Floor, Denver, CO 80203 (303) 866-1300

Detroit District Office, Patrick V. McNamara Federal Building, 477 Michigan Avenue, Room 1540, Detroit, MI 48226

(313) 226-7636

El Paso Local Office, 700 East San Antonio Street, Room B-406, El Paso, TX 79901 (915) 534-6550

Fresno Local Office, 1313 P Street, Suite 103, Fresno, CA 93721 (209) 487-5793

Greensboro Local Office, 324 West Market Street, Room B-27, Post Office Box 3363, Greensboro, NC 27401 (919) 333-5174

Greensville Local Office, 211 Century Drive, Suite 109B, Greensville, SC 29607 (803) 233-1791

Houston District Office, 405 Main Street, 6th Floor, Houston, TX 77002 (713) 226-2601

Indianapolis District Office, Federal Building, U.S. Courthouse, 46 East Ohio Street, Room 456, Indianapolis, IN 46204

(317) 269-7212

Jackson Area Office, New Federal Building, 100 West Capitol Street, Suite 721, Jackson, MS 39269 (601) 965-4537

Kansas City Area Office, 911 Walnut, 10th Floor, Kansas City, MO 64106 (816) 374-5773

Little Rock Area Office, Savers Building, 320 West Capitol Avenue, Suite 621, Little Rock, AR 72201 (501) 378-5060

Los Angeles District Office, 3660 Wilshire, 5th Floor, Los Angeles, CA 90010 (213) 251-7278

Louisville Area Office, U.S. Post Office and Courthouse, 601 West Broadway, 6th Floor, Louisville, KY 40202 (502) 582-6082

Memphis District Office, 1407 Union Avenue, Suite 502, Memphis, TN 38104 (901) 521-2617

Miami District Office, Metro Mall, 1 NE First Street, 6th Floor, Miami, FL 33132 (305) 536-4491

Milwaukee District Office, 310 West Wisconsin Avenue, Suite 8000, Milwaukee, WI 53203 (414) 291-1111

Minneapolis Local Office, 110 South Fourth Street, Room 178, Minneapolis, MN 55401 (612) 348-1730

Nashville Area Office, 404 James Robertson Parkway, Suite 1100, Nashville, TN 37219 (615) 736-5820

Newark Area Office, 60 Park Place, Room 301, Newark, NJ 07102 (201) 645-6383

New Orleans District Office, F. Edward Hebert Federal Building, 600 South Maestri Place, Room 528, New Orleans, LA 70130 (504) 589-2329

New York District Office, 90 Church Street, Room 1505, New York, NY 10007 (212) 264-7161

Norfolk Area Office, Federal Building, 200 Granby Mall, Room 412, Norfolk, VA 23510 (804) 441-3470

Oakland Local Office, Wells Fargo Bank Building, 1333 Broadway, 4th Floor, Oakland, CA 94612 (415) 273-7588

Oklahoma City Area Office, Alfred P. Murrah Federal Building, 200 NW Fifth Street, Room 703, Oklahoma City, OK 73102 (405) 231-4911

Philadelphia District Office, 127 North Fourth Street, Suite 300, Philadelphia, PA 19106 (215) 597-7784

Phoenix District Office, 4520 North Central Avenue, Suite 300, Phoenix, AZ 85012 (602) 261-3882

Pittsburgh Area Office, Federal Building, 1000 Liberty Avenue, Room 2038A, Pittsburgh, PA 15222 (412) 644-3444

Raleigh Area Office, 127 West Hargett Street, Suite 500, Raleigh, NC 27601 (919) 856-4064

Richmond Area Office, 400 North Eighth Street, Room 7026, Richmond, VA 23240 (804) 771-2692

San Antonio District Office, 5410 Fredricksburg Road, Suite 200, Mockingbird Plaza, Plaza II, San Antonio, TX 78229 (512) 229-4810

San Diego Local Office, San Diego Federal Building, 880 Front Street, Room 4S-21, San Diego, CA 92188 (619) 293-6288

San Francisco District Office, 901 Market Street, Suite 500, San Francisco, CA 94103 (415) 995-5049

San Jose Local Office, U.S. Courthouse & Federal Building, 280 South First Street, Room 4150, San Jose, CA 95113 (408) 291-7352

Seattle District Office, Arcade Plaza Building, 1321 Second Avenue, 7th Floor, Seattle, WA 98101 (206) 442-0968

St. Louis District Office, 625 North Euclid Street, St. Louis, MO 63108 (314) 425-6585

Tampa Area Office, 700 Twiggs Street, Room 302, Tampa, FL
   33602                                                    (813) 228-2310
Washington Area Office, 1717 H Street, NW, Suite 400, Washington, DC 20006                                           (202) 653-6197

## APPENDIX II. STATE LAWS ON RECORDS INSPECTION

There are now almost two dozen states which have laws on the books
allowing employees to inspect their own personnel files, and in some
cases, to copy the contents. Keep in mind that even though a state
does not have a specific law, the courts may rule against a company
for what it sees as an abuse.

*Arkansas* Arkansas has no statute governing access to employee
records. A federal judge there has ruled that an employer's practice
of placing memos of misconduct and poor performance in an employee's file, without notice to the employee, was "highly suspect"
and supported the employee's claim of sex discrimination.

*California—inspection only* Employees can inspect their personnel
files at reasonable times and at reasonable intervals within a reasonable period after an employee's request. Such personnel files must
include: qualifications for employment, promotions, performance
appraisals, compensation and bonuses, and termination and other
disciplinary notes and letters. *Note:* Under California law, employee
medical records are kept separately from personnel files. However,
employees are entitled to review those files as well.

*Connecticut—inspection and copying* Employees can inspect their
personnel files within a reasonable time after a written request, but
no more than twice a year. However, the employer may request that
the inspection occur in front of a designated official.

Such personnel files must include: eligibility for employment, promotions, compensations, transfers, termination, discipline notes or
any adverse personnel action, and other work-related details. Medical
records are not included in these files, but such records can be
inspected by the employee.

The employer must provide copies of any of the material requested
by the employee and may charge any fee reasonably related to the
cost of copying.

If the employee disagrees with anything that is filed, and the employer refuses to remove it and/or modify it, the employee may submit a written statement with his or her position and then ask to have that statement included in the file.

The employer may not disclose any information from the personnel file to any third party without the employee's written authorization, except for verification of employment, job title, salary, or disclosures pursuant to judicial subpoena or collective bargaining agreements.

*Delaware—inspection only* Employees can inspect their personnel files at reasonable times, but normally not more than once a year. All employee materials, including application forms, warning or disciplinary notices, employment history, and other work related information, is open to review by the individual employee. However, there are some exceptions, such as reference letters and Fair Credit Reporting Act information, which are not open to review.

Corrections of the file data by the employee may be allowed if the employer agrees. If there is no such agreement, written statements by the employee may be submitted and kept within the file.

*District of Columbia—inspection only* Employees have access to their personnel files while in the presence of an employer representative. All personnel material is open to inspection, with certain exceptions including materials received on a confidential basis.

Employees may put new information in their file and can seek to have any irrelevant, immaterial, or untimely data removed. Untimely is defined as more than three years old.

*Illinois—inspection and copying* Any current or laid-off employees can request to inspect their personnel files, although the request may have to be in writing. The employer must grant the request within seven working days.

The employee can check such personnel file material as qualifications for employment, promotions, transfers, compensation, discharge, and other disciplinary items. Exceptions to this inspection include any materials regarding letters of reference, test documents, management planning materials, or information of a personal nature relating to another employee.

Employees can obtain a copy of the personnel file, but the employer may charge a small fee for such copies. In terms of making corrections, the employee may place supplemental materials in his or her file if there is some question as to the accuracy of file material.

Personnel file material may not be distributed to third parties without written notice to the employee first. Personnel material that is over four years old must be deleted from the employee's file.

*Maine—inspection only* An employee or former employee must make a written request to see personnel files. Inspection must be allowed within ten days after the receipt of the request. All personnel records covering employee evaluations, character, work habits, and compensation are open for inspection.

*Massachusetts—inspection and copying* Employees can see their personnel files by making a written request. The employee can also make copies of the file.

Materials that are incorrect or wrong can be deleted from the file if requested by the employee and approved by the employer. Without the employer's sanction, the employee may prepare his or her written statement which is then placed in the file.

*Michigan—inspection and copying* Any employer with four or more employees is covered by the statute. Employees must make requests in writing, no more than twice a year.

Personnel records open for review include qualifications for employment, promotion, transfer, compensation, and disciplinary actions. Exceptions that are not open for review include management planning materials and records of a personal nature about other employees.

An employee can make a copy of the files and must pay a limited copying fee. If the employee disagrees with anything in that file, he or she can submit a statement not exceeding five pages which is then placed in the file.

The employer must delete all records of a disciplinary nature which are more than four years old.

*Nevada—inspection and copying* After an employee makes a request, the employer must provide the personnel files within a reasonable time. Terminated employees can inspect their files within sixty days of their dismissal.

Employees can inspect and make copies of their files of all materials, with the exception of confidential reports from previous employers and information regarding arrests or convictions.

An employee can ask the employer to correct any information that he or she believes is wrong. The employer must allow any changes that are, indeed, factual and correct.

*New Hampshire—inspection and copying* Once an employee makes a request, the employer must provide the files within a reasonable period of time. All materials within the files can be inspected and copied by the employee. The employee can also put his or her own statement in the file which then becomes a part of the file.

*New York* New York has no statute which grants employees access to their personnel files. A ruling by the state's highest court might confer that right, depending on later interpretations. The court ruled in favor of a police officer who had been discharged on the basis of records in his file that he had never seen. The court said the employer's practice lacked "fundamental fairness," and the employee should have had the right to inspect and rebut the records. It is not certain whether this public-sector decision will also apply to private employers.

*Ohio—medical records and copying* The employer must furnish, upon written request, any medical records including examination results that the employee wants, unless the employer's physician feels that the release of the information would cause the employee serious harm. The employee must pay for the cost of the copying up to twenty-five cents a page.

*Oregon—inspection and copying* Employee can inspect any personnel files regarding employment, promotions, compensation, termination, and other work-related actions. Major exceptions include criminal conduct investigations and confidential reports about other employees. The employee can copy these records, but must pay a reasonable fee.

*Pennsylvania—inspection* Current employees plus laid-off employees can inspect the personnel files. There must be a written request for such review, and a designated official of the employer will be present at the time of the inspection.

Records regarding employment application, salary, disciplinary memos, benefit information, and similar materials are open for review by the employee. The exceptions include criminal investigations, reference letters, and exceptions under the Fair Credit Reporting Act.

Copying is not allowed but the employee can make notes of the files. The employee can also add his or her own statement of rebuttal to the file.

*Rhode Island—inspection only* On the employee's written request and with seven days' notice. The inspection must be at a reasonable time, other than the employee's work hours. Maximum of three inspections in a calendar year.

Employees can inspect all personnel files including medical records and those that are or have been used to determine qualifications, promotion, compensation, termination, or discipline.

The exceptions are records of criminal investigations, records prepared for use in court proceedings, recommendations and letters of reference, managerial records and planning records kept by the employer, and confidential reports.

*South Carolina—state employees* Only employees of the state are entitled to inspect their personnel files, and that includes only job grade, job description, and salary information.

*South Dakota—state employees* The statute simply says state employees can inspect their personnel files during working hours.

*Tennessee—state employees* Employees of the state can inspect and receive copies of their files.

*Utah—state employees* With the exception of confidential documents, state employees can inspect and make copies of their personnel files.

*Vermont—state employees* State employees can inspect personnel files on information regarding hiring, evaluations, compensation, and medical and psychological records.

*Washington—inspection only* Employees can inspect their personnel files at least once a year and up to two years after termination. All materials are open to the employee with the exception of criminal investigations and those materials involved in preparation for pretrial discovery.

If an employee wants to protest a record, the employee can file a rebuttal in writing which will be placed in the file.

*Wisconsin—inspection and copying* All employees and former employees can inspect the personnel records, but no more than twice a year. The employer must make files available within seven working days of the request.

The employee can inspect all records regarding qualifications for employment, promotions, transfers, compensation, disciplinary actions, and termination. Exceptions include materials regarding criminal investigations, letters of reference, and management staff planning documents.

Under an amendment passed in 1982, the employee can also make copies of the file. The fee is paid by the employee. If the employee disagrees with the contents of the file, the employee may add a statement to the file.

# Glossary of Employee Rights Terms

Act. One of the laws enforced by the EEOC, as Title VII of the Civil Rights Act, the Age Discrimination in Employment Act, the Equal Pay Act.

ADEA. The Age Discrimination in Employment Act.

Affirmative action. A program of remedy for the present effects of past discrimination usually involving analysis of the work force to determine areas where minorities and women are underutilized, and providing preferential treatment for persons falling into previously underutilized categories. Usually affirmative action programs use goals and quotas to meet stated aims.

(the) Agency. Refers to the Equal Employment Opportunity Commission.

Area office. The smallest EEOC field office, reports to a District Office. Its directors have limited authority.

Benefits. In equal employment opportunity law, refers to nonsalary items provided to employees, such as vacation pay, sick pay, health and life insurance, pensions, etc.

Bona fide occupational qualification. One of the legally permissible defenses to a Title VII charge.

Bona fide seniority system. A lawfully constituted seniority system

Cause. An EEOC term meaning an employer is believed to have discriminated against the charging party, as in "this is a cause case" (as opposed to No cause, which means no discrimination).

CHARGE. An EEOC form 5, the form used by the agency to structure the charges which come before it. The letter with which the person files his or her complaint.

CLASS ACTION SUIT. A legal action brought by one or more persons on behalf of themselves and a much larger group, all of whom have the same grounds for action.

COLLATERAL ESTOPPEL. A bar to litigating the issues between the parties, in which the facts in question have been previously determined.

COMMON LAW. Refers to judicial interpretation.

COMPLAINANT. The person who files a charge or brings a complaint. The term used to refer to a charging party in a charge of discrimination against a federal agency.

COMPLAINT. The cause or subject of complaint, a grievance. In law, a formal charge or accusation.

CONTINGENT FEE BASIS. Refers to an arrangement between client and lawyer where the lawyer does not receive payment unless the client's case prevails, or where the lawyer's fee is based upon the settlement.

DEFAMATION. Damage to one's reputation either by the spoken or written word, including slander and libel.

DEFENDANT. In law, the defending party, one who is sued or accused; opposed to PLAINTIFF.

DE MINIMUS. A term meaning of little cost, literally of the smallest possible cost.

DEPOSITION. The testimony given under oath and recorded verbatim by a court reporter, usually in connection with court proceedings.

DISCRIMINATION. In equal employment law, the basing of employment decisions on unlawful considerations of the personal characteristics or beliefs of employees or applicants for employment.

EEOC. The Equal Employment Opportunity Commission.

EMPLOYMENT-AT-WILL. Employment which can be terminated at any time for any reason is at-will.

EQUAL OPPORTUNITY SPECIALIST. The term used within EEOC to refer to its investigative staff members.

EXECUTIVE ORDER 11246. A presidential order aimed at eliminating employment discrimination by contractors with federal government contracts in amounts exceeding $10,000.

FIELD OFFICE. An EEOC office reporting to a district office and smaller in size and scope of authority than a district office.

FRAUD. False representation of fact designed to deceive the other party into relying on it.

INTAKE. The function at the EEOC where members of the public are interviewed for the purpose of drafting formal charges, preparing them on the proper form, and notifying employers that a charge has been filed.

LIBEL. Defamation of character expressed by writing, or picture.

LITIGATION. The act or process of litigating or carrying on a suit in a court of law or equity; also a lawsuit.

LITIGIOUS. Given to carrying on lawsuits, quarrelsome. In equal employment opportunity law, sometimes used to describe a charging party who has filed a number of charges against employers with the EEOC, or the atmosphere surrounding employer-employee relations.

MINORITY. A racial, religious, national, or political group smaller than and differing from the larger, controlling group of which it is a part.

NO CAUSE. The EEOC term used to mean "not guilty." Shortened from "No reasonable cause was found to believe the employer engaged in practices prohibited by Title VII of the Civil Rights Act of 1964, as amended."

NLRB. National Labor Relations Board: the federal agency which enforces the Fair Labor Standards Act.

OFCCP. The Office of Federal Contracts Compliance Programs: This agency administers Executive Order 11246 which prohibits federal contractors from employment discrimination.

PLAINTIFF. A person who brings suit before a court of law; a complainant; opposed to DEFENDANT.

PRIMA FACIE. In law, adequate to establish a fact or raise a presumption of fact unless refuted: said of evidence; at first sight; at first view; before further examination.

PROMISSORY ESTOPPEL. Enforcement of a promise which was binding when made and acted on by the person promised.

PUBLIC POLICY. A principle of law which restricts individuals from acting against the public good.

REPRISAL. Adverse action in violation of Section 704(a) of Title VII because a person filed a charge or otherwise participated in an EEOC investigation.

RES JUDICATION. Legal doctrine which bars relitigation of a cause of action. A plaintiff (that's you) chooses his or her forum and all potential causes of action are merged in that choice of forum. A final judgment in this forum bars any litigation between parties regarding any issue which could have been raised in that forum.

RESPONDENT. The employer, the entity that is the object of a charge, the responder to the complaint.

RETALIATION. Adverse action taken in violation of Section 704(a) of Title VII because a person protests unlawful discrimination.

REVERSE DISCRIMINATION. Discrimination against a person or a class of persons not usually in the minority class. A typical instance of this would be a white male filing because a person in a minority group or a woman obtained employment preference.

SEXUAL HARASSMENT. To harass an employee or applicant by impermissable touching, proffering unwanted social or sexual invitations, or making sexually based comments because of that employee's gender.

SLANDER. Defamation by spoken word.

STANDING TO FILE. Legal qualification which provides that only certain people may file.

STATE AGENCY. Refers to agencies established as deferral agencies by Section 706 of Title VII, agencies which enforce state or local laws banning discrimination in employment.

STATUTE. A law, an established rule, passed by a legislative body and set forth in a formal document.

STATUTE OF FRAUDS. Traditional legal principle which states that a verbal contract is invalid if it can't be fulfilled within a certain time frame, usually a year.

STATUTORY LAW. Refers to legislative actions.

SUMMARY JUDGMENT. A decision by a judge that there is no factual or legal issue in the case, so therefore it is decided without the necessity of a trial.

TIMELY FILED. A charge which is filed within the time limits imposed by the law; a charge filed in time, before the expiration of legal limits.

TITLE VII. Refers to Title VII of the Civil Rights Act of 1964.

# Index of Cases Cited

# General Index